Voices from Vilcabamba

Voices from Vilcabamba

Accounts Chronicling the Fall of the Inca Empire

Brian S. Bauer,
Madeleine Halac–Higashimori,
and Gabriel E. Cantarutti

UNIVERSITY PRESS OF COLORADO
Boulder

© 2016 by University Press of Colorado

Published by University Press of Colorado
5589 Arapahoe Avenue, Suite 206C
Boulder, Colorado 80303

 The University Press of Colorado is a proud member of
Association of American University Presses.

The University Press of Colorado is a cooperative publishing enterprise supported, in part, by Adams State University, Colorado State University, Fort Lewis College, Metropolitan State University of Denver, Regis University, University of Colorado, University of Northern Colorado, Utah State University, and Western State Colorado University.

∞ This paper meets the requirements of the ANSI/NISO Z39.48-1992 (Permanence of Paper).

ISBN: 978-1-60732-425-6 (pbk)
ISBN: 978-1-60732-426-3 (ebook)

Library of Congress Cataloging-in-Publication Data
Bauer, Brian S.
  Voices from Vilcabamba : accounts chronicling the fall of the Inca Empire (1572) / Brian S.
  Bauer, Madeleine Halac-Higashimori, and Gabriel E. Cantarutti.
      pages cm
  Includes bibliographical references and index.
  ISBN 978-1-60732-425-6 (paperback : alkaline paper) — ISBN 978-1-60732-426-3 (ebook)
  1. Incas—Peru—Vilcabamba Mountains Region—History—16th century. 2. Incas—
  Peru—Vilcabamba Mountains Region—History—16th century—Sources. 3. Vilcabamba
  Mountains Region (Peru)—Colonization—History—16th century. 4. Vilcabamba
  Mountains Region (Peru)—Colonization—History—16th century—Sources. 5. Peru—
  History—Conquest, 1522-1548. 6. Peru—History—1548-1820. 7. Peru—History—Conquest,
  1522-1548—Sources. 8. Peru—History—1548-1820—Sources. I. Halac-Higashimori,
  Madeleine. II. Cantarutti, Gabriel E. III. Title.
  F3429.1.V48B283 2016
  985'.02—dc23

                              2015013218

Cover illustration: The meeting between Sayri Tupac and Lope García de Castro, in a drawing by Guaman Poma de Ayala

Contents

Figures

Acknowledgments

Major funding for this work was provided by the Office of the Dean (College of Liberal Arts and Sciences) and the Department of Anthropology at the University of Illinois at Chicago. Additional support was given by the Institute for New World Archaeology. We also thank David Drew, Jean-Jacques Decoster, Vincent Lee, Carmen Halac, Donato Amado, Jesus Galiano Blanco, Laura Nussbaum-Barberena, Javier Fonseca Santa Cruz, John Monaghan, and Miriam Aráoz Silva, who helped us in various stage of the research and manuscript preparation.

In the translations we have tried to remain true to the original authors; yet we have also taken certain liberties to make the manuscripts more accessible to a wide readership. For example, we have corrected mistakes in tense and plural forms, and we have made minor changes in punctuation and capitalization to clarify meaning. When needed, we have also added paragraph breaks within some of the longer passages. We have also attempted to standardize toponyms, personal names, and the more common Quechua terms to match the Hispanic spelling found in other Spanish chronicles and on modern maps. Scholars who are interested in the subtleties of the spellings and the orthography of these manuscripts can consult the originals or reproductions that are available. We provide translations for Quechua and Spanish words on their first appearance.

Voices from
Vilcabamba

1

*Vilcabamba and the Fall
of the Inca Empire*

The 1572 Spanish raid into the Vilcabamba region of
present-day Peru, resulting in the capture and execution of the last Inca, Tupac Amaru, marks a unique
moment in Andean history. The Spaniards had successfully invaded the Andes forty years earlier, but
the Vilcabamba region remained as the final bastion
of indigenous resistance against European hegemony.
Manco Inca, who first aided the Spaniards in occupying the imperial capital, Cuzco, and then rebelled
against them, established a stump state in this mountainous region while he attempted to regain control of
the realm. After Manco Inca's death, his sons (Sayri
Tupac, Titu Cusi Yupanqui, and Tupac Amaru) negotiated with the Spaniards while also leading indigenous
resistance against them. For their part, the Spaniards
sent diplomats, priests, and at times military expeditions into the Vilcabamba region in an effort to bring an
end to the conflict and establish absolute control over
the Andes. Then in 1572 Viceroy Francisco de Toledo
declared a war of "fire and blood" against the Incas and
launched a massive raid into the region. The last living son of Manco Inca, Tupac Amaru, was captured
during this raid and subsequently executed in Cuzco;
bringing an end to organized resistance to Spanish rule.
This volume presents an overview of the major events
that occurred in the Vilcabamba region during those
final decades of Inca rule and English translations of
several major documents that were produced during
that period.[1] In organizing these materials we hope to

DOI: 10.5876/9781607324263.c001

provide an enhanced narrative on the nature of European-American relations during this time of important cultural transformations.

MANCO INCA AND VILCABAMBA

Manco Inca first retreated down the Urubamba River into the vast, mountainous region of Vilcabamba after his unsuccessful 1536 siege of Cuzco.[2] The young Inca ruler must have viewed Vilcabamba as an impenetrable region where he could live while attempting to reorganize his loyalists against the Spaniards. The Incas had occupied the Vilcabamba area for at least two generations and had already constructed four major installations (Machu Picchu, Choquequirao, Vitcos, and Vilcabamba) and dozens of smaller settlements within the region.

To enter the Vilcabamba region, Manco Inca and his forces crossed the Chuquichaca Bridge, at the modern settlement of Chaullay, on the central road that leads to the town of Vitcos. After crossing the bridge, Manco Inca ordered it destroyed in hopes that this would prevent the Spaniards, who were in hot pursuit, from entering the region (figure 1.1). The Spanish raid into Vilcabamba had been ordered by Diego de Almagro and led by Rodrigo Ordóñez and Rui Díaz.[3] These Spaniards were supported by Manco Inca's half brother, Paullu (Topa) Inca, as well as a host of indigenous allies. This group was forced to stop for a few days at the river's edge as they rebuilt the bridge (Pizarro [1571] 1921: 365, [1571] 1986: 169). However, upon its reconstruction, the Spanish-led forces quickly traveled on horseback as far as Vitcos. No Spaniard had entered this region before, and what they found surely amazed them.

Near the center of the Vilcabamba region, on a high hill at the intersection of three different valleys, was the town of Vitcos. This sprawling town included an impressive central plaza, various elite dwellings, dozens of domestic clusters, and a large shrine complex (Bauer, Aráoz Silva, and Burr 2012). The settlement was also surrounded by large, well-watered terrace systems. However, by the time that the Spanish arrived in Vitcos, Manco Inca had fled into the dense forests of the surrounding mountains. Unable to capture the Inca, the Spanish troops returned to Cuzco with a large hoard of gold and silver taken from the town.

During this first raid into the Vilcabamba region, the Spaniards captured a son of Manco Inca, Titu Cusi Yupanqui, and two of the Inca's daughters. Titu Cusi Yupanqui was sent to live with Pedro de Oñate[4] in Cuzco and was well cared for (Titu Cusi Yupanqui [1570] 2005: 118). Within two years, however, Titu Cusi Yupanqui returned to live in Vilcabamba with his father and was

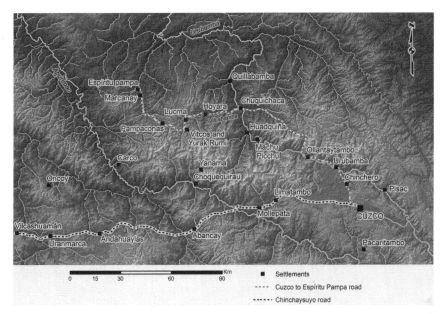

FIGURE I.I. *The Vilcabamba region. Map by Gabriel E Cantarutti.*

there to witness his death in 1545. Years later, when he became ruler, Titu Cusi Yupanqui would negotiate with the Spaniards for an end to hostilities.

Manco Inca won a few encounters against the Spaniards during the early years of his exile from Cuzco. The most decisive occurred in 1538 near the town of Oncoy, in the province of Andahuaylas, where the Inca surrounded a contingent of Spaniards who had advanced too quickly and were caught, exhausted and isolated. Raids by Manco Inca over the Apurímac River were so frequent that the Spaniards were forced to build a new town, called San Juan de la Frontera de Huamanga (modern Ayacucho), along the trade route between Cuzco and Lima.

In 1539 Gonzalo Pizarro led the second Spanish raid into the Vilcabamba region. As in the first raid, by the time the Spaniards reached the town of Vitcos, Manco Inca had already fled into the mountains. This time, however, the Spaniards pushed on and followed the Inca road to the village of Pampaconas and then further into the lowlands. A battle took place at a small ridgetop settlement called Huayna Pucará,[5] about two days from the Inca town of Vilcabamba, in which several Spaniards and their indigenous allies were killed. Following this battle, Manco Inca again escaped into the forested mountains. Although Spanish forces stayed in the Vilcabamba region for over two months, they were unable to learn the whereabouts of Manco Inca.[6]

It was during this raid, however, that Gonzalo Pizarro captured Manco Inca's principal wife, Cura Ocllo. As they pulled back from Vilcabamba, the Spaniards met Francisco Pizarro in Ollantaytambo. Frustrated by the failure of the expedition, Francisco Pizarro had Cura Ocllo tied to a stake and killed with arrows. News of this great cruelty even reached Bartolomé de Las Casas ([1552] 1992: 119), who, describing it in his book *The Devastation of the Indies*, wrote: "A few days ago . . . they took the queen, his wife, and against all justice and reason killed her, even though it is said that she was with child, for the sole reason to cause suffering to her husband."

Over the next five years, there was only sporadic contact between the Incas of Vilcabamba and the Spaniards. It may have been during this time that Manco Inca began to expand a small settlement, likewise called Vilcabamba, that the Incas had already established three to four days further down the eastern slope of the Andes. The Spaniards had, after all, invaded the Vilcabamba region two times within just a few years and both times had quickly reached Vitcos. It was clear to the Inca that additional arrangements had to be made further into the interior.

This was also a time of considerable confusion across the Spanish-held territories, as various factions fought for control of Peru. Francisco Pizarro was murdered in Lima in 1541 by supporters of Diego de Almagro, his original partner in the conquest, who had himself been killed three years earlier. Later, in 1546, Gonzalo Pizarro, one of Francisco Pizarro's half brothers, would lead the colonists in an uprising against the king of Spain and would even kill the newly appointed viceroy of Peru. This rebellion proved unsuccessful, and soon afterward Gonzalo Pizarro was captured and beheaded in Cuzco.

These revolts are of relevance to the history of Vilcabamba, since Manco Inca granted a small group of Spaniards who had fought on the losing side of an uprising, refuge in Vitcos (in 1544 or early 1545). Although well treated, the renegade Spaniards soon grew tired of life in exile and plotted to kill Manco Inca, hoping that this deed would win them favor with Spanish authorities when they left Vilcabamba. Titu Cusi Yupanqui, who witnessed the death of his father, describes the assassination:

> . . . the said Spaniards were in my father's company in his own house in Vitcos, my father, they, and I were enjoying ourselves by playing a game of *herron*.[7]
> . . . When, in the course of the game, my father went to pick up the iron with which they were playing, they all fell upon him with daggers, knives and some

swords. . . . When I, still being very young, saw them treat my father this way, I tried to rush to his aid, but they angrily turned on me and threw at me my father's personal lance, which happened to be there, thus almost killing me as well. (Titu Cusi Yupanqui [1570] 2005: 126)

The traitorous Spaniards did murder the Inca, stabbing him in the plaza of Vitcos; however, they were all killed in turn before they could leave the province. As was customary among the Inca, the body of Manco Inca was preserved. Manco Inca's mummy remained in Vilcabamba until 1572, when the Spaniards stormed the city. It was then burned in Cuzco under the orders of Viceroy Toledo.

SAYRI TUPAC AND THE RULE OF VILCABAMBA

With the death of Manco Inca (ca. 1544), a small contingent of Inca nobility continued to live in the Vilcabamba region, and the rule was passed down to his eldest son, Sayri Tupac, who was born just after the Spaniards first entered Cuzco (figure 1.2). Sayri Tupac first ruled with the aid of a regent but later took full control of the region.[8] After many meetings and years of prolonged negotiations, Sayri Tupac agreed to leave the Vilcabamba region and to reside in the wealthy *encomienda*[9] of Yucay, which included the former country estate of his grandfather, Huayna Capac.[10]

The *encomienda* of Yucay was located in what is now referred to as the Sacred Valley. It was the most recent of all the royal Inca estates in the Cuzco region, and Huayna Capac had built various amenities within it and improved its large tracts of terraces. The *encomienda* was also populated with a large number of resettled people, as many as 2,000, from across the empire who were dedicated to its maintenance (Covey and Amado Gonzáles 2008: 21–22). Being one of the most productive estates in the Cuzco region, it was large enough to support Sayri Tupac and his descendants at a high lifestyle.

In October of 1557 Sayri Tupac left Vilcabamba with a large entourage and at great expense to travel to Lima to meet Viceroy Lope García de Castro. The Inca then returned to Cuzco, where he received a spectacular welcoming by the indigenous people, and took up residency in Yucay. Sayri Tupac and his sister/wife Cusi Huarcay were baptized, and, as part of a previously signed treaty, dispensation was granted so that they could marry (figure 1.3). The departure of Sayri Tupac from Vilcabamba and the establishment of an accord between him and the Spaniards did not, however, bring much relief to the crown since Sayri Tupac died only a few years later (ca. 1560).[11]

FIGURE 1.2. *Viceroy Andrés Hurtado de Mendoza, Third Marquis of Cañete, meeting with Sayri Tupac in Lima. Drawing by Guaman Poma de Ayala ([ca. 1615] 1980, vol. 2: 420 [442]).*

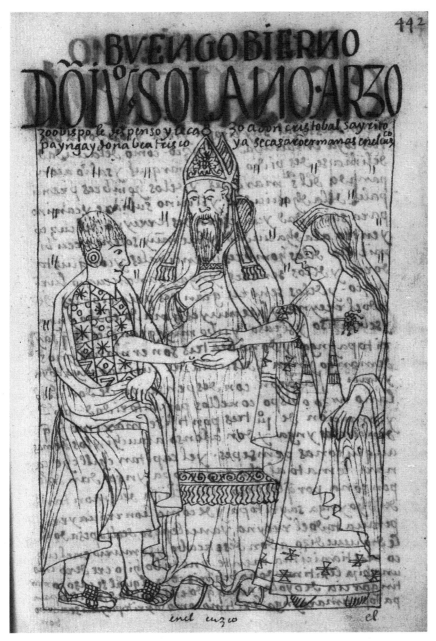

FIGURE 1.3. *Don Juan Solano marrying Sayri Tupac and Cusi Huarcay. Drawing by Guaman Poma de Ayala ([ca. 1615] 1980, vol. 2: 442 [444]).*

THE BRIEF RULE OF TITU CUSI YUPANQUI

The death of Sayri Tupac had major repercussions for the history of Vilcabamba. With the death of the Inca, the Yucay *encomienda* passed from Sayri Tupac to his only offspring, Beatriz Clara Coya. As she was a child at that time, a prominent citizen of Cuzco, Atilano de Anaya, was placed in charge of her holdings.[12] Furthermore, with the death of Sayri Tupac the focus of independent, indigenous power turned once again toward Vilcabamba, where Manco Inca's second son, Titu Cusi Yupanqui, still ruled.

Since the fate of Titu Cusi Yupanqui was not included in the extensive discussions held between the Spaniards and Sayri Tupac, negotiations between Vilcabamba and the crown had to begin anew. Juan Polo de Ondegardo, who was the corregidor of Cuzco at the time of Sayri Tupac's death, immediately sent an envoy into Vilcabamba to explain the circumstances of the Inca's death. Martín Pando, a mestizo,[13] and Juan de Betanzos, a Spaniard, both fluent Quechua speakers, agreed to go on the mission. While Betanzos returned to Cuzco after the mission, Pando stayed to serve as a secretary and advisor to Titu Cusi Yupanqui (Guillén Guillén [1977] 2005: 572–573).[14]

Over the next five years a series of meetings was arranged between various representatives of the crown and the Inca. García de Melo, the royal treasurer in Cuzco, made at least two separate trips into Vilcabamba to negotiate with the Inca on behalf of the viceroy.[15] An even more successful trip took place in April and May of 1565 by Diego Rodríguez de Figueroa (see document 3, this volume). When Rodríguez de Figueroa, who recorded his extraordinary journey into Vilcabamba in a detailed report, arrived at the bridge of Chuquichaca, he had to wait several days to establish contact with the Inca and gain permission to enter the region. When he did enter, Rodríguez de Figueroa crossed the river in a hanging basket supported by a rope, as the suspension bridge had been destroyed. Several days later, as he passed Vitcos, he saw the heads of the men who had killed Manco Inca many years before, still impaled on stakes.

Rodríguez de Figueroa met Titu Cusi Yupanqui in the remote village of Pampaconas. The meeting lasted several days and was extremely successful. In the end, the Inca agreed to meet with a number of high-ranking officials at the bridge of Chuquichaca to continue peace negotiations. The Chuquichaca Bridge meeting took place in June of 1565, with Titu Cusi Yupanqui, Rodríguez de Figueroa, Melo, and the powerful judge of the Audiencia of Charcas, Juan de Matienzo, all attending.[16] Although the negotiations were tense, with Titu Cusi Yupanqui and Matienzo meeting armed but alone, an outline of a settlement was drawn up and agreed upon (Guillén Guillén 1977a; Titu Cusi Yupanqui 1916a). Matienzo and his men then returned to Cuzco while Titu

Cusi Yupanqui and his forces returned to Vilcabamba. The Chuquichaca Bridge, which had been rebuilt for this meeting, was destroyed as each side left the negotiations.

In late August of 1566, under the orders of Viceroy Lope García de Castro, several Spaniards met with Titu Cusi Yupanqui to sign what has become known as the Treaty of Acobamba (Nowack 2004; Guillén Guillén 1977a, 1977b, 1981, [1977] 2005: 543–588). The Spaniards were represented by Melo, Rodríguez de Figueroa, and a priest named Francisco de las Veredas. The Inca himself attended, along with his two most important advisors, Yamqui Mayta and Rimachi Yupanqui, as well as Martín Pando (Guillén Guillén 1977a). Under the terms of this treaty, Titu Cusi Yupanqui conceded to Spanish rule and accepted a Spanish overseer (corregidor) for the Vilcabamba region. This position was filled by Rodríguez de Figueroa. The Acobamba treaty also specified that Titu Cusi Yupanqui was to become a Christian and that missionary work could begin in the Vilcabamba region. In turn, Titu Cusi Yupanqui was granted amnesty by the crown, and, equally important, arrangements were made to have his son, Quispe Titu, marry Beatriz Clara Coya; an arrangement that would give Titu Cusi Yupanqui access to the Yucay estate.

In response to these demands, priests were allowed to enter the Vilcabamba region in July 1567 to baptize Quispe Titu, the son of Titu Cusi Yupanqui. Witnesses to this event included Father Antonio de Vera, Father Francisco de las Veredas, Diego Rodriquez de Figueroa, and Diego de Olivares as well as Yamqui Mayta, Rimachi Yupanqui, Martín Pando and Chimbo Ocllo Coya, the mother of Quispe Titu (Guillén Guillén 1977a).

After the Spanish ratification of the Acobamba treaty, Titu Cusi Yupanqui showed no eagerness to leave the Vilcabamba region; nevertheless, he did continue to respect its obligations. For example, in 1568, Titu Cusi Yupanqui wrote to Father Juan de Vivero, the prior of the San Agustin Convent in Cuzco, inviting the Augustinians to enter the Vilcabamba region so that he, along with his principal wife, could be baptized. In response, Vivero, one of his friars, Marcos García, and two lay citizens of Cuzco journeyed to Vitcos and the nearby community of Huancacalle[17] (Hemming 1970; Titu Cusi Yupanqui [1570] 2005).[18] After the baptism, Fray García remained in the region to establish a mission while the others returned to Cuzco (Titu Cusi Yupanqui 1916a, 1916b, 1916c, [1570] 2005). About a year later, a second Augustinian, Diego Ortiz, received permission to join García in the Vilcabamba area. While Ortiz was generally tolerated by the indigenous communities, it seems that García, because of his harsher temperament, encountered various problems (Hemming 1970; Calancha [1638] 1981). Nevertheless, Ortiz and García were able to establish churches in two separate villages, Huancacalle and Puquiura,[19] both of which are near Vitcos. They also occasionally made trips further into the interior to establish churches, raise crosses, and seek converts. Apparently, sometime in 1569, García grew tired of the missionary work in the region and attempted to return to Cuzco. However, the Inca sent a group of solders to force him to return.

In February of 1570, Titu Cusi Yupanqui agreed to take the two Augustinians to the town of Vilcabamba. The three- to four-day trip from Vitcos to Vilcabamba was made at the height of the rainy season, which added to the difficulties of the journey. While the priests were not allowed to enter the city proper, they stayed on its outskirts for about two weeks. On the eve of their departure, Titu Cusi Yupanqui dictated a long account of his life and that of his father's. This famous account was recorded by Martín Pando, who by that time had spent more than ten years in the Vilcabamba region working with the Inca.[20] Witnessed by the two priests, García and Ortiz, as well as various Inca captains, this account forms the core of most of what we know occurred in the Vilcabamba region from 1536 to 1570 (Titu Cusi Yupanqui [1570] 2005).

After signing Titu Cusi Yupanqui's account, the two priests left the town of Vilcabamba and traveled back to Puquiura. Soon after they arrived, the Augustinians gathered a group of followers and marched to the nearby shrine of Yurak Rumi (figure 1.4). Perhaps angered by what they believed to have been poor treatment in the town of Vilcabamba, they then covered the shrine with firewood and burned it to the ground.[21] In the wake of this provocative act, Titu Cusi Yupanqui had to travel to Puquiura to restore order. Marcos García was immediately expelled from the Vilcabamba region; however, Ortiz was allowed to remain.

THE DEATH OF TITU CUSI YUPANQUI AND THE TRIALS OF DIEGO ORTIZ

Sometime after the burning of the Yurak Rumi shrine, Titu Cusi Yupanqui became sick while visiting the town of Vitcos.[22] That evening, Ortiz and Pando, who were both in the nearby town of Puquiura, were asked to come and see the Inca. Years later, several eyewitnesses reported that Pando had given the Inca something to drink, perhaps a whipped egg, to ease his stomach (Bauer et al. 2014). After the Inca's unexpected death the next morning, the two foreigners were accused of poisoning the Inca.[23] Pando was immediately killed; however, Ortiz was kept alive for about a week (see document 5, this volume).

Following the logic of his many sermons, the Inca loyalists demanded that Ortiz hold a mass and resurrect the dead Inca. After Ortiz had held the mass

Figure 1.4. *The shrine of Chuquipalta (now called Yurak Rumi). Photograph by Brian S. Bauer and Miriam Aráoz Silva.*

and announced that he did not have the power to bring the Inca back to life, the disappointed loyalists forced the priest to walk several days toward the town of Vilcabamba, where the successor to the kingship, Tupac Amaru, was residing. The group stopped at a small town called Marcanay,[24] within a day's walk of Vilcabamba, and sent word to the Inca that they were near. When Tupac Amaru denied the loyalists entrance to the city, Ortiz was killed with a blow to the head, and his body was buried feet up in a deep hole. Saltpeter and a colored *chicha* (a fermented drink made from maize) were offered over the grave. Parts of his habit were saved and made into *chuspas* (small coca bags). Furthermore, the earth from below where Ortiz said mass was dug up and thrown into a river to lessen any danger that he might still present.

Within a year of Ortiz's death, Spanish forces aided by native allies overran the Vilcabamba region and captured Tupac Amaru. Soon afterward, Ortiz's body was retrieved, and the Spaniards were surprised to see that, despite the tropical climate, it remained well preserved. The corpse was carried back to the newly established Spanish town of San Francisco de la Victoria de Vilcabamba. Under the direction of Martín Hurtado de Arbieto and the priest Diego López de Ayala, the body of Ortiz was paraded through the town and buried near the altar of the church. Almost immediately small miracles began to be associated with the corpse. Many years later, in 1595 and 1599–1600, the Augustinians supported investigations into the death of Ortiz, hoping that through his sufferings and miracles he would be recognized as a Christian martyr and be named as a saint (see document 5, this volume).

However, a review of the Ortiz case documents (Aparicio López 1989; Bauer et al. 2014) also indicates that the bones of Ortiz were stolen in 1595 by Fray Pedro de Aguiar as he completed his investigation into the death of

Ortiz. Apparently, Aguiar had requested that the bones of Ortiz be moved to the Augustinian monastery in Cuzco, and when the citizenry of Vilcabamba denied his request, Aguiar arranged for the church to be broken into and Ortiz's remains removed. Aguiar himself then received the stolen relics and carried them to Cuzco. The theft of Ortiz's bones from the Vilcabamba region caused considerable outrage among its citizens, especially since their removal was widely perceived to have caused the sudden return of mosquitoes to the region. In 1607, long after Ortiz's nomination for sainthood had come to an unsuccessful close, his remains were buried in the Augustinian convent in Cuzco near the main altar.

THE FALL OF VILCABAMBA

With the death of Titu Cusi Yupanqui, communication between Vilcabamba and Cuzco suddenly stopped. Unaware of the dramatic events that had occurred in the region, the newly arrived viceroy, Francisco de Toledo, attempted to reestablish communication with the Inca. He first sent a group of men to enter the Vilcabamba area by crossing the Apurímac River. When they were barred from entering, Toledo sent Atilano de Anaya to the Urubamba River crossing to establish communication with the Inca. Anaya was a logical person to send on this mission, since he already knew the Vilcabamba region, having witnessed Titu Cusi Yupanqui's baptism in August of 1568, and served as caretaker for Beatriz Clara Coya. However, when Anaya crossed into the Vilcabamba region, he was killed by Inca loyalists.

The death of Anaya provided Viceroy Toledo with the justification to organize a massive raid into the Vilcabamba region with the aim of capturing Titu Cusi Yupanqui and bringing the region under the firm control of the crown. As Spanish troops, led by Martín Hurtado de Arbieto and aided by indigenous allies, crossed the Urubamba River, they must have learned that Titu Cusi Yupanqui was dead and that the title of Inca had passed to the third and last son of Manco Inca, Tupac Amaru.

Among Hurtado de Arbieto's troops were many men who were the sons of Spanish men and noble Andean women and who could trace their lineages back to rulers before the Spanish invasion. The aid of these mestizos was critical to the fall of Vilcabamba, and many personally benefited by the elimination of their cousins. Many members of the Cañari and Chachapoya ethnic groups were also among those who entered the Vilcabamba region. Later Toledo granted these groups a tax-exemption status because of the important role they had played in the fall of Vilcabamba.

FIGURE 1.5. *The site of Huayna Pucará (now called Tambo) is situated on top of a narrow ridge. Note the narrow curving trail along the slope of the ridge. Photograph by Brian S. Bauer and Miriam Aráoz Silva.*

Fighting a number of skirmishes, the Spaniards soon took the town of Vitcos and then pushed on to Pampaconas. There Hurtado de Arbieto's troops rested and were reinforced by those of Arias de Sotelo, who had entered the region via another route. The combined force then pushed on toward the town of Vilcabamba. As had occurred many years earlier at the time of Gonzalo Pizarro's raid into the region, the Incas took a stand at the hilltop site of Huayna Pucará (figure 1.5), hoping to ambush the Spaniards. This time, however, their position was revealed by an informant who may well have remembered, or had been told of, the battle that had occurred along that same trail in 1538.

On 24 June 1572 several hundred Spaniards and their Andean allies stormed the last Inca stronghold of Vilcabamba.[25] One of the first to enter the town was Pedro Sarmiento de Gamboa, who planted a flag in the central plaza, claiming the town for Spain. However, as the Spaniards occupied the final capital of the Inca, they found it in ruins; still smoldering from fires lit the night before.[26] The royal court and the townspeople had abandoned the settlement, set it on fire, and fled into the surrounding mountains in an attempt to escape the invaders. The inhabitants no doubt hoped that the Spaniards would soon leave the area, as they had under Gonzalo Pizarro when his troops eventually ran low on supplies.

Three days after taking the town of Vilcabamba, Hurtado de Arbieto wrote a short field report to Viceroy Toledo, detailing the events that had occurred since their entrance into Vilcabamba. News of the victory traveled fast, and only a few days later Toledo wrote a letter in which he named Hurtado de Arbieto the governor, captain general, and royal justice of the newly won region.[27] In a second letter, written the next day, Toledo detailed the extent of Hurtado do Arbieto's new powers. Both of the letters arrived in Vilcabamba a week later, and Hurtado de Arbieto immediately held a meeting in Vilcabamba's plaza on 8 August to announce his governorship of the region (Maúrtua 1906: 199–204, 218–219).[28]

The Spaniards occupied the settlement of Vilcabamba for about two months as they sent search parties in different directions looking for the leaders of the resistance. Within a short time, the Spaniards hunted down and captured most of the important members of the royal court. Then Martín García Oñaz de Loyola was selected to pursue Tupac Amaru and his uncle (Huallpa Yupanqui), who had escaped by fleeing down the Urubamba River toward the remote settlement of Momorí. When García Óñaz de Loyola reached Momorí, he learned that the Incas had left the river and were attempting to travel overland to the territory of the Pilcosuni. The next day, García Óñaz de Loyola captured Huallpa Yupanqui. Traveling with his pregnant wife, Tupac Amaru also moved slowly, and eventually García Óñaz de Loyola came upon the lone pair in a clearing in the jungle. The exhausted royal couple, not wishing to take their chances in this remote region, surrendered to the Spaniards.

Following the capture of Tupac Amaru, Hurtado de Arbieto and his forces left the scorched Inca city and moved with their prisoners toward Cuzco (figure 1.6). They stopped near the modern settlement of Hoyara to establish a new Spanish town that they named San Francisco de la Victoria de Vilcabamba. Hurtado de Arbieto then stayed in the Vilcabamba region while García Oñaz de Loyola returned to Cuzco with the prisoners (figure 1.7). Several of the leading Incas were killed on their arrival in Cuzco, while Tupac Amaru underwent a hasty trial. The last of Manco Inca's sons, Tupac Amaru was beheaded in the central plaza of Cuzco on the orders of Viceroy Toledo on 24 September 1572, just three days after arriving in Cuzco. That same day, as a reward for capturing Tupac Amaru, Toledo signed a decree

FIGURE I.6. *Martín García Oñaz de Loyola leading the captured Tupac Amaru. A second Spaniard holds the golden sun idol, Punchao (Daylight). Drawing by Guaman Poma de Ayala ([ca. 1615] 1980, vol. 2: 449 [451]).*

FIGURE 1.7. *The execution of Tupac Amaru. Drawing by Guaman Poma de Ayala ([ca. 1615] 1980, vol. 2: 451 [453]).*

allowing García Oñaz de Loyola to marry Beatriz Clara Coya, the last of the noble Inca bloodline (Maúrtua 1906: 65–67). The marriage gave García Oñaz de Loyola access to the Yucay landholdings, which had been at the center of the peace negotiations with the Incas, and in many ways marks the end of independent indigenous rule in the Andes.

NOTES

1. Parts of this introduction also appear in Bauer, Fonseca Santa Cruz, and Aráoz Silva (2015).

2. There are many insightful books describing the collapse of the Inca Empire from the arrival of the first Europeans to the invasion of Vilcabamba. The highest level of scholarship has been set by John Hemming (1970) in his book *The Conquest of the Incas*. Other important books and articles have been produced by Guillén Guillén (1994), Nowack (2004), Nowack and Julien (1999), and Lee (2000), to name a few.

3. Diego de Almagro was a partner, and later a rival, of Francisco Pizarro in the invasion of Peru. He was captured in the battle of Las Salinas, outside Cuzco, and soon executed under the orders of Hernando Pizarro in 1538. In 1541 loyalists to Diego de Almagro's son (Diego de Almagro, the younger) killed Francisco Pizarro. This revolt came to an end in 1542, when the son was defeated in the Battle of Chapas and subsequently executed.

4. Oñate died in 1542 during the failed revolt of Diego de Almagro (the younger).

5. Another battle took place at Huayna Pucará when the Spaniards entered the Vilcabamba region in 1572.

6. It is possible that the Spaniards visited the Inca town of Vilcabamba during this period.

7. A throwing game similar to horseshoes.

8. This little known Inca regent, named Atoc Supa, is mentioned by both Murúa and Titu Cusi Yupanqui ([1570] 2005: 125) as an adviser to Manco Inca. He is also mentioned in testimonies by Felipe Pomaunga and Francisco Condorpuri concerning the death of Diego Ortiz (Bauer et al. 2014).

9. *Encomiendas* were large landholdings given to Spaniards by the crown as rewards for their services. After 1548 many of these were reconfigured into smaller land units that were called *repartimientos*.

10. After the Spanish invasion, the Yucay *encomienda* was taken by Francisco Pizarro, and it was later passed down to his two sons. It was subsequently claimed by Francisco Hernández Girón; however, upon his death the Yucay *encomienda* returned to crown control. The crown then gave it to Sayri Tupac in return for his abdication.

11. Cusi Huarcay survived her husband/brother for many years and was an important political voice in Cuzco.

12. Court cases and legal disputes over the Yucay estate lasted for generations (see Covey and Amado González 2008). Clara Coya's inheritance rights became the focus of the Acobamba treaty negotiations between Titu Cusi Yupanqui and the Spaniards (Nowack 2004; Guillén Guillén 1977a).

13. A child of European and Native American descent.

14. Juan de Betanzos was no doubt asked to go since he had played a critical role in convincing Sayri Tupac to leave Vilcabamba. Betanzos is also the well-known author of a chronicle titled *Narrative of the Incas* (Betanzos [1557] 1996). This work ends on the eve of Betanzos's departure for Vilcabamba.

15. These trips were complicated by the death of a viceroy and the need to restart the negations afterward (Hemming 1970: 291–292).

16. Several interesting documents have survived from this meeting (see Rodríguez de Figueroa [1565] 1910, [1565] 1913; Titu Cusi Yupanqui 1916a; Lohmann Villena 1941; Julien 2006).

17. Also spelled as Gurancalla and Arangalla.

18. Gonzalo Pérez de Vivero and Atilano de Anaya, who was at that time the guardian of Titu Cusi Yupanqui's niece Beatriz Clara Coya, also made the journey (Hemming 1970: 309).

19. Also spelled Puquihura.

20. Martín Pando was first sent to Vilcabamba in 1557, under the direction of Polo de Ondegrado (Guillén Guillén 1979). Both literate and fluent in Quechua, Pando continued to survive as the secretary to the Inca and as an important intermediate between the Incas of Vilcabamba and the Spaniards in Cuzco until his death in 1570. Long after the fall of Vilcabamba, Pando's wife, Juana Guerrero, provided information on the events that occurred in the town of Vilcabamba and the subsequent burning of the Yurak Rumi shrine (Bauer, Aráoz Silva, and Burr 2012; Bauer et al. 2014; Bauer, Fonseca Santa Cruz, and Aráoz Silva 2015).

21. Yurak Rumi, the largest and most important shrine of the Vilcabamba region, is less than an hour's walk from Puquiura. There is no doubt that the priests would have known about this prominent shrine long before their return from Vilcabamba. Thus, the burning of the shrine may have been motivated by the Augustinians' unsuccessful, and perhaps humiliating, trip to Vilcabamba. The burning of the shrine is recounted in Angelina Llacsa Chuqui's 25 January 1595 testimony (Bauer et al. 2014). For archaeological information on the destruction of Yurak Rumi, see Bauer, Aráoz Silva, and Burr (2012).

22. The settlement of Vitcos is located on a low ridge, and the village of Puquiura is situated at the base of the same ridge.

23. It is not surprising that the foreigners were suspected of poisoning the Inca. Titu Cusi Yupanqui's brother, Sayri Tupac, had mysteriously died while in Spanish-controlled Cuzco in 1560, and his father, Manco Inca, was assassinated by Spaniards in the town of Vitcos in 1544. Titu Cusi Yupanqui's grandfather, Atahualpa, had also been killed by the Spaniards in 1532.

24. Also written as Marcabay.

25. The Spanish entered the Inca city of Vilcabamba on the day of John the Baptist (24 June). Accordingly, San Juan was selected as the city's patron saint. He continues to be the patron saint of the modern settlement of Espíritu Pampa.

26. Currently the archaeological remains of the Inca town of Vilcabamba are called Espíritu Pampa.

27. For a comprehensive overview of postcolonial events in Vilcabamba, using many of the same documents that are reviewed in this work, see Regalado de Hurtado (1992).

28. Witnesses to this act included Juan de Ortega, Gaspar de Córdova Moreno, Juan Alvárez Maldonado, Antonio de Gatos, Simón Domínguez, Diego Galo, Luis Arias, Pedro de Orúe, and Father Diego Escudero (Maúrtua 1906: 219–220).

2

For most students of Inca studies, the history of the Vilcabamba region ends with the 1572 Spanish-led raid into the region and the subsequent capture and execution of the Inca ruler Tupac Amaru. In contrast, this chapter examines the Spanish colonization of the Vilcabamba region from 1572 to 1600. To discuss this period, we focus largely on the life of Martín Hurtado de Arbieto, who was named governor of Vilcabamba by Viceroy Francisco de Toledo. Hurtado de Arbieto's major achievement as governor of Vilcabamba was the founding of the town of San Francisco de la Victoria de Vilcabamba. However, his governorship also included disastrous expeditions down the Urubamba and the Apurímac Rivers.

HURTADO DE ARBIETO AND THE GOVERNORSHIP OF VILCABAMBA

As governor, captain general, and royal justice of Vilcabamba, Hurtado de Arbieto held sweeping powers. For example, he was to appoint all the lower officials needed to rule the newly won territory.[1] He was also authorized to collect tribute—in the form of taxes—from the indigenous people. Furthermore, he was instructed to establish a new town in the region and to give land and labor grants to other Spaniards who wished to settle in the area. Toledo writes:

> You will also give and assign house lots, lands, *chacras* (fields), orchards, high pasture lands, stables, and

DOI: 10.5876/9781607324263.c002

other properties to the persons that take part with you in this expedition and rule, as well as to the others that may go and live there, helping you with its conquest, settlement and maintenance. [You will do this] according to your will, depending on how [much] you think each [person] deserves and what is most convenient to serve God, our lord, and His Majesty. (Maúrtua 1906: 202; authors' translation)

The governorship of Vilcabamba came with an annual salary of 2,000 pesos, paid from the royal treasury in Cuzco. In turn, Hurtado de Arbieto was obligated to defend and watch over the natives and to provide for two priests.[2] The governorship was granted for two lifetimes: that of Hurtado de Arbieto's and that of his son, Juan. Toledo, ever the mindful administrator, notes in his letters to Hurtado de Arbieto that the appointment would have to be approved by the king, a process that he indicated would take three to six years (Maúrtua 1906: 201), and that in the meantime his actions would be evaluated. Hurtado de Arbieto's rule seems to have met with the viceroy's approval, as several years later, writing on 3 November 1575 while in the town of Quilca, the viceroy increased Hurtado de Arbieto's annual salary by 1,000 pesos from the *repartimento* of Tina (Toledo [1575] 1899g).[3] Then on the next day, writing from Arequipa, Toledo filed the paperwork necessary for the permanent appointment of Hurtado de Arbieto as governor of Vilcabamba (Maúrtua 1906: 207–213).

THE BRIEF OCCUPATION OF SAN JUAN DE VILCABAMBA

Since the Inca settlement of Vilcabamba marked the edge of Spanish-controlled territory in the lowlands and there were many hostile groups within the surrounding areas, Hurtado de Arbieto felt that a small garrison of men should remain in the settlement to establish an outpost.[4] On 4 September 1572, Hurtado de Arbieto selected Francisco de Camargo y Aguilar[5] to serve as the mayor of what was briefly called San Juan de Vilcabamba. The office was granted for two lifetimes and included an annual salary of 1,000 pesos. While this initially may have seemed a favorable position to hold, within a year Camargo y Aguilar was petitioning that his salary did not cover the basic costs of the office (Maúrtua 1906: 81). Claiming that the occupation of Vilcabamba required a large amount of work and that items had to be brought in from Cuzco at a considerable expense, Camargo y Aguilar pleaded with Cuzco officials for a raise in his annual salary (Maúrtua 1906: 71–98).[6] The occupation of the Inca city does not appear to have lasted much longer, as Toledo signed a document on 25 September 1575 granting Francisco de Camargo y Aguilar's request for funds to support missionary work in San Francisco de la Victoria de Vilcabamba (Toledo [1575] 1899c). It is possible that Camargo y Aguilar had already given up his position in the Inca city and returned to the newly established Spanish town.

THE FOUNDING OF SAN FRANCISCO DE LA VICTORIA DE VILCABAMBA

After the capture of Tupac Amaru, Hurtado de Arbieto established a new Spanish town, called San Francisco de la Victoria de Vilcabamba, near the modern settlement of Hoyara.[7] Baltasar de Ocampo Conejeros, a longtime resident of the area, describes its founding:

> After capturing the Inca and his captains and Indians, taking them well guarded and in an orderly manner, [the Spanish army] returned to the Hoyara Valley. There they settled the Indians in a large town and they founded a Spanish city [that they] named San Francisco de la Victoria de Vilcabamba.... This city was founded on a very large plain with a marvelous climate, next to a river, [from] where they dug canals for the service of the city. The water from the river is particularly sweet because it passes through gold ore. (Ocampo Conejeros [1611] 2013: 35–36; authors' translation)

The town of San Francisco de la Victoria de Vilcabamba was built in a rich agricultural region, at an elevation of approximately 2,000 meters, in the Vitcos Valley.[8] It was located about midway between the former Inca stronghold of Vitcos and the bridge of Chuquichaca (figure 2.1). According to Ocampo, Hurtado de Arbieto used his newly established powers not only to found the city but also to divide the region's 1,500 natives among its Spanish citizens: "After General Martín Hurtado de Arbieto delineated the limits of the [new Spanish] city and began building the foundations for the city, he named the citizens who would be *encomenderos*. He distributed among these more than 1,500 Indians for personal service until Lord Don Francisco de Toledo intervened" (Ocampo Conejeros [1611] 2013: 37; authors' translation).

Hurtado de Arbieto remained in the town of San Francisco de la Victoria de Vilcabamba while Martín García Óñaz de Loyola returned to Cuzco with the captives and the loot from the raid, which included the golden sun idol Punchao (Daylight), a lesser known idol called Pachamama (Earth Mother), as well as the mummies of Manco Inca and Titu Cusi Yupanqui (Toledo [1575] 1899g).

About a month later (15 October 1572), Toledo sent Hurtado de Arbieto additional instructions detailing how the pacification of the Vilcabamba region should take place (Maúrtua 1906: 205–207). By that time, Tupac Amaru

FIGURE 2.1. *The modern settlement of Hoyara. The first Spanish town in the Vilcabamba region was established near this community. Photograph by Brian S. Bauer and Miriam Aráoz Silva.*

had already been executed in Cuzco, and Toledo had left the city and was on his way to Lake Titicaca. Stopping for several days in the town of Checacupe, Toledo instructed Hurtado de Arbieto to work slowly and with great care for the general welfare of the inhabitants of the region. Understanding that the natives would be weakened by war, the viceroy told Hurtado de Arbieto that their tribute obligations should be light, no more than they were able to pay, "giving them time to work in their fields and things, to cloth and feed themselves and their wives, children and family" (Maúrtua 1906: 207).

Hurtado de Arbieto remained in firm control over the Vilcabamba region for many years. Later testimonies credit him with recruiting Spaniards to settle the region and covering the cost of many of the supplies needed to maintain the settlement (Maúrtua 1906: 267–281). He was also successful in petitioning the viceroy to provide stipends for some of the veterans of the Vilcabamba war who remained in the region to help secure what was then the crown's frontier. For example, writing from Arequipa on 20 October 1575, Toledo ([1575] 1899d) responded to a request by Hurtado de Arbieto and committed a total of 800 pesos to be given annually to Juan de Ortega (250 pesos), Juan de Arbieto (250 pesos), Alonso Juárez (200 pesos), and Francisco Pérez Fonseca (100 pesos).[9]

The Mercederian Order was interested in working in the Vilcabamba area, and on 21 July 1576 Toledo ([1576] 1899e) tried to encourage priests to work in the region by ordering the royal treasury of Cuzco to pay a salary of 600 pesos per year to two priests (Mercederian or from any other order) to reside in and indoctrinate the people of the region. As governor, Hurtado de Arbieto also played a large role in supporting the church. Under the initial terms of his governorship, he agreed to support two priests in the region. Furthermore, during the construction of the local church he oversaw the gathering of stones and the making of adobes, and he personally provided the roof tiles. Furthermore, he gave an altar cloth embroidered with gold, tablecloths, a silver lamp, and a silver tabernacle to the church when it was completed (Maúrtua 1906: 268, 272, 277).

Hurtado de Arbieto's time in office was not, however, without controversies, and there was at least one period during which he appears to have been under the close watch of the viceroy. This is suggested by a stern letter written on 13 January 1580 in which Toledo states that since Hurtado de Arbieto has left the province without his permission, Hurtado de Arbieto is not to be awarded his salary unless he can prove when he was present in the province (Toledo [1580] 1899f).

THE RESETTLEMENT OF SAN FRANCISCO DE LA VICTORIA DE VILCABAMBA

Sometime during the term of Viceroy Luis de Velasco (1596–1604), perhaps around 1596, the city of San Francisco de la Victoria de Vilcabamba was moved from its original location near Hoyara to a higher (3,450 meters), somewhat marshy valley, which the Incas called Oncoy but the Spaniards had renamed Villa Rica de Argete.[10] Although the area was agriculturally less productive, the new settlement was located closer to the mineral deposits that were becoming increasingly important for the region. Ocampo, who was a citizen of Vilcabamba at the time of the resettlement, provides details on the move:

> In consideration of the rich silver mines that were discovered in the hills of Huamani and Huamanate, this city was [later] relocated from where it was [originally founded] to the small town of Villa Rica de Argete in order to be close to the mines. . . . In this council meeting it was decided that they would

FIGURE 2.2. *The colonial church at San Francisco de la Victoria de Vilcabamba, 1983. Photograph courtesy of David Drew.*

send a Procurator General to ask for permission and consent from Lord Don Luis de Velasco, who was viceroy of the kingdom at the time. For this negotiation, I, Baltasar de Ocampo was named as the Procurator, and I came to this city and I met with the Lord Viceroy. [Changing the location of the town] appeared to be an action beneficial to the service of our Lord God and His Majesty, raising the royal taxes, and advantageous for the citizens and inhabitants of the city. Having examined, addressed and consulted the stipulations and justification provided for moving it, the Lord Don Luis de Velasco gave his approval and authorization [for the city to] move to the place where it is now. He ordered that [the new settlement] should be given the [same] title and name of the original settlement, San Francisco de la Victoria de Vilcabamba. (Ocampo Conejeros [1611] 2013: 36; authors' translation)

When the governorship was first established in the Vilcabamba region in the town of San Francisco de la Victoria de Vilcabamba (a.k.a. Hoyara), Martín Hurtado de Arbieto played a major role in the construction of its first church. With the relocation of the township, another church had to be built (figures 2.2 and 2.3). This project appears to have been organized by Ocampo, who writes:

FIGURE 2.3. *The interior of the restored church in Vilcabamba de la Victoria, 2009. Photograph by Brian S. Bauer and Miriam Aráoz Silva.*

In this move, I, Baltasar de Ocampo, did a great service to God, our lord, and to Your Majesty because, as a result of my labor, requests and care, a very good, large church was built with a main chapel and large doors. [This was necessary] because there was [only] one small chapel in the whole town, where one could not fit more than just the citizens and miners. The *mita* [forced rotational labor] Indians had to stand outside [exposed to] the sun and water when it rained. (Ocampo Conejeros [1611] 2013: 37; authors' translation)

The town of San Francisco de la Victoria de Vilcabamba reached its maximum population during the early colonial era, when it served as the mining center for the Vilcabamba region. It then experienced a gradual depopulation, as much of the mineral wealth of the region was exhausted. Its position remains marked on numerous maps produced in the 1700s and 1800s; however, its importance lapsed as Quillabamba (Santa Ana) slowly emerged as the center of wealth in the region.

HURTADO DE ARBIETO AND HIS
CAMPAIGNS BEYOND VILCABAMBA

San Francisco de la Victoria de Vilcabamba served as a center for religious conversions as well as the point of contact between the Spaniards and the tribal groups located in the interior. For example, one of the leaders of the Manarí, Alonso Guanenciue,[11] came to the city, along with his wife and brother, to be baptized. Likewise, a leader named Sanarua,[12] from the area of Momorí, came to request that priests visit his tribe, and a leader of the Pilcosuni, named Quinonte, also visited the town (Maúrtua 1906: 269, 273, 278–279).

Nevertheless, during the approximately sixteen years that Hurtado de Arbieto held power in Vilcabamba, he led several organized raids against different Amazonian groups in the surrounding territories. The incursions were authorized by Viceroy Toledo, who himself had barely survived an ill-fated attempt to conquer the Chiriguanos in what is now northwestern Argentina. Writing to the king of Spain from Arequipa on 4 November 1575, Hurtado de Arbieto and Toledo optimistically suggested that Hurtado de Arbieto had already pacified a number of groups beyond Vilcabamba, including the Guanucomarca,[13] Manarí, Pilcosuni and Momorí (Maúrtua 1906: 207–213). However, Hurtado de Arbieto was well aware of Juan Alvárez Maldonado's failed expedition into the Madre de Dios region (1556–1560), and he did not want to undertake a similar journey without a large number of men and supplies (Maúrtua 1906: 274, 280).

While contact with some of these groups began before the Spanish gained control of Vilcabamba, large-scale expeditions into their territories did not take place for several more years. When they did occur, it is difficult to describe the expeditions as anything other than military and financial failures.[14] Acosta, writing in 1590, summarizes the hardships that were endured in these lowland expeditions in general: "And did not the flower of Peru, with such quantities of arms and people as we witnessed, go against the Chunchos and Chiriguanos and Pilcosuni? What happened? With what victory did they return? They returned happy to have escaped with their lives, almost all of them having lost their equipment and horses. Let no one believe that by saying Indians, he means weak men; if he does, let him go and find out" (Acosta [1590] 2002: 446–447).

Information on Spanish contact with the indigenous groups that occupied the peripheries of Vilcabamba is provided in a set of testimonies dating to 1579 in which Hurtado de Arbieto and others recount the accomplishments that occurred in the province since he took power (Maúrtua 1906: 266–281).[15] Additional references to the largest raids against the Pilcosuni and other neighboring tribes are recorded in a series of interviews that took place in 1590 concerning Hurtado de Arbieto's governorship (Maúrtua 1906: 227–260).[16] Other details are offered in additional documents produced by Juan Hurtado as he was attempting to inherit his father's position and in a 1611 account written by Baltasar de Ocampo Conejeros to the Viceroy Mendoza (see document 2, this volume). While there is a great deal of overlapping information in these sources, they each contain unique details and together offer a compelling narrative of these otherwise poorly documented excursions.[17]

The Manarí were among the most important of the tribal groups contacted by Hurtado de Arbieto. They are described by several early colonial writers involved in the Vilcabamba campaigns as a large native group living in the vast tropical region east of Quillabamba along the lower Urubamba. They are said to have been brought under Inca rule during the campaigns of Tupa Inca Yupanqui (Sarmiento de Gamboa [1572] 2007: 41, 159), although how much control the highland state actually imposed on any lowland group is questionable.

The Spaniards and the Manarí began negotiations even before the Europeans entered the Vilcabamba region. On 20 September 1571 Alonso Chiri, the leader of two large Manarí towns, Catinte[18] and Cáyar, met with Father Santa Cruz and a representative of Viceroy Toledo (Maúrtua 1906: 1–2). This early meeting, which resulted in the Manarí recognizing Spanish rule, may explain the largely neutral role that the Manarí held in García Oñaz de Loyola's hunt for Tupac Amaru across their territory the following year.

There was frequent contact between the Manarí and the Spaniards in the decade following the fall of Vilcabamba. Various Manarí visited the town of San Francisco de la Victoria de Vilcabamba, and different Spaniards traveled into Manarí territory. For example, Hurtado de Arbieto and his fellow compatriots stated that peaceful relations had been established with the Manarí when Alonso Juárez, accompanied by an Inca captain, Luis Chuimasa,[19] were sent into their region sometime before 1575 (Maúrtua 1906: 268–269, 272, 277–278). Under Juárez's leadership, a principal lord of the Manarí named Timana and his wife, Biri, subsequently came to San Francisco de la Victoria de Vilcabamba to be baptized and married.[20] The lowlanders then returned to their villages, accompanied by several Spaniards,[21] who built at least one church in the area (Maúrtua 1906: 125, 268). Ocampo describes this early encounter between the Spaniards and the Manarí:

They gave [the Spaniards] much food: tapirs, peccaries (whose navels are on their backs), turkeys, ducks, and other game and a great quantity of river fish (i.e., shad), [as well as] yuca [cassava], peanuts, toasted and boiled corn, and many delicious fruits of these lands, especially [fruit] from their many orchards, including avocados, guavas, pacays, and a great quantity of almonds, much larger and better than those of Castile, and cacao.

The Indians showed themselves to be so affable and friendly, that the four Spaniards brought an image of Our Lady painted on a canvas. To entrust themselves to God, the soldiers instructed the Indians to construct a small chapel, which they built, where they hung her image. [They also erected] a large cross outside of the chapel on a stone pedestal and other small crosses inside the chapel. [The Spaniards] went to pray there each morning and [pledged] to commend themselves to God. They did the same in the afternoons. Seeing this devotion, the Indians went to the chapel to pray; kneeling and raising their hands towards the sky, they [then] struck their chests. With this the Spaniards rejoiced; seeing them so friendly and desirous of being Christian. (Ocampo Conejeros [1611] 2013: 46; authors' translation)

Later the Spaniards convinced another important Manarí, named Guarin-quirabe,[22] and some ten other leaders as well as more than fifty villagers to visit Cuzco (Maúrtua 1906: 268–269, 272, 278). While in Cuzco, they visited the churches and monasteries and were treated to a range of food and clothing. The same was done with other leaders of the Manarí, including a local leader named Luis Saco (Maúrtua 1906: 269, 272–273). As a result of this alliance, the Manarí offered to help the Spaniards in raids against the Pilcosuni and the even more remote Asháninka.[23]

THE FIRST RAID AGAINST THE PILCOSUNI (1582)

The Pilcosuni were an especially feared lowland group concentrated near the junction of the Apurímac and Mantaro Rivers.[24] Despite their remote location, the Pilcosuni had relatively early contact with the Spaniards.[25] For example, in November of 1568 some thirty Pilcosuni entered the Vilcabamba region and met with the Jesuit priest Marcos Garcia[26] to express their willingness to give up the worship of *huacas* (shrines) and convert to Christianity.[27] A short time later, writing from the village of Pampaconas to Juan de Vivero, the prior of the Augustinian monastery in Cuzco, Titu Cusi Yupanqui noted that other aspects of Pilcosuni culture would need to change as well: "[The Pilcosuni] have only one fault, and that is that they eat human flesh. When an *aule* [relative?][28] dies, they make a *chicha* to eat the flesh of the dead, and they burn the bones and finely grind them to drink with the *chicha*. This ceremony that they have is very easily ended" (Titu Cusi Yupanqui 1916b: 122; authors' translation).

Much later, in 1582, Hurtado de Arbieto requested permission from Viceroy Enríquez de Almanza to attempt a conquest of the Pilcosuni.[29] The apparent plan was to travel down the Urubamba River to Momorí and then cross overland to enter Pilcosuni territory. Hurtado de Arbieto's forces included some fifty to seventy Spaniards,[30] two Jesuit priests,[31] a Jesuit brother, and an unspecified number of natives, blacks, mestizos, and mulatos.[32] Hurtado de Arbieto covered the cost of the expedition, offering varying sums to recruit solders and paying off the debts of others.[33] He also provided the arms, footwear, clothing, munitions, food (including corn flour, biscuits, ham, lard, and beef jerky), and all the other supplies required to maintain the troops. Hurtado de Arbieto even bought the materials needed by the priests for the journey.[34]

The expedition began with Hurtado de Arbieto's troops traveling from San Francisco de la Victoria de Vilcabamba to Quillabamba, where they spent several weeks preparing for the river journey. They entered the Urubamba River on 2 August in a large group of canoes and rafts. The first day of the passage did not go well. Within less than a league, three rafts overturned in the rapids and several other vessels were damaged. The expedition fared no better during the rest of the week. On the second day, two boats were damaged and their contents lost. Three more rafts broke up on the rapids during the third and fourth days. A Spaniard named Miguel de Andueza drowned when his canoe hit a boulder in the river, and other members of the expedition survived only by clinging onto debris and floating to safety. In less than a week from having left Quillabamba, the expedition had lost much of its supplies and had advanced only a few leagues.

Following these ills on the river, Hurtado de Arbieto ordered his troops to continue on foot, but their advancement was hindered by nearly continuous rain. After sending some villagers back to Vilcabamba for fresh supplies and reinforcements, the men continued cutting a trail through the difficult terrain for several more days. Ocampo, who had been recruited by Hurtado de Arbieto to take part in the expedition, tells of the difficult conditions: "[W]e convened a war council, and it was agreed that we would make a path through the mountains using our axes and machetes. [We] suffered from great hunger, exposure and cold, getting stuck on tree branches that shredded our clothing. We were left without any covering and in need of food, as this is an uninhabited land without paths to travel along" (Ocampo Conejeros [1611] 2013: 48; authors' translation). The troops then stopped at a place called Yuqua for several weeks to build new rafts.[35] When the rafts were finished, the troops continued downriver for a few more days, even though a reconnaissance group headed by Juan de Plata reported that there was no end in sight to the rapids.

The sick, starving, and disabled party stopped on 18 September at what they called the port of the Simaponte River. Exhausted by the terrain and fearing that they would drown if they continued by boat, the beleaguered troops petitioned Hurtado de Arbieto to return to Vilcabamba. Having lost the majority of his boats as well as nearly all of his food and equipment, Hurtado de Arbieto agreed to end the ill-fated trek. When he began the long journey back to Vilcabamba, he ordered a few Spaniards, accompanied by a small group of natives, to continue explorations and to reestablish contact with the Manarí. Miraculously, these men arrived back in San Francisco de la Victoria de Vilcabamba some eight to twelve months later, accompanied by forty to fifty Manarí who were willing to continue the campaign against the Pilcosuni.

THE SECOND RAID AGAINST THE PILCOSUNI (1583)

Within a year of his failed trip down the Urubamba River, Hurtado de Arbieto decided to enter the area of the Pilcosuni by traveling down the Apurímac River. Knowing that he needed additional troops, he gathered a range of soldiers from Potosí, Cuzco, and elsewhere. As in his earlier expedition, he used his own personal wealth to supply the troops on the Apurímac expedition.[36]

Hurtado de Arbieto's company again consisted of some 50 to 75 Spaniards and perhaps as many as 150 natives. Among the participants were the 40-odd Manarí who had recently arrived in the Vilcabamba region. The same three Jesuits who had been involved in the failed Urubamba expedition also participated. Using both horses and llamas provided by Hurtado de Arbieto, the troops first traveled from San Francisco de la Victoria to the Apurímac River, where they built about thirty log rafts and various canoes. The expeditionary force then traveled some 120 leagues downriver under difficult conditions. Several members, including a Spaniard, a native, and one of the four black slaves that the governor had brought to serve him, drowned during the voyage.

The forces left the river at the first sign of a Pilcosuni village. Having established relations with the local Pilcosuni through gift-giving, the Spaniards then claimed the territory in the name of the king. As they attempted to introduce the Christian faith, the Spaniards also promised the Pilcosuni protection from the nearby Asháninka.

Hurtado de Arbieto and his forces then pressed further into Pilcosuni territory and constructed a fortified community called Jesús.[37] Peaceful relations between the Spaniards and the natives existed for more than six months, during which the foreigners planted crops and continued to build structures within the palisade. The fragile peace was, however, broken when the Pilcosuni killed four Spaniards and ten to twelve natives who were on a reconnaissance trip. This event was certainly emotional for Hurtado de Arbieto because one of the fallen Spaniards was his son-in-law, Francisco de Mariaca (Maúrtua 1906).[38]

The source of the discontent is unknown, but it seems that the Pilcosuni continued to gather warriors, and two months later, in the early morning of 24 November 1583, from 300 to 500 Pilcosuni, armed with bows, arrows, darts, and clubs, attacked the Spanish outpost. The inhabitants of the town of Jesús were poorly equipped for the battle since some thirty were already ill with fever. The Pilcosuni burned the town, including the church, with flaming arrows wrapped with cotton, and only three of the twenty-odd structures within the settlement remained intact. The height of the battle is described in the 1590 testimony of Esteban Pérez:

> The armed Governor, with the soldiers and people that he had, fought with their harquebuses and weapons doing all that was possible. In that battle, which lasted more than four hours, the Governor received seven wounds, six in his face and one in his right arm. Eighteen other soldiers and some allied Indians were also wounded. And when the Indian enemies saw that the Governor was injured they started to shout loudly in their language "*ya Apu guanu*," which in Spanish means "the Governor has already died." In this way, the Indians would be inspired to fight. Noticing this and that he was bathed in blood from his wounds, the Governor asked this witness [i.e., Esteban Pérez] if I had some flour or other things to cover the blood, so that the Indians could not see it and get encouraged. This witness went to a hearth and scooped up a handful of ashes which he used to cover the [governor's] blood. Having done this the battle ended. Since the Indians noticed that they were winning nothing, they ran and escaped, leaving the houses as well as a large pit, which was full of food and provisions for the Governor and his people, burning. (Maúrtua 1906: 230; authors' translation)

With their town burned and many of their men badly wounded, Hurtado de Arbieto's troops retreated from Pilcosuni territory to the city of Huamanga.[39] Eventually Hurtado de Arbieto traveled to the Yucay Valley, near Cuzco, where he spent many weeks recovering from his wounds. More than one witness noted that Hurtado de Arbieto still had arrowheads, made from black palms, embedded in him when he arrived in Yucay. Nevertheless, he survived his wounds and was able to maintain his governorship over the Vilcabamba region until his death in Lima six years later.

THE DEATH OF MARTÍN HURTADO DE ARBIETO AND THE LITIGATION FOR THE GOVERNORSHIP OF VILCABAMBA

During his years in power, Hurtado de Arbieto proved to be an ineffective overseer of the Vilcabamba province. His two failed expeditions against the Pilcosuni cost him dearly, with estimates ranging as high as 80,000 pesos, and may have left his wife and six children in debt. Hurtado de Arbieto borrowed at least 30,000 pesos from his son-in-law Diego de Gamarra, further reducing the wealth of the extended family. These financial misadventures may have increased Hurtado de Arbieto's desire to squeeze more income from the indigenous inhabitants of the region.

Complaints against Hurtado de Arbieto as an inept administrator slowly mounted, and an investigation was begun by Viceroy Fernando de Torres y Portugal (1584–1589). Antonio Pereyra was placed in charge, and he traveled into the Vilcabamba province in 1588 (Levillier 1925, II: 68). Pereyra, Portuguese by birth, was an interesting choice as inspector for the crown since he had served under Hurtado de Arbieto in the Vilcabamba campaign and was personally responsible for the capture of several important Inca generals and high nobility. Like many prominent Spaniards, Pereyra was also the holder of several *encomiendas* and understood how to manage large territories (Cook 1975). Pereyra's investigation indicated that the administration of the Vilcabamba province was in complete disorder and suggested a long history of misconduct. The allegations filed by Pereyra against Hurtado de Arbieto included excessive taxes, the personal use of native labor, and the failure to collect the king's fifth from the silver mines of the region. Hurtado de Arbieto may have been especially abusive in his relations with the natives.[40] For example, the inspection revealed:

> . . . so he could personally be better served by the Indians as well as to keep them better under control, the Governor had the bridge, which was the only entrance to that province, closed with guards so that no Indians could run away. All of them personally served their *encomenderos* in sugar and ore mills, disgraced and exploited, as if they were slaves. Many Indians frequently died or were disabled during this very dangerous work. (Maúrtua 1906: 182; authors' translation)·

Surprisingly, Pereyra also suggested that Hurtado de Arbieto did not play a critical role in the conquest of the Vilcabamba region and failed to expand the reach of the crown into the surrounding regions.[41]

Working from Pereyra's report, the viceroy reported Hurtado de Arbieto's offensive practices and questionable rights-of-conquest to the king in a letter written on 12 May 1589. The viceroy recommended that Hurtado de

Arbieto be removed as governor for failure to comply with the official duties of the office. A year later the king addressed this issue in a letter to the newly appointed viceroy, García Hurtado de Mendoza (1590–1596), revoking Hurtado de Arbieto's governorship.

Meanwhile, Hurtado de Arbieto had objected to the charges filed against him and at first had refused to give up the governorship of Vilcabamba. He then traveled to Lima, armed with his own documents, to argue his case in the Royal Council of the Indies (Maúrtua 1906: 184). The king's order to remove Hurtado de Arbieto from office arrived in Lima too late to directly affect the Vilcabamba situation since Hurtado de Arbieto died on 12 November 1589 as his appeal was working its way through the council (Maúrtua 1906: 139).

With the death of Martín Hurtado de Arbieto, Viceroy García Hurtado de Mendoza named Antonio Luis de Cabrera as chief magistrate and justice of the Vilcabamba region. Cabrera moved quickly to implement changes in the province. For example, on 16 August 1590 the viceroy granted Cabrera permission to build a Mercedarian church in Villa Rica de Argete and to set aside agricultural land to support the expected priests (Barriga 1942: 280–281).[42]

The governorship issue was not, however, fully settled. Soon after Hurtado de Arbieto's death, his teenage son, Juan, and his widow, Juana de Ayala Ponce de León,[43] requested that the governorship be given to Juan, stating that Viceroy Toledo had originally granted the governorship for two lifetimes. Accordingly, they argued that at the time of Hurtado de Arbieto's death, the governorship should have been given to Juan.[44] In 1591 García Hurtado de Mendoza granted the governorship to Juan, with the condition that it be reconfirmed by the king in four years (Maúrtua 1906: 213–215).[45] However, Juan survived his father by only a few years and died while rights of inheritance were still under review (Maúrtua 1906: 195–290). After the death of Juan, the governorship was transferred to Pedro de Ledesma (Maúrtua 1906: 292), and the crown took full control of the Vilcabamba region.

NOTES

1. His powers were not, however, unlimited. For example, in 1582 Hurtado de Arbieto was banned from dividing the lands of Maranura while it was being determined if they fell within the jurisdiction of Cuzco or of Vilcabamba (Maúrtua 1906: 170–171).

2. According to Toledo's instructions, one of the priests was to be stationed in the newly established town, and the other was to travel across the region teaching the gospel.

3. *Repartimentos* were later forms of landholdings (*encomiendas*) granted to individual Spaniards.

4. It is logical that the troops would have occupied one of the former buildings, and archival documents suggest that Hurtado de Arbieto planned to house the garrison within the former Temple of the Sun: "For its security, it was agreed that a town would be established in Vilcabamba, which is twelve leagues from the site of Vitcos, being on the route of the Manarí Indians and other warring Indians, who usually come to the site of Vilcabamba, [and] that a fort should be made in the Houses of the Sun, and that a garrison stay there" (Maúrtua 1906: 90; authors' translation).

5. Francisco de Camargo y Aguilar served under Martín de Menses during the conquest of the Vilcabamba region. He was also among the troops who captured the Idol of the Sun after the fall of Vilcabamba and was among the men who aided García Óñaz de Loyola in capturing Tupac Amaru. The only other named resident of San Juan de Vilcabamba is Luis de Alvin (Maúrtua 1906: 80–84).

6. During his time in Vilcabamba, Camargo y Aguilar led successful negotiations with a number of indigenous leaders and neighboring groups (Maúrtua 1906: 79).

7. Bingham (1912a) reports seeing ruins near the town of Hoyara; however, these remains have been destroyed by the growth of the town.

8. The earliest city contained several blockhouses, "unas casas fuertes de mucha autoridad y seguridad, donde poca gente se pueden sustentar y prevalecer contra toda la suma de indios que de las provincias" (Maúrtua 1906: 268).

9. Earlier, on 8 June 1574, Toledo had granted Antón Álvarez 300 pesos a year for his service to the crown and for remaining in the Vilcabamba region (Toledo [1574] 1899a, [1575] 1899b).

10. Ocampo indicates that the mining settlement of Villa Rica de Argete was established during the rule of Viceroy García Hurtado de Mendoza. References to Villa Rica de Argete can be found in several other colonial-period documents (e.g., Maúrtua 1906: 226, 289; Bauer et al. 2014).

11. Also spelled Guaneuçidi.

12. Also spelled Sabara.

13. The Guanucomarca are a little-known group, mentioned in a small number of earlier colonial documents related to the Vilcabamba region (e.g., Maúrtua 1906: 267–281). They may have been first contacted by García Óñaz de Loyola during his long pursuit of Tupac Amaru. Then, sometime before 1579, an expedition of a dozen soldiers was led by the lieutenant governor of Vilcabamba, Antón de Álvarez, into Guanucomarca territory. Following the route taken by García Óñaz de Loyola, Álvarez entered the region by way of the Inca town of Vilcabamba and traveled downriver toward the modern town of Kiteni along what is now called the Cosireni River. On reaching the Urubamba River, he continued an unknown distance downriver before turning around

and returning to the town of San Francisco de la Victoria de Vilcabamba by way of the Chuquichaca Bridge. Álvarez reports that during this trip he identified some possible placer gold deposits as well as two villages occupied by the Guanucomarca (Maúrtua 1906: 271, 275–276). The Guanucomarca were later visited by Juan de Arbieto, who brought many of them back with him to San Francisco de la Victoria de Vilcabamba (Maúrtua 1906: 276, 280).

14. Other ethnic groups were located relatively near Vilcabamba, including the Paros, Satis, Sacapaqui, Simapontes, Otayvas, Pauquis, and Mapacaro. However, as spellings of the names of these groups differ greatly, their exact relationship with each other is not known (e.g., Maúrtua 1906: 79; Matienzo [1567] 1910: 193; Titu Cusi Yupanqui 1916a: 125).

15. Within these documents Francisco Pérez Fonseca states that Hurtado de Arbieto recruited many Spaniards and their families to settle in the region, including Pedro Sánchez, Andrés Gómez Marron, and Antonio Gonzáles. Vasco Gudino, a bachelor from Lima, was also convinced to settle in the region (Maúrtua 1906: 276).

16. The 1590 interviews took place in November in the town of Lucma on the 23rd (with Andrés Gómez Marrón), 24th (with Estevan Pérez), and 26th (with Toribio de Bustamante and Diego García Moreno) as well as with Martín Pérez de Aponte on 23 December in the town of San Francisco de la Victoria de Vilcabamba (Maúrtua 1906: 227–246, 254–261). In each testimony, Antonio Luis de Cabrera was the lead questioner, and Luis Garrido de Billena served as scribe.

17. Nevertheless, the exact number of expeditions, raids, and missions that were sent into the lowlands from Vilcabamba is not clear, nor are the names of the native groups with whom they came into contact. While we offer a series of dates and tribal affiliations, the data are disparate enough that other scenarios can be developed. For a similar, although not identical reading of the documents, see Regalado de Hurtado (1992).

18. Perhaps modern Kiteni.

19. Also spelled Chimaes (Maúrtua 1906: 134).

20. Timana took the name Francisco de Toledo while Biri took the name Juana de Figueroa (Maúrtua 1906: 268).

21. Alonso Juárez, Juan de Arbieto, and Alonso de la Cueva are mentioned in several testimonies (e.g., Maúrtua 1906: 268–269, 272, 278, 127–131) as being sent to contact the Manarí, while Ocampo suggests that Alonso Juárez, Antón de Álvarez, Pedro Gudiño, and one unnamed soldier entered the region. They may be describing two different events, or there may be some confusion in the names of the Spaniards involved.

22. Also spelled Guarinquiraue.

23. The Asháninka, spelled in various ways, were located further downriver from the Pilcosuni. Their name appears on early maps of the region, and they are mentioned

by various different writers, including Ocampo Conejeros ([1611] 2013) and Oricain ([1790] 2004: 73). For information on their history, see Varese (2004).

24. Also spelled Piliocuni, Pilcomu, Pillcosuni, Pilcoçone, Pilcozone.

25. The Pilcosuni are also named in various Vilcabamba-related documents (e.g., Maúrtua 1906), in letters written by Viceroy Toledo (e.g., Toledo 1906: 102), and by different chroniclers. For additional information on the Pilcosuni, see Hemming (1970: 330–331, 595) and Varese (2004: 43–49).

26. The encounter took place in the village of Carco near the Apurímac River and included Martín Pando. The leader of the Pilcosuni was Juan de Procho (Titu Cusi Yupanqui 1916b: 121–122).

27. It seems that sometime before 1575 Hurtado de Arbieto also sent several natives with gifts to the Pilcosuni, hoping to establish better relations with this more remote and less well known group (Maúrtua 1906: 269). Among the first of these messengers was an individual named Opa (or Oparo). He was followed by another person named Cayao, who traveled with a group of other lowlanders with the idea that some of them would help to settle the town of Mapacaro (Mapocoro, Mapacaso), which was located near the halfway point between the area of Vilcabamba and that of the Pilcosuni (Maúrtua 1906: 269, 273, 278).

28. The text contains the unknown term *aule*.

29. Several different dates are given for raids beyond Vilcabamba, including 1572 (Maúrtua 1906: 247), 1578 (Maúrtua 1906: 255), and 1582 and 1583 (Maúrtua 1906: 241, 283–286); as such, it is difficult to sort out what events occurred during each raid.

30. Baltasar de Ocampo Conejeros was one of the Spaniards who was recruited to participate in this raid.

31. The Jesuits included Doctor Montoya Romano, Father Pedro de Cartagena and Brother Madrid (Maúrtua 1906: 288). It seems that Montoya was included very early in the planning stages for these expeditions (Maúrtua 1906: 269, 273, 279), and he may have even already visited the region.

32. A person of mixed African and European descent.

33. For example, Diego García Moreno (Maúrtua 1906: 247) was paid 200 pesos and provided with clothing and arms.

34. A collection of documents provided in Juan Hurtado's petition to inherit his father's governorship chronicles the disastrous events that took place during this raid in unusual detail (Maúrtua 1906: 195–290).

35. They also left one raft at Yuqua to ferry down the supplies that were en route from Vilcabamba. This raft was later lost in the river because of heavy rains.

36. For example, on this trip Diego García Moreno was paid fifty pesos and provided with clothing, arms, and other things (Maúrtua 1906: 248).

37. The settlement was established in what the Spaniards called the Manylle Valley (Maúrtua 1906: 229, 249).

38. Francisco de Mariaca married Mencia de Salcedo Hurtado de Arbieto in 1582.

39. Some left via the river, while others went overland. One witness indicates that Hurtado de Arbieto would not have arrived at Huamanga had he not been helped by reinforcements headed by his brother-in-law, Juan Ponce de León (Maúrtua 1906: 242).

40. Pereyra claimed that Hurtado de Arbieto received word of the upcoming inspection and increased his demands on the Vilcabamba natives to make up for the missing crown funds (Maúrtua 1906: 182). As a response, many of the natives had fled the townships and were hiding in the mountains when the inspector arrived.

41. There is no question that Hurtado de Arbieto did play a critical role in the conquest of the Vilcabamba region and that he led several expeditions to expand the rule of Spain into the Andean lowlands. As such, these charges are patently false and call into question many of Pereyra's other accusations. For example, all eight witnesses who spoke on behalf of Juan Hurtado's claim to the governorship in 1590 stated that the tax burden placed on the Vilcabamba natives was reasonable and even low in comparison with that of other areas (Maúrtua 1906: 226–260).

42. Early that year, on 14 May 1590, land had been set aside near Lucma to support the Meridians living in San Francisco de la Victoria de Vilcabamba (Barriga 1942: 278–279).

43. Juana de Ayala Ponce de León and Martín Hurtado de Arbieto had one son, Juan Hurtado, and several daughters, including Leonor Hurtado de Mendoza (who married Diego de Gamarra and, after his death, Miguel de Otaça de Mondragón) and Mariana Hurtado de Mendoza (who married Luis Catano de Cazana). Martín also had an illegitimate daughter named Mencia de Salcedo Hurtado de Arbieto (who married Francisco de Mariaca). His wife and his daughters were living in Cuzco in 1595 and 1599–1600 (see Bauer et al. 2014).

44. At the time of the initial petition, Juan was sixteen and not yet of age, so his mother represented him as his legal guardian. Martín Hurtado de Arbieto's will stipulated that Juan should become governor of Vilcabamba when he reached twenty-four. During the interim, Martín wanted his son-in-law, Diego de Gamarra, to oversee the region.

To support his case, Juan asked a series of men to testify concerning the achievements of his father. Juan also included within his petition a group of documents recording the original conditions of the Vilcabamba governorship presented to his father. These documents provide a record of the postconquest events of the Vilcabamba region that are not recorded with clarity elsewhere.

45. It appears that at the time of this appointment, García Hurtado de Mendoza was not aware of the long court case against Martín Hurtado de Arbieto. In response to the appointment of Juan as governor, the king asked Juan to submit copies of additional documents and testimonies to prove that his father was an adequate governor.

Document 1

*Martín de Murúa and
the Fall of Vilcabamba*

The Mercedarian priest Martín de Murúa lived much
of his life in Peru. He is best known for writing two
illustrated works on the history of the Incas and the
Spanish invasion of Peru (Ossio 2008a, 2008b).[1] The
first of these works, Murúa ([ca. 1590] 2004) dates to
between 1590 and 1598, a period when Murúa was living in the Peruvian highlands.[2] The manuscript, titled
*The History of the Origin and Royal Genealogy of the Inca
Kings of Peru* (*Historia del origen y genealogía real de los
reyes Inças del Perú*), is relatively short, but it contains
over 100 illustrations. A second manuscript, much
larger but less lavishly illustrated, was written by Murúa
([ca. 1616 [2008]) sometime before 1616 while he was
residing in Spain. Generally known by the title *General
History of Peru* (*Historia general del Perú*), Murúa's second work is one of the most comprehensive overviews
of the Incas produced during the early colonial period.
Many of our most renowned historians, from Bernabé
Cobo ([1653] 1956) to John Hemming (1970), have used
Murúa's *General History of Peru* as a major source for
their own overviews of Inca history.

Murúa's *General History of Peru* devotes more than a
dozen chapters to the Vilcabamba region and presents
a comprehensive description of the events that occurred
in the region between 1536 and 1572.[3] His account of
Vilcabamba begins with Manco Inca's failed siege of
Cuzco and concludes with the capture and subsequent
execution of Tupac Amaru. Rivaling the famous mem-
oir of Titu Cusi Yupanqui in detail, Murúa's history

DOI: 10.5876/9781607324263.c003

43

reflects his access to the works of other writers, Viceroy Toledo's archives, investigations conducted by different religious orders in Cuzco, and local residents. We know that Murúa lived in the Mercedarian monastery of Cuzco for three years, from 1585 to 1588, perhaps even longer, and that he was also stationed as the parish priest of Curahuasi on the southern edge of the Vilcabamba region in 1595 (Ossio 2008a: 436). So Murúa had plenty of opportunity to learn about the fall of Vilcabamba from eyewitness; both Andean and European.

Because Murúa's *General History of Peru* has never been translated, his insightful descriptions of the final decades of Inca rule remained largely inaccessible to non-Spanish readers. In this work we offer the first English version of chapters 70, 72–85, which focus on the extraordinary events that occurred in the Vilcabamba region. Within our translation we have also included the margin notes that are found in the document and the sections of the document that the royal censors crossed out during their review of the manuscript for publication. In most of the censored passages, we were able to read the original text; however, in a few cases where we can no longer identify individual letters we mark spaces with a boldface dot (●).[4]

CHAPTER 70 (PARTIAL TRANSLATION)

*That Don Diego de Almagro, on returning from Chile, tried
to relocate Manco Inca and what happened to him*

[We begin our translation halfway through chapter 70 as
Murúa describes Manco Inca fleeing to the Vilcabamba
region after his failed 1536 siege of Cuzco.]

During this time, Manco Inca did not rest; on the contrary, he roamed about doing much harm and [committing] robberies, destroying everything he could. When this news reached the Spaniards, [who] wanted to be done with him for once and for all, since he was disturbing the kingdom, they went out to where he was and fought bravely, killing many of his Indians. They thwarted and wounded him, pursuing him as far as the province of Vitcos, which is in Vilcabamba. Paullu Topa[5] followed them, and one day they had [Manco Inca] in such a tight spot that they took the litter on which he was [being carried] and the *tiana* (which is the chair on which he was seated), but he escaped into the forested mountains, where he hid with many Indians.[6] The other [warriors], who were not able to follow him, were so exhausted that they did not have the will to continue. [So] they went to Cuzco, and from there, each went to his own land, and the Spaniards, since they saw that Manco Inca had escaped from their grasp, returned to Cuzco. With the people he had left, Manco Inca went [first to] Huamanga, where he did all the harm he could, [and then to Vilcabamba].

Seeing that he did not stop, [the Spaniards] tried sending [troops] to capture him again.[7] Gonzalo Pizarro, [Francisco de] Villacastín,[8] Captain Orgón[ez] [de Valencia], Captain [Pedro de] Oñate,[9] and Juan Balsa [the elder][10] entered [the Vilcabamba region]. Thirteen Spaniards and six horses were killed, although they killed many relatives of Manco Inca and [other] important people who were with him. Captain [Francisco de] Villacastín went with a large number of Spanish soldiers as well as many Indians, whose captains were Inquill and Huaipar.[11] Manco Inca gathered as many people as he could [and] suddenly attacked the Indians and found and captured Huaipar. Inquill, who had escaped and fled, fell off a precipice. In order to make everyone else fear him, [Manco Inca] ordered that Huaipar be killed in front of his sister, who was the wife of Manco Inca. Afterward, a battle was fought[12] [in which] Villacastín with the Spaniards defeated Manco Inca and captured his wife.[13] She fell into their hands because she remained in their hiding place, angry, and did not want to follow her husband because he had killed her brother, Huaipar, in front of her. As we have said, Villacastín and Gonzalo Pizarro brought her to [Ollantay]tambo, where the Marquis [Francisco] Pizarro was, having just returned from Lima.[14] With unusual cruelty, not appropriate to inflict upon a woman who was not responsible for her husband's uprisings and rebellion, [Francisco Pizarro] ordered that she and other captains of Manco Inca be shot with arrows. In grief and despair [over] the death of his wife, [Manco Inca] cried and expressed great sorrow for her, because he loved her very much, and he therefore retreated to the site of Vilcabamba.[15]

CHAPTER 72

How Manco Inca killed many Spaniards who were coming to capture him, and [how] Diego Méndez and others entered where [the Inca was] living in peace

At the time when these uprisings were taking place in Collao and Charca, we have seen [that] Manco Inca was given a respite. As the Spaniards were occupied with the [uprising] in Collao, he founded the town of Vilcabamba in the province of Vitcos. He told his vassals and captains who were with him: "It seems to me now that it will be necessary to live here, as the Spaniards have proven themselves more powerful than us and they have taken and forced us out of much of our lands. [They have taken away] what my grandparents and ancestors possessed and won. Let us settle here until times have changed." So he rested for several days without going anywhere or trying to harm or attack the regions where the Spaniards were.

This was the situation when he received news that the Spaniards were entering through Rupa Rupa, intending to capture him, because they thought that an expedition against him would fare far better if they came in from behind[16] rather than through the usual trail, which [the Indians] had fortified.[17] As he knew why they were coming, he sent Paucar Huaman and Yuncallo with many Indians to defend the entrance at the most difficult pass along the trail by which [the Spaniards] were coming. These two captains went to find the Spaniards, who were 160 [in number], not counting the many Indian allies who were with them. In Yuramayo, which is behind Jauja, toward the Andes, they gave battle. The Spaniards were tired and worn down from the rough trails and forested slopes that they had cut and traversed, crossing rivers and suffering a thousand necessities, as is common on such expeditions that diverge from the beaten path and where there are [no] supplies. Since the Indians came rested and eager to fight, they defeated [the Spaniards] without much difficulty and killed most of those who were unable to escape.[18] Only a few [escaped] and these left from there and reached Christian lands after [experiencing] great hunger and dangers, crossing a thousand cliffs. Of Manco Inca's people, Yuncallo died in this battle, which caused [the Inca] great sadness and pain, because [Yuncallo] was a brave Indian, a great counselor and courageous in war, and [the Inca] missed him. Also, he had great affection for him, for through all his trials and tribulations, Yuncallo had always been loyal.

Paucar Huaman, having killed so many Spaniards, gathered all the spoils he found after the battle was won and returned very content with his [forces] to Vilcabamba. Manco Inca received him with great honor and applause. After this event, the captains and people of Manco Inca occupied themselves in going, from time to time, to the royal roads of Abancay, Andahuaylas, Limatambo, Curahuasi, and [Ollantay]tambo and other places, where they knew they could find lone Spaniards, to kill them and steal what they found, such that nothing was safe from them, nor could any [Spaniard] travel unless there were many together. Manco Inca discussed with his followers the following: that they go to Quito, which was a fertile and abundant land where the Spaniards would be less able to harm them. And there they could more easily fortify themselves against their opponents. Furthermore, there was an infinite [number] of people in those provinces, more than up here [i.e., in the Cuzco highlands], because the Spaniards had not drained [their numbers] as they had [done] to [Manco Inca's people]. After he discussed it with his captains, who agreed, he put [his plan] into effect, leaving Vilcabamba with all his army and all the things he had and those that had been taken from the Spaniards, and they arrived at Huamanga, where there were then few Spaniards, and they robbed and destroyed it, doing every ill deed they could. Once there, Manco Inca concluded that many Spaniards were already there, and that [more] were coming from Castile every day, and thus their forces were growing. Therefore, it would not be good for him to pass in front [of them] because they could come out from Lima and other places in large numbers and wait for him in some place that was well suited for the horses and there undo and capture him. So he judged it more advantageous to return to Vitcos, from where he had left. On conveying this to his [people], he did so and upon arriving there, he said that they should stay in [the] Vilcabamba [region], as they could not safely go to other places, as the Spaniards occupied everywhere else.

At this time, the widespread and notoriously known rebellions occurred in the kingdom. They were caused by Captain Juan de Herrada and other friends of his as they sought to avenge the sorrowful death of Diego de Almagro [the elder] in Lima. Don Diego de Almagro, [the] son of the deceased, conspired with them, and one day they left Don Diego locked in the house where they lived—because he was very young and they did not want to put him in such danger—they went to the houses where the Marquis Don Francisco Pizarro lived, which are now owned by the crown [and] where the Viceroy and the [Royal] Audiencia reside. [Pizarro] had just finished eating with Captain Francisco de Cháves,[19] who was his compatriot, when [the rebels] entered the dining room. [Pizarro] went into a side room where he defended himself at the door with a halberd for a long time, as he was [a] man of great courage. Realizing that if they delayed, the people of the city would be attracted by all this noise and the conspirators' intentions would be thwarted, they thrust a black man to the front, making him enter by giving him a push. As the Marquis dealt a blow to him with his halberd, they were able to enter [the room], where they killed [Pizarro] and Captain Francisco de Cháves. They removed the body of the Marquis, dragging it through the plaza. Many people gathered there as a result; all those of Don Diego de Almagro's faction accepted his son as their [new] leader.

[Cristóbal] Vaca de Castro of the Royal Council of the Emperor, our lord, of the Order of Santiago, then arrived, and he seized control of those who were loyal to the service of His Majesty.[20] [Vaca de Castro] confronted Don Diego de Almagro, the younger, in Chupas, two leagues from Huamanga, with the King's army. There Captain Francisco de Carvajal,[21] who was later Gonzalo Pizarro's *maese de campo* [chief of staff] against Your Majesty, served and was even [responsible] in a large part for the victory. The battle was fought and

Don Diego de Almagro was defeated. He fled to Cuzco, where he was taken prisoner, and Vaca de Castro meted out justice to him, beheading him. Other things occurred that I do not intend to discuss at length, as I am only focusing on, as I have said, the succession of the Inca Indians.

When Don Diego de Almagro, the younger, was defeated, Diego Méndez, [a] mestizo, and Barba Briceño y Escalante and other soldiers fled from the battle of Chupas. In all, they were 13 companions, and they found themselves in opposition to Your Majesty. Seeing that those who were responsible for the rebellion were assiduously being captured, they fled into the mountains, until reaching Vilcabamba, where Manco Inca was. [He] received them very well and with great generosity, [in sympathy] for all they had suffered. They told him that many Spaniards would enter there to serve him, and with them, he would return to recover his land and would defeat and cast out those Spaniards who were in it. They told Manco Inca this, fearing that he would have them killed and to help and please him. He treated them well in every way, without a thought of harming them, which reassured them and [thus they] lost their fear.

A few days later, Manco Inca found out through the spies he had in Cuzco and other places, how a *curaca* [local lord] named Sitiel had mocked Manco Inca in front of many Christians. [Sitiel] told Caruarayco, the *cacique* [leader] of Cotomarca:[22] "We are going to Vilcabamba to capture Manco Inca and Caruarayco will be Inca and lord, and we will all obey him, and Manco Inca will serve him and bring him the *tiana*, which is the seat where the *curacas* and important lords sit. When Manco Inca learned of this, he was deeply hurt, and he set about devising a plan to avenge the impudence and mockery that Sitiel had shown to him, as he considered it a great affront that one of his Indian vassals had the nerve to say such a thing, whether in the presence of the Spaniards or anyone. [Manco Inca] said to Diego Méndez and the others: "We are going to capture those people so that they may know our mettle and not underestimate us." Diego Méndez and the others agreed and apparently offered [their assistance] very willingly. Afterward, Manco Inca changed his mind, saying: "We are not going there, because you're still tired from the arduous trip you have made; it will suffice if the bravest of my people go. They will capture him." Thus, in accordance with this, he sent [for] all the captains and all the Indians who were with him, and [the Inca] charged them to go with great haste before they could be detected and to attempt to bring Sitiel and Caruarayco back alive, so that [Manco Inca] could exact revenge upon them as he pleased. With this they went to fulfill their order with utmost speed such that only 500 [warriors] remained as his guard.

CHAPTER 73

How Diego Méndez and the other Spaniards traitorously killed Manco Inca

No one would deny that ingratitude is an ugly and abominable vice. To do good to he who did me wrong is a Christian act that follows in the footsteps and example of Christ, our redeemer, who taught this through [his] words and deeds until the end of his life. All men who have [even] a little understanding of natural law reward good with good. But to [not] reward he who helped me, who freed me from risk and danger, who gave me food and drink when I was in need, and who gave me clothing when I had none, is [the act] of a malign soul, blind and barbaric in understanding. Even wild animals recognize and respect those who have helped them and have done them good. We have a thousand examples of this in books and, as the Spanish philosopher Séneca put it well, [saying] that in calling a man ungrateful, with this name alone, they had spoken the worst of him, since all the shame and insults possible are included and subsumed in this single term. I say this because of Diego Méndez Barba and his companions. They had fled [a situation] from which they, like others who committed a sinful crime, would not have escaped with their lives if they had been caught. Instead of treating them like enemies who had done so much harm to [the native peoples], Manco Inca helped them. He took them in and gave them food and drink, and kept them in his company. He helped them in every way possible. [Yet] they repaid [Manco Inca's] hospitality and welcome by taking his life, under the false hope that [the Spaniards] would show them mercy. They did not take into account what an ugly and vile act, too base to be imagined by noble hearts, they had committed against those who had, in fact, helped them [figure 3.1].

After dispatching his captains and people, Manco Inca stayed with the Spaniards, whom he treated very well and courteously in every way. He had a table for them, and there he gave them abundant food and drink. He gave them many gifts, as though they were in their own towns. [Yet] it seemed as though the Spaniards were angered by so many courtesies and [growing] tired of being there; they wanted to leave the interior and go to Cuzco. They did not know, however, how to do it safely, in such a way that Vaca de Castro would not catch them. They discussed among themselves a terrible betrayal, that of killing Manco Inca in whatever way they could. Then having killed him, they would flee [Vilcabamba], [since] there was no doubt that, having committed such a noble service [and having] pacified the region, Vaca de Castro would forgive them and show them mercy. After they conferred among themselves, Diego Méndez was in favor of killing [Manco Inca] when the occasion presented itself, before the Indians who had gone to capture Sitiel

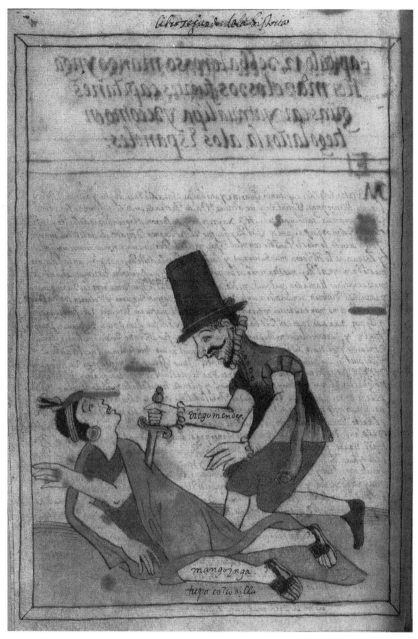

FIGURE 3.1. *The death of Manco Inca. Drawing by Guaman Poma de Ayala; in Murúa ([ca. 1590] 2004: 47v).*

and Caruarayco returned, because once they returned it would be more difficult, as there would be so many people with Manco Inca. Therefore, they continued, carefully waiting for an opportunity to carry out their harmful and perverse act.

One day, while Manco Inca and Diego Méndez were playing a game of *bolos*,[23] Diego Méndez won some money from Manco Inca, which was then paid to him. Having played for a short time, [Manco Inca] said that he did not want to play anymore, as he was tired. He ordered food, which was brought to him, and Manco Inca said to Diego Méndez and the others, "Let us eat." They agreed and happily sat down and ate what had been brought to the Inca. [Manco Inca] was suspicious of the Spaniards, because he saw them carefully going about, carrying concealed weapons. As a result, he became worried that they might intend to commit treason, as he had few companions [to protect him]. So when they finished eating, he told [the Spaniards] to go rest, as he wanted to relax for a while with his Indians. [The Spaniards] said that they would then leave, but [instead] started to fool around and made fun of each other, trying to make Manco Inca, who liked it when they enjoyed themselves, laugh. They amused themselves like this for a while, until Manco Inca, having drunk, got up to give a drink to the captain of his guard—because it is customary among them to grant this honor to those whom they like very much—and he gave him a drink. Standing up, he drank another glass, which was given to him by one of his Indian women [who was] behind him. At this moment, Diego Méndez, who was carefully waiting to seize the opportunity if it arose, seeing that [the Inca's] back was turned toward them, attacked with great fury and stabbed him from behind with a dagger.[24] Manco Inca fell on the ground and then Diego Méndez stabbed him two more times. The Indians who were there [were] all unarmed, [and] were surprised by this unforeseen event. They tried to defend Manco Inca, [so that the Spaniards] would not injure him any further. The other Spaniards [then] grabbed their swords and counterattacked to free Diego Méndez. They then ran very quickly to their stables and saddled their horses. They took with them the supplies that they had there, and they loaded their personal property as best they could in their rush. They then took the trail to Cuzco without stopping anywhere. They marched all that night without sleeping. As it was mountainous and they could not easily find the trail, they became lost, staggering about from one place to another. So they were delayed.

After Diego Méndez and the others had wounded Manco Inca and fled, the prominent Indians who were [in Vitcos], [filled] with an understandable sorrow and grief, did not dare follow the Spaniards with the people that Manco

Inca had there. They were fearful that the betrayal had been conducted in concert with more people from Cuzco who had come to help. Instead, with utmost haste, they sent word to Manco Inca's captains and people who had gone to capture Sitiel and Caruarayco, telling them that Diego Méndez and the other Spaniards had stabbed the Inca and fled toward Cuzco. [The captains were told] that they should drop everything and return to see if they could catch the Spaniards before they could escape, because if [they] did not return, the Spaniards would get away. The Indians who went to relay this [information] had such good luck that they came across [the captains] on the road, as they were already returning, bringing Caruarayco [as a] prisoner.[25] They had captured Sitiel at the same time, but being fast on his feet, he had slipped through their fingers.

Upon hearing the sad news, the captains and hundreds and hundreds of other people [headed toward Vitcos]. The bravest and quickest ran ahead at great speed and arrived at where Manco Inca was; who was mortally wounded but had not yet died. Seeing their lord in this condition [and] wanting to avenge him and tear to pieces those responsible for this betrayal, [the captains] returned to where they knew the Spaniards had gone. They were so eager in their pursuit that they caught up to them the next day. [The Spaniards] had taken shelter in a big *galpón* [large building] along the trail and were resting, thinking that no one was following them and they were safe and sound. The Indians who were following them arrived at where the Spaniards were resting [with] their horses [sheltered] inside, before dusk. However, the Indians did not want to attack them immediately so that none of them would escape while there was still daylight. So they hid in the woods, without showing themselves until the middle of the night. Then, after gathering a large quantity of firewood from the woods where they had hidden, they went to the *galpón*, encircled it, and placed the firewood at the doors so that [the Spaniards] could not get out, and they set it on fire with straw. When the Spaniards heard the noise they woke up. As some of them tried to escape through the fire, the Indians speared them, while the others burned there with their horses. No one or anything they had inside escaped, as the *galpón* was completely burned. Having done this [and] being very happy to see the murder of Manco Inca, their lord, avenged, they returned to Vitcos, where they found him about to expire, because the medicines they had given were not sufficient to save him.

When [the Inca] found out that the Spaniards were dead, none being able to escape, and his murder punished, he was very pleased. So that the people of the region would not be distressed and rebel, [the Inca] told them not to cry for him. He named one of his sons, the oldest, named Sayri Tupac, as heir, although [he was] still young. He [also named] Atoc Supa as governor, until [Sayri Tupac] came of age to rule and take the lordship upon himself. [Atoc Supa] was an *orejón* [nobleman] captain from Cuzco who was there with them. He was a man of valor, great prudence, and bravery in war. [Manco Inca] told them to obey him and not to abandon the Vilcabamba region, and that his curse would fall upon them if they did anything to the contrary, as he had discovered and founded the region through such hard work and sweat from his people, and so many of them had died in conquering it, and they had defended it from the Spaniards with such courage and determination. Having explained these reasons, [Manco Inca] died. With as much emotion as they were permitted show, they embalmed his body according to their customs.[26] Following his orders, they took him, without crying or demonstrating sadness, to Vilcabamba, where they remained under the governorship of the *orejón* captain Atoc Supa.

This was the end of Manco Inca Yupanqui, [a] son of Huayna Capac, [the] universal lord of this kingdom. Since he left Cuzco, because of the abuses and rebellions of Hernando Pizarro and his [men], [the Inca had] suffered infinite hardships and misadventures, [traveling] from one place to another, followed and pursued by the Spaniards. Sometimes defeated by and other times defeating [the Spaniards], he escaped on millions of occasions, all to maintain his liberty. What the Marquis Pizarro, his brothers, and other captains had failed to do with so many soldiers and Indian allies, Diego Méndez, a mestizo whom Manco Inca had taken in, aided, and hosted in his house along with his companions, achieved and concluded. Thus we see the extent to which a betrayal can go.

CHAPTER 74

How Sayri Tupac traveled to Lima and swore
obedience to Your Majesty, and of his death

[When] Manco Inca Yupanqui died, as discussed above, his son, Inca Sayri Tupac Inca Yupanqui, succeeded him in office, although his entire dominion and lordship encompassed the province of Vilcabamba and the Indians and *orejones* who were with him. [This was] because the Spaniards had been gaining strength and power every day, and they had been taking possession of the kingdom, such that the Inca had become secluded in that corner [of the realm]. Lacking strength and authority, he was contented with the small area of land they had left him, more because of its ruggedness than out of goodwill. The Chunchos, Indians from the other side of the large river commonly called the Marañon, and [other groups] from other provinces of which the Spaniards still know little about, also came to support him. In this manner, without taking the governorship itself, Sayri Tupac came under the tutelage of [the] *orejón* Ato[c-Sopa].

During this time, the famous wars that occurred between the Spaniards took place. [They] resulted from the New Laws that His Majesty, the Emperor, our lord, established for this kingdom of Peru and that of New Spain, at the insistence of Don Fray Bartolomé de las Casas, [a] cleric of the Order of Santo Domingo, [and the] bishop of Chiapas.[27] He was an apostolic man [and a] vigorous defender of the liberty of the Indians, in whose aid and protection he spent many years showing in Spain the harm that was being done to them by the Spaniards and *encomenderos*. [He showed] the insolence and tyranny with which they [the Indians] were ordered [about] and humbled, the greed and covetousness with which they were defrauded of their estates, [and] the contempt with which they were treated, as if they were wild animals from the forests. Through these [actions] and abuses, the governors and lords of the *repartimientos* severely impeded the spread of the Holy Gospel and the indoctrination and teaching of these miserable [people], [treating them] as if they had not been created in the image and semblance of God and [as though their salvation] had not been bought with the blood of the most innocent lamb. [Las Casas] therefore wrote a book wherein he describes thousands of events that occurred in this kingdom,[28] never seen or heard among barbarians, all for the purpose of obtaining money, gold, and silver—and more gold and more silver—[such that] if the mountains turned into gold and silver, the Spaniards' greed would not be satisfied. With persuasive and theological logic, [he] asserts that the Indians are not as barbaric as they have been made out to be. There were some [Spaniards] who dared to say that they were not real men, [and] thus those who wanted to take over their estates and strip and deprive them of their rightful property defamed them. In the end, through his holy zeal and indefatigable diligence, he accomplished so much that some new laws were passed by the Emperor, our lord. [These New Laws were] very holy and advantageous for the benefit, advancement, and conversion of the natives of this kingdom.[29] To enforce them, [the Emperor] sent Blasco Núñez Vela, a gentleman from Avila, with the title of viceroy of this kingdom, and he sent the Royal Audiencia [to uphold] his authority, defend the poor who were oppressed, and promote justice, which was downtrodden and dejected. Thus, he left nothing unattended to in this kingdom.

Viceroy Blasco Nuñez Vela put the New Laws into effect, throwing the kingdom into turmoil. Because [the New Laws] were [intended to] curb the insolence of so many rich and powerful men, who were inflamed and made arrogant by the quantity and abundance of gold and silver, [these men] did not want to obey them or suffer the yoke of the law, [which was] based upon good reasoning. Gonzalo Pizarro rebelled in Cuzco, where he was [living], with the intention of going to Castile with [the] 500,000 pesos he had. Under the title of *procurador*, he went to Lima and from there to Quito, where he fought the good and loyal viceroy [Blasco Núñez Vela]. [Pizarro] defeated [the viceroy] and cut off his head, putting it on the gallows for some time as [a] trophy of [the viceroy's] loyalty [to the crown]. To pacify Peru, President Pedro de la Gasca came from Spain in the year 1548, defeating Gonzalo Pizarro at Jaquijahuana, four leagues from Cuzco. He beheaded [Gonzalo Pizarro] and pacified the region. Believing that [Peru] would remain calm and at peace, [the viceroy then] returned to Spain.

[However,] new disturbances arose, born of unbridled ambition and the greed of many malcontents, because their insatiable desire for rich *repartimientos* had not been fulfilled. Even if each one were given the entire kingdom, it would not have been enough to fill their insatiable appetite. Don Antonio de Mendoza [then] came to this kingdom as viceroy, having governed in New Spain.[30] God brought him at the most opportune time, for the greater punishment of this kingdom. In the city of La Plata, in the province of the Charcas, Don Sebastián de Castilla rebelled.[31] However, within a few days the same people who moved and incited him to this [act] killed him. Francisco Hernández Girón rose up in Cuzco, at first successfully, [but] he was ultimately defeated by the army of the king in Pucará, [which was] governed by the Judges [of the Royal Audiencia].[32] [He] was captured by Captains [Juan] Tello and [Miguel de la] Serna and the people of Huánuco in Jauja and put to death in Lima. The rebellions and seditions raised by the malcontent were [then] over. As a book has [already] been written about them, I touch upon all these things briefly, since my intention here is to discuss only the Incas.[33]

At that time, Your Majesty sent Andrés Hurtado de Mendoza, Marquis of Cañete, as viceroy of this kingdom. Seeing Peru peaceful and moods calmer, he tried to convince Sayri Tupac to [pledge] obedience to Your Majesty and [thus] subdue the province of Vilcabamba, so that the gospel would be preached and the Indians of that [province] would convert to the fellowship of the Catholic Church. For this purpose, he sent Diego Hernández, [the] husband of Doña Beatriz Quispe Quipi Coya,[34] [a] daughter of Huayna Capac, and Juan Sierra[35] and Alonso Juárez[36] and others as messengers [to] beg [Sayri Tupac] to come out in peace and to give obedience to Your Majesty. At the time when they went, Sayri Tupac had not [yet] received the tassel.[37] So he did not send a reply until he received it and had time to see if the embassy was well intentioned. Reassured, he discussed the matter with his captains. After many agreements, judgments, and contradictions made by the sorcerers he had with him, and a lukewarm response from many of his [captains], he decided to depart and go to Lima. Therefore, he embarked [upon his journey], taking 300 prominent Indians, *caciques*, *orejones*, and captains and a sister, named Cusi Huarcay, with him. They arrived in Lima, where the Marquis of Cañete received him, doing him a great honor.[38] Several days later, Sayri Tupac abdicated [his kingship], giving Your Majesty, the Emperor, our lord, the right to this kingdom. In [the King's] name, the Marquis of Cañete granted [Sayri Tupac] a favor, [giving] him the *repartimiento* and Indians that had belonged to Francisco Hernández Girón[39] for his maintenance, which was known to yield 17,000 pesos *ensayados* [figure 3.2].

After staying several days in Lima, Sayri Tupac returned to Cuzco, where the Indians of Chinchaysuyo and Collasuyo received him as Inca, because the Marquis of Cañete had ordered it so. He wore [the] tassel and rode on a litter as his ancestors had done.[40] The *orejones*, from Hanan Cuzco [Upper Cuzco] and from Hurin Cuzco [Lower Cuzco], also obeyed him, as he represented the descendant of Huayna Capac, his grandfather. All the Spaniards liked and respected him, calling him Inca. Sayri Tupac and his sister, Cusi Huarcay, were baptized there, because the Marquis of Cañete sent word to [Juan] Bautista Muñoz, who was corregidor of the city of Cuzco at the time, to have them baptized, to which they gladly consented. Upon being baptized, Sayri Tupac took the name Don Diego de Mendoza,[41] for love of the viceroy, and his sister was named Doña María Manrique. Being baptized, [the matter of] their marrying was discussed, as they were siblings. It was an inviolable custom kept by the Incas to marry their sisters, so that the son who would succeed his reign would be the son of [an] Inca and Coya, of royal blood through [both] the paternal and maternal line. Therefore, they say that the bishop of that city, Don Juan Solano, granted them special permission to marry. Others [say] that the archbishop of Lima, Don Jerónimo de Loayza, [a] learned and eminent man of great prudence and conduct, dispensed [permission] by [the] apostolic authority and mandate of Pope Julius III.[42] Although it is extremely difficult to gain such dispensations. [Crossed out in text: "for its validation, as there are many learned scholars of theology wiser than us who know for certain that such a matrimony is prohibited by natural law. •••• ••• •• ••• •••••••••• put his will before without faults or any violence •• of marriages."][43] [The following is in the margin: "It is certain that there was a dispensation or (that) it was done with (the) authority and commission of the

Figure 3.2. *The meeting between Sayri Tupac and Andrés Hurado de Mendoza. Drawing by Guaman Poma de Ayala; in Murúa ([ca. 1590] 2004: 49v).*

Pope."] Born of that marriage was Doña Beatriz Clara Coya,[44] their legitimate daughter, who, in time, became the wife of Martín García [Oñaz] de Loyola, [a] Knight of the Order of Calatrava and [the] captain of Viceroy Don Francisco de Toledo's guard.

Unfortunately, Sayri Tupac was not able to enjoy the quiet and peace he had in Cuzco among his kin, since he lived for only one year after he and his sister were baptized and married.[45] They say that [Francisco] Chilche, [a] Cañari, [the] *cacique* of Yucay, killed him with poison; for this sin he was in prison for a year in Cuzco. In the end, he escaped without any new revelations concerning the [circumstances] of [Sayri Tupac's] death. Sayri Tupac made a will, in which he declared his brother, Tupac Amaru, who was in Vilcabamba [and who was] the legitimate son of Manco Inca, his father, as his successor in the lordship. When news of Sayri Tupac's death reached Vilcabamba, the older bastard brother of the young Tupac Amaru, Cusi Titu Yupanqui,[46] [who was also a] son of Manco Inca, took away [Tupac Amaru's] litter and rulership, making himself lord. With the intention that his son would succeed him, [Cusi Titu Yupanqui] made Tupac Amaru a priest and sent him to guard his father's body in Vilcabamba, where Manco Inca was kept. So it was until we return. In Chapter 93, I will also tell of a remarkable event that happened to this Prince Sayri.[47]

CHAPTER 75

How, during the governance of Cusi Titu Yupanqui, two clerics of the Order of Saint Augustine entered Vilcabamba and what happened to them, and of the death of the Inca

Cusi Titu Yupanqui was inducted as the lord of the Incas in Vilcabamba. He did not leave from there, staying with the *orejones* and Indians of that province.[48] So a few years passed during which President Castro,[49] the Count of Nieva, governed, until the cautious and prudent gentleman, Don Francisco de Toledo, came to be viceroy of this kingdom. At this time, two clerics of the Order of Lord Saint Augustine entered the province of Vilcabamba to preach to the Indians and to instruct them in the Catholic faith. One of them was named Friar Marcos [García][50] and the other Friar Diego Ortiz,[51] [a] native of Seville.[52] With a fervent desire to save souls and set them on the path to heaven, they started to practice such holy work, [as they had been] sent by their prelate [to do]. They preached and indoctrinated Cusi Titu Yupanqui and the Indians who were with him. They willingly listened to [the friars], because, in general, many of the Indians rejoiced at having priests and clerics to instruct them in the faith of the Redeemer, since there were no Spaniards with them. These two clerics would catechize and baptize [the Indians], and many of them learned the necessary things [and] received the water of holy baptism. One of [these clerics], Friar Marcos [García], baptized Cusi Titu Yupanqui and named him Don Felipe.[53] After some time had passed Friar Marcos decided to leave the province, and he requested permission from his prelate to [return to] the city of Cuzco. Having sent it, [Marcos] left [the province] where the Inca was [residing] without informing him where he was going, because he was afraid [the Inca] would send someone to kill him, as he had shown signs of ill will.

When Cusi Titu Yupanqui learned that Father Fray Marcos was leaving, he sent Indians after him to bring him back to where he was and, when [he] arrived, [the Inca] roundly scolded him with great arrogance, asking him why he left the land without permission. By way of explanation [Fray Marcos] replied that he was not leaving, but was just traveling about. He told [the Inca] this because he realized that [Cusi Titu Yupanqui] would later have him killed. Cusi Titu Yupanqui told him not to leave from there until another cleric replaced him. Later his companion, Friar Diego Martín [*sic*], came and they stayed in Puquiura, working for a month with the Inca, who had already abandoned the goodwill with which he had received holy baptism. [The Inca] took the two clerics with him to [the town of] Vilcabamba and, along the way, he made [them] wade across a river, where the water reached to their waist. [He] did this with cruel and perverse intentions, so that the trail would seem difficult and the land rough and rugged, so that they would not want to stay there with him or remain in that province.

Not satisfied with this, Cusi Titu Yupanqui ordered, when they arrived at the town of Vilcabamba, for the *yunga* [lowland] Indian women to come out in pairs, dressed as friars, to speak with the clerics. [He did this] to mock and ridicule [them] since he held them in little esteem. When they arrived at the town, [he] did not want [the clerics] to lodge within it, so that they would not see the *huacas* and *mochaderos* [holy places] he had there, or reprimand him for the rites and ceremonies that he held [there].[54] After spending eight days with the Inca, the clerics returned to the town of Puquiura, leaving him in Vilcabamba. They had been there a month when, some Indians came to the clerics, telling them that next to Vitcos, at a place named Chuquipalta, there was a house dedicated to the Sun, [and] a large[55] and rough stone above a spring.[56] [They said] that many evils redounded from this [stone] that astonished and frightened them and killed many Indians. Therefore, they said the devil was in that stone and, for this reason, they did not worship or offer gold and silver as they used to in the past. They pleaded with the two clerics, begging them to go and exorcise the stone so that from then on it would not harm or frighten them and so that they would be free from the danger that was there.

Hearing this, the clerics went there, taking many Indians and young men of the parish with them, loaded with a [great] amount of firewood, and they burned the stone. Since this event, nothing was ever seen again that would cause the Indians fear, nor did they feel any harm. This further confirmed the faith that was preached among those who were satisfied with it. They knew that the devil was fleeing and was afraid of the clerics and the holy words that they spoke, and [that the Devil] shunned the cross and did not return to [the places] where they sprinkled holy water.

Within eight days of this, Father Fray Marcos set out for Cuzco from Puquiura, and Father Fray Diego stayed [there] alone, administering the Holy Sacraments and preaching the Gospel to the Indians because he knew the common language of the Indians very well, so they willingly listened to him.[57] [Soon afterward] a Spaniard named [Antonio] Romero entered the province alone, stating that he was a miner and had come in search of mines. (There are very rich ones in that province, as was revealed to Governor Don Fernando de Torres y Portugal, Count of Villar, [of] this kingdom, [in] the year 1587.)[58] This Spaniard asked Cusi Titu for permission to look for silver and gold mines, which he then granted. [The Spaniard] went from place to place looking for mines until he found them, and he returned to the Inca very pleased. He brought [samples] of the metals to show [the Inca], demonstrating that there was much gold and silver to extract. Once the Inca saw this, it weighed upon his mind, because he knew that if it was publicly known that there were gold and silver mines in that province and [this] news reached the Spaniards in Cuzco, many of them would enter. [They] would send soldiers to conquer the province and would seize the entire region, and the Indians who lived there in seclusion would come to lose their freedom and kingdom. [The Inca] therefore ordered that the Spaniard be killed and his head cut off and thrown in the river. At this time the Inca was in Puquiura. When Father Fray Diego heard the commotion in the Inca's house he rushed there to see what was the matter and [if] he could resolve it. When he understood that they were killing the Spaniard, he begged the Inca not to kill [him]. Since Cusi Titu heard him, he sent word to Father Fray Diego not to go to or enter his house, [but rather] to let him kill the man, and if [Fray Diego] kept interfering, he would have him killed, like the Spaniard. Seeing that he was already dead and he could not remedy [the situation], [Fray Diego] returned home very saddened with great regret and remorse at not having been able take the man's confession. Wanting to carry out a final act of mercy, he sent a young man of the parish to speak with the Inca. Since the Spaniard was already dead, he implored [the Inca] to give him the body so that [the Spaniard] could be buried like the Christian he was. The Inca sent word that he did not want to give [the body] to him, no matter how much he insisted, and he ordered that it be thrown in the nearby river.

Unsatisfied with this, the Father wanted to be diligent and [see] if he could find the body in the river, [so] he secretly went out at night with some young men and looked for the body in order to bury it. However, he could never find it. When the Inca heard what the Father was doing, he sent word to the Father not to try to [find] the Spaniard's body or to leave his house to look for it, because if he [did so, the Inca] would have him killed. With this, the Father stopped the holy work that he was doing.

God did not want to leave Cusi Titu Yupanqui unpunished for the murder of the Spaniard and the threats he had made to the good cleric, [or for] the scorn and mockery that he had ordered [through] the Indian [women] dressed in friars' habits. Within five days after the [abovementioned] event, the Inca went to a *mochadero* that he had [in Vitcos], where [the] mestizo Diego Méndez killed his father, Manco Inca. There he was mourning with other Indians, and [when he was] tired of mourning, [he] returned to his house. That night, tired and sweaty, [he] ate a lot and drank a great quantity of wine and *chicha*, from which that very night he contracted a deadly illness, which included a terrible pain in his side together with pronounced bleeding through his mouth and nose. The illness worsened as his mouth and tongue became swollen. The disease was so severe that he died within 24 hours, leaving the Indians very sad and inconsolable.

CHAPTER 76

*How the captains of Cusi Titu Yupanqui captured and
killed Father Fray Diego in a very cruel manner*

Everyone meets his end according to his deeds. This we have seen in [the case of] Cusi Titu Yupanqui Inca, [a] son of Manco Inca, who [mis]treated the clerics who entered the province where he lived to grant him the good deed of putting his soul on the path to [eternal bliss].[59] When Cusi Titu Yupanqui died, a young Indian woman who was with him when he passed away, [named] Mama Cona Suya, [also] called Angelina Polan Quilaco,[60] [was] moved by some evil spirit that entered her heart. As [this evil spirit] had [long] held [the province] under his will, and in the palm of his hand, he wanted to kill the blessed friar, by whose words and deeds he was now losing ground in the conquest of that province. [She] came out screaming to the captains and Indians who were there with the Inca to capture the friar, since he along with Martín Pando, his mestizo secretary, had killed the Inca [by] giving him poison. [However, the fact went] unnoted that the blessed father had not entered the house of the Inca nor had he been close enough to him to give him the poison when he became ill. The captains who were there, especially Guandopa, Macora, Sotic, [and] Palloc,[61] motivated [by] that infernal Indian, went screaming like insane people without thought or reasoning, with many others to the house of the priest. They grabbed him and, in an instant, put a rope around his neck and, with another, tied his hands and forearms behind [his back]. They squeezed him so forcefully and violently that they made some of his ribs move forward and become dislocated. Taking him out into a patio, they started to say thousands of offensive words. Punching and clubbing him, they [accused the friar] of killing their Inca and demanded him back. And to cause him even more pain, they kept him out all night in the cold, naked, wearing only a loose, white breechcloth, surrounded by many Indians. From time to time [these Indians] would throw water on the ropes so that they would cut him more and cause him additional pain.

In the morning, the captains and other Indians met, and the Father, tied as he was, asked why they were abusing him so cruelly, for he was their Father, who had indoctrinated and taught them with much love and desire for their well-being. [He said] that if the Inca was dead, they [should] tell him [and] he would pray to God for him and his soul; and if he was alive and ill, he would say masses for his health so that he would recover. To these words, they replied that Cusi Titu Yupanqui, their Inca and lord, was dead, [and] that [Ortiz should] say mass and resurrect him, since he had said and preached that his God was able to resurrect the dead. The holy Father responded to this, [saying] that he was [but] a sinful priest [and] that only God could resurrect the dead; however, [he agreed] that he would say mass and commend [the Inca] to God and that his majesty would do with [the Inca] what he deemed best. With this, they then told him to say the mass.

Because of the torments that he had endured that night and the pain that the so tightly tied ropes caused him, and especially due to his ribs, which were dislocated, the father was not able to turn around. So one of the captains who was there tormenting him knocked him to the ground and, standing on the Father's chest and pulling his hands forcefully, he kicked him many times in his chest to set his bones back into place. This caused still greater pain. With this mistreatment and cruelty, they took him to the church that the priests had built in the town of Puquiura. There he went to the altar and donned his robes to say mass, which he started to say very slowly [and] with much devotion. The mass lasted such a long time and he shed so many tears that he soaked the missal and corporals with them. He let out load sighs and moans throughout the mass, because he understood well the broken hearts of the Indians and their evil plans to kill him afterward, such that every time he said the Dominus Vobiscum, they threatened him with the spears they held in their hands, gesturing their intent to kill him.

When he had finished saying mass, [the Indians] returned, screaming and shouting loudly; they returned to take him and tie him like before. When they asked why he had not resurrected the Inca as they requested, he responded that the creator of all things, who was God, could do that, but [the Inca] did not revive because it was not God's will, [and] that it must not suit [Him] that the Inca return to this world. Then they took [Ortiz] out of the church and tied him around the waist. They tied him to a cross that was in the cemetery, and there they whipped him very cruelly for a very long time and warned him that he would walk into the interior with them to Vilcabamba. Tired and tormented, the good friar asked, for the love of God, that they give him something to eat, as he was hungry and very thirsty. They went to his house and brought two crusts of cake that he had in a pouch. He started to eat them, but when he could not swallow them, as his thirst had increased with the strain and pain, he asked that they give him some water. But instead of water, the Indians brought him urine and saltpeter, mixed with some bitter and disgusting concoctions, in a glass. As the blessed father tasted it and realized that it was so bitter and foul-smelling, he spit it out of his mouth, not wanting to drink it. Then many of those ministers of Satan got up from where they were sitting and threatened him. They pressed their spears to his chest, telling him to drink it immediately, otherwise they would kill him. Therefore, lifting his hands to heaven, with great humility, he drank it, saying: "Be it for the love of God, what more do I deserve than this?" He said [this] in the common language of the Indians, such that they all understood him, whereupon they untied him from the cross to walk to Marcanay.[62] Sometime after they untied him, he sat down next to [the cross] to rest. But he could not get up as quickly as the Indians ordered him, so an Indian named Juan Quispe, to show and amuse everyone with his boldness, or, better said, his insolence, raised his hand and hit the holy father [in the face]. The omnipotent Majesty of God wanted to punish the insolence and lack of respect [that Quispe] had for his minister, so little by little, his hand and arm withered to serve as proof and a demonstration of divine justice. This Indian lived many years longer than the others who were there with him.[63] Through the withered arm and hand, he publicly showed the wonders of God and how deeply He feels the affronts that are committed against His priests, as we will later explain.

To lead [Ortiz], they pierced his cheeks and pulled through them a rope of cut *ichu* [Andean bunchgrass], which is very rough, and they pulled him as with a bit, making much blood flow from his wounds. So they left with him, walking barefoot and naked, in only a white tunic. Along the trail, they shoved him, [hit him with] sticks and slapped him, saying a thousand hurtful words. On the first day that they were walking in this way, there was such a downpour of rain that streams of water ran along the trail. Because of the mud, water, and the readiness with which they would kick, slap, and push him, he sometimes fell to the ground, but they made him get up immediately. In the meantime, with unusual patience and profound humility, all he would say was: "Oh, God!" There is no doubt that, on this occasion, the Supreme Lord came to His priest's aid with supernatural help and assistance so that, in imitation of Christ, our lord, he [endured these trials] with joy and patience. He would raise his eyes to heaven and, with great humility, ask for forgiveness for his sins. The Indians mocked and ridiculed him for this and started [beating] him again.

When they arrived that day at their resting place, they put him in a cave under a rock where a lot of water dripped on him. [Ortiz] meekly asked the Indians why they treated him so badly and with such cruelty, for he was fond of them and loved them like his children. [He] had indoctrinated and taught them, and it was only for their good that he had stayed in the province, as he could have gone to Cuzco. The Indians replied that he was a lying deceiver who had not resurrected the Inca. Thus, administering a thousand tortures and torments along the way, they took him to Marcanay. There they dragged him along the ground, his hands and feet bound, and tied him to a pole. Having removed the habits he usually wore, and having terribly [and] inhumanely whipped him, they put native palm thorns in his fingertips. They forced him to smell foul-smelling things, which left him breathless and unable to speak. Finally, they finished him off with a blow to the back of his neck with a copper axe.[64] [With this] his holy soul went to enjoy, in the presence of God, the reward merited by his holy zeal, [as well as] the patience and humility with which he suffered death at the hands of those whose spiritual well-being he had come to oversee. They should have guarded his physical life by any means possible in order to have a refuge for their souls in that land so lacking in priests. But since they did not value the blessing that they had, one should not be shocked that they took his life, thus to better it in heaven.

CHAPTER 77

*Of the cruelty that the Indians committed against the
dead body of the blessed Friar Diego Ortiz*

When the Indian *caciques* concluded that terrible cruelty and inhuman sacrilege, bloodying their dirty hands in the blood of he who was anointed by God and was their own spiritual father, who had paid with his sweat and toil to stay among them to win them [over] into His divine grace, they were not content or satisfied in their diabolical intent and fervor. Not satisfied with having taken the Father's life, and to please the devil, who moved invisibly among them soliciting their evil (as it seemed to him that with [the death of Ortiz] he would have the field secured and he would return to rejoice at having possessed their souls) [they] took the body and trampled it as a greater demonstration of their rage.[65] Laying [it] on the ground, they ordered all the Indians who were there, men, women, and youth, to walk on him to further scorn and mock him. So they stepped and trampled on him, thus satisfying their barbaric cruelty. Then they made a very deep and narrow pit and there they placed him, head down and feet up. To inflict further iniquity upon the dead body, they shoved a palm lance through his anus, passing it through his entire body to his head. Then they filled [the grave] with earth, saltpeter, and *collpa*, which is a [type of] colored earth with which they dye, and they threw a lot of red *chicha* and other things over him, according to their diabolical rites and ceremonies. Thus, they covered his body in the pit that they [had] made under the roots of a huge tree, and with a great din and screaming, they left him, overjoyed at having fulfilled their infernal desire and having killed the priest of their souls, these blind and unfortunate, being unaware of the great punishment that divine justice had in store for them.

The reason they put his body in the pit feet up and head down was that, according to what those same Indians said, since the holy Father lifted his eyes to heaven with every step, asking God for forgiveness for his sins and help in enduring those torments and hardships, the barbarians believed that God would, through his importuning and groans, hear him and take him out of the pit if he had his head up. Therefore they cast him [in] head down, so that, in the pit, he would not lift his head up to heaven and call [out] to God, but Oh! [what] blind men without reasoning or understanding![66] Did not He who could take him out of the hole [if he] was head up have the power to take him out [if he] was head down? Perhaps He has limited power? Do you not think that if I saw him from heaven [positioned] in one way, that I would [not] also hear him and take him out if he were [facing] the other? But their malice and wickedness blinded them, and the devil, who led [them] to this heinous sacrilege, had them senseless and lacking judgment to see the iniquity they were perpetrating against Christ, our lord.

Having done this, the confusion and sadness born of their sin began to fall on them, as the *caciques* and captains, seeing how unjustly they had laid their hands on a priest, and how contrary to reason, without any cause or provocation, they had taken the life of an innocent [person]. Fearful of the punishment that loomed in their hearts, they held a meeting of all the sorcerers and diviners in the province, and together they asked them what was going to happen and occur in the future as a consequence of the death of Father Friar Diego Ortiz, because it weighed very heavily upon them. For several days, the diviners and sorcerers conferred among themselves over the answer, asking questions of the devil, whose vassals and subjects they were, and they finally came to the conclusion that the creator of all things was very angry at them over what they had planned and done; laying their hands on and taking the life of that priest, who was innocent of the offense that had been attributed to him. [The fortunetellers stated] that because of this egregious sin, much ill and misfortune would befall them, and God would punish them and destroy this generation of the Inca and all his people. This reply left the Indians more confused and distressed over the deed they had committed. Adding to their fears, the next day, in the evening, without forewarning, a large house that was there, where they and the Inca held their drunken revelries and where the aforesaid matter had been discussed, suddenly burned down. As they came to put out the fire, which was impossible to stop no matter how hard they tried, and as the house was burning, they saw[67] a large snake moving through the fire, from one place to another, without being burned. Seeing that it did not burn frightened and terrified everyone. [They therefore] departed from there even sadder and more pensive.

The *curacas* and captains agreed to consult again with the priests of their *huacas* and the diviners and sorcerers. [Once they had been] summoned, they asked them what had happened and what was the meaning of the house having burned and such a large snake moving through the fire without being harmed or injured. The diviners responded that they foresaw a time of great misfortune, calamity, and a cruel war of fire and blood would soon fall upon that province, destroying everyone, because the blood of the priest that they had killed was crying and calling out before God for vengeance for his unjust death.

Believing that [by] removing any memory of the priest, they would avoid those evils and threats, they scraped [away] the earth from the altar where he had said mass and where he used to sit down and walk around, and where he prayed the Divine Office[68] at the church they had there. Gathering the scraped-up earth, they threw it into the river to remove any trace of it. The more daring distributed his habits among themselves, making *chuspas*, which are small bags that they carry hanging on their left side, where they put the coca they chewed.[69] [They] took the vestment with which he said mass and, carrying it to a place a few days from there that is called the Gallows of the Inca, threw it onto the ground and stepped on it, out of contempt for the Christian religion and the priests who celebrated [mass] with it.

But You are just, Lord! Your judgments are righteous and justified. In the punishment of sinners You give the world an example of Your essential attribute that is justice, and [show] that You keep and fulfill Your holy word, through which You said that no one [may] touch Your Christians and [Your] anointed.[70] Therefore, these barbarians, lacking supernatural faith, paid the price through the punishments with which You punish those who lay their hands on Your priests or speak badly of them. They themselves confessed that an infinite [number] of hardships and misfortunes befell them for having committed such a great evil. Because a little over a year later, the Spanish entered the area [of] the town where this sacrilege had been committed, leveling, depopulating, and burning it, such that it has not been rebuilt to this day, appearing as if the curse of God and fire from heaven had descended over it and [upon] everyone who was involved in the death and martyrdom of the blessed friar. The fact that they all quickly came to a miserable end, of various sad deaths and misfortunes, is widely known.[71] And only the man who hit him, named Juan Quispe, whose arm became withered, lived for more than 30 years, to further shame him and demonstrate Divine Justice. This has served as a lesson to many to desist from sin and to respect and venerate the priests and ministers of the Gospel of Christ.

Their misfortune did not simply end there, because God later sent them all pestilence, hunger, massacre, hardships, misery. And the vermin of the earth, as ministers and implementers of divine punishment, destroyed their foods and *chacras* [fields] and cornfields, such that they could palpably know that it came from the heavens, and they cursed at one another, especially those who had advised and encouraged that they kill the blessed father who indoctrinated them because they clearly recognized that, as the most culpable, these curses and hardships were primarily directed at them. There was an Indian among them, named Don Diego Aucalli,[72] who, as a consequence of all this, converted wholeheartedly to God and turned to Him, asking for forgiveness for his sins, reforming his life, and performing the works of a good Christian. [He] became a preacher [among] those peoples, persuading them to do penance, telling them that this was the true [way] and the path to heaven, because their superstitions and idolatry were lies and deceit and trickeries of the devil. And if they did not [believe this], they should see how God came back for His priest, punishing those who had killed him. ['They should] take note because, although in the past the Inca martyred and administered cruel torments to his pontiffs and diviners, hanging them and leaving them thus for four or five days until they finally died, they had never [before] seen such signs and hardships and calamities as those [that] they saw clearly and evidently after having committed the crime of killing the priest. Glory to the omnipotent Lord of Heaven, who draws emendation out of the sins and missteps of sinners, and who through His punishments draws fear and true repentance from sin[ners].

One cannot assume or conclude [that] they suddenly conspired to kill the good Father Friar Diego for having mistreated and shamed the Indians. First, because the punishment we have described, sent from the hand of the exalted one onto those who killed [Friar Diego], highlights their injustice and lack of reason. And second, [as] the Spaniards entered and taught the Manarí Indians, [who lived] more than 200 leagues inland, the Christian doctrine, they were told that Father Friar Diego had taught them the same thing and had preached to them when they went to Vilcabamba to see Cusi Titu Yupanqui Inca. [They say] that he was a very good priest, who, with great love and sincerity, gave them gifts of what he had in his home, and when they fell ill, he healed them with great care. He himself made porridges for them to eat and visited them and stayed to console them, telling them many times that God sent hardships and illness for [their] sins and so that they would remember Him and mend their lives, and desist from the offenses they committed against Him. Upon hearing of his death and the cruel manner in which it had occurred, being infidels, they showed [such] emotion and deep [concern] over it that they were almost crying, and they said this was why so much harm had befallen the Inca and his generation. It was because of the memory of the good Father that they did not harm the Spaniards who entered [their territory], fearing that another [punishment] would come upon them, and they therefore came out in peace. They gave [the Spaniards] food for the road and many Indians who would accompany them [back] to Vilcabamba.

All that I have relayed about the death and events [of the life of] the blessed cleric has not been [based on the] knowledge of solely one person, nor from confusing accounts from the aforementioned Indians, who so easily lie. Rather, all of this [information] and what occurred next when the Spaniards took over that province and transferred his remains to the church of San Francisco de la Victoria was drawn from an investigation that the clerics of the Order of St. Augustine conducted with the Indians who were present, and with Juana

Guerrero, [the] wife of Martín Pando, [the] secretary of Inca Cusi Titu, who saw it all firsthand, as she was in the province, and with many Spaniards who received news of it and swore to it.[73] And what later occurred, as we will tell in Chapter 84, provides clear evidence of the unjust death and blessed martyrdom of this holy cleric, which occurred in the year 1570 or 1571, because the Indians often erred since they do not know how to track time.[74]

CHAPTER 78

How Viceroy Don Francisco de Toledo sent messengers to
Cusi Titu Yupanqui, and how they were killed

As previously mentioned, Don Francisco de Toledo, commander of Acebuche of the Order of Alcántara, [the] brother of Don Juan de Toledo, Count of Oropesa, governed these kingdoms at the time when the events that we have discussed occurred, concerning the death of Inca Cusi Titu Yupanqui and that of Father Friar Diego Ortiz, Augustine cleric. [Toledo] wanted to succeed in the governance and administration of this kingdom, as even here disorder and injustices remained and were not entirely extinct. He wanted to carry out a general inspection of the whole kingdom of the Indians and reduce them into towns under Christian policing and order, for this was the only way for them to be completely indoctrinated and for them to learn the things of our Holy Catholic faith, and for their ancient rites and ceremonies to be extirpated. Through the presence of their [Catholic] priests and ministers, which experience has shown to be most favorable for the salvation of these natives' souls, [the Indians] would abstain from many vices, such as drunkenness and other harmful and abominable [sins]. In contrast, [where] the *reducciones* [resettled populations] have been dismantled, the towns have grown through the work carried out by men of little conscience or fear of God, corrupted by the Indians. This has been seen, and continues to be seen, every day that there is a decline in the spiritual well-being of these souls. Moreover, many die without confession or sacraments for this reason.

The viceroy decided to go out in person to the cities of this kingdom, to see with his own eyes what would be helpful for good governance. [He] passed some laws and ordinances through which justice would be administered; the Indians were not to be troubled or humiliated by their *encomenderos* or by anyone else who lived among them causing them problems, and they should pay their tributes and taxes equally and justly without the excesses and irregularities of the past, [with] reliable counts and quantities in everything being established. Thus, he put [his plan] into effect, which was very acceptable to

God and very much in the service of our lord the King. [Furthermore,] it was good and useful throughout the kingdom, such that if today all remained as he had ordered, commanded, and reformed, one would only have to wish, and [the kingdom] would be in peace and justice. Therefore, the viceroy set out and after going to Huamanga, he went up to the city of Cuzco, the principal city of this kingdom, which had been in ancient times the place and residence of the Incas, [the] natural lords of [this kingdom], although now fallen from its old glory. When he arrived, he learned about the [regional] government, giving many orders that were necessary for its purpose and functioning.

Among other things, he proposed that it would be good to relocate Cusi Titu Yupanqui, who governed in Vilcabamba, on behalf of his brother Tupac Inca, as the Marquis of Cañete had done in the case of Sayri Tupac, [who was also] his brother. [Toledo] did not know that [Cusi Titu Yupanqui] had died because the Indians of Vilcabamba hid it very carefully, not letting anyone from Cuzco leave or enter that region. After [Toledo] discussed and conferred with many people who had information of the interior [i.e., Vilcabamba] and had experience in the affairs of this kingdom, he decided to send an ambassador to discuss the matter with [Cusi Titu Yupanqui] and to induce him to leave in peace, as Sayri Tupac had done, [so] that that land would come under the domain of Your Majesty, since [Cusi Titu Yupanqui] was resisting the crown. [The viceroy] therefore selected Atilano de Anaya, a highly esteemed nobleman [and] citizen of the city of Zamora in Spain. [He picked Anaya] believing the negotiations would be easier [if conducted] through him because [Anaya] knew [Cusi Titu Yupanqui, as he] collected the tributes and taxes that belonged to the Incas in the *repartimientos* of Yucay and Jaquijahuana under the Inca's orders, keeping track of the tax money and other things for him. So [Toledo] ordered him to prepare to go to the province of Vilcabamba to [visit] Cusi Titu Yupanqui, who, as previously stated, ruled and was [the] absolute lord in place of Tupac Amaru, his legitimate brother. Once the necessary things and money were ready, almost at the start of Lent, [Anaya] left Cuzco accompanied by many Indians. When Atilano de Anaya arrived at the entrance of Chuquichaca, which is 20 leagues from the town of Puquiura, where the previously mentioned cleric was killed, and crossed the bridge, the *orejón* captains, named Paucar Unya and Colla Topa, as well as Curi Paucar Yauyo,[75] who the Inca had garrisoned there so that nobody would enter or leave, went out to [meet] him. They asked him what he was bringing the Inca and why he had come, and if he was bringing the taxes and tribute list from Yucay, because it had been four or five years since they had brought them.[76] In this manner, without giving him a chance to respond, and fearful that he, or one of the various Indians who had accompanied him there, might learn of the death of Cusi Titu Yupanqui, which had occurred over a year before and was [still] being kept secret, they speared [Anaya] and the Indians with him to death. They also took the money, tribute, and other things that the viceroy had sent the Inca. Only four or five Indians and one black man, named Diego, who belonged to Atilano de Anaya, escaped, [as] they fled upon seeing what was happening. With great haste and fortune they left the bridge and went quickly to Cuzco, where Viceroy Don Francisco de Toledo was, to relay the news. They arrived on the fifth Sunday of Lent, which was on what is commonly called [Saint] Lazarus Day in the year 1572.

After the viceroy heard the news, it weighed upon his soul and he deeply felt the death of Atilano, who was a highly honored and esteemed man. Moreover, as he had been sent by [the viceroy] under the title of ambassador, and seeing that the Indians, like barbarians and without respect, had broken the inviolable law awarded to ambassadors by all the nations of the world, [Toledo] wanted to punish Inca Cusi Titu, and everyone with him, at once, and to level and reduce that province to the service and obedience of Your Majesty, thus bringing the matter [of the Incas] to a close. [Therefore,] he sent Juan Blasco and Tarifeño, harquebusiers of the Royal Guard, who were close to him along with others. [He also sent] Father Diego López de Ayala,[77] who was the priest of the [Ollantay]tambo and Amaibamba Valley at the time, and Diego Plaza, [a] mestizo [and the] son of Juan de la Plaza, who was one of the first conquistadors of this kingdom [and] who was in the Amaibamba Valley at that time. They went with Don Pedro Pazca, [the] Indian leader of the abovementioned valley, to the bridge of Chuquichaca, accompanied by many Indians, and tried to find the body of Atilano de Anaya. They finally found it, as the Inca's captains who killed him had only thought of robbing him of the possessions he was carrying and had thrown him down a ravine, a very long way from where they had killed him, so that he would not be found easily. After they retrieved the body, they took him to the church of Amaibamba Valley, [which is] two leagues from the bridge. [There] they buried him, 10 days after he had been killed. It was certain that it was God's will that [the Indians] killed ambassador Atilano de Anaya without cause, thus provoking the ire of the viceroy, Don Francisco de Toledo, [who would then] try to take revenge on them in order to thus more completely punish the murder of Father Fray Diego, which they were covering up, fearful over what had happened.

Consequently, by sending Juan Basco and the others, the viceroy proclaimed full-scale war and started to gather people to move against Tupac Amaru and the other Incas who were hiding with him. On Quasimodo

Sunday,[78] they assembled, and he sent Governor Juan Alvárez Maldonado, a citizen of the city of Cuzco, and nine soldiers to go with him to the bridge of Chuquichaca.[79] These [soldiers] were Gabriel de Loarte, nephew of Doctor [Gabriel] Loarte, chief justice of Lima; Captain Juan Balsa, nephew of these Incas [and the] grandson of Huayna Capac, [who was] the legitimate son of Coya Doña Marca Chimbo[80] and Pedro de Orúe, [a] citizen of Cuzco; Juan Zapata, [a] servant of the viceroy; Juan de Ortega; and Galarza *alguaciles* of Cuzco. [The viceroy] ordered that they rebuild the bridge, as there was news that the Indians had burned it, and that when it had been [re]built, they [should] guard it with 50 Cañari Indian allies, without abandoning it until the viceroy sent them troops. Thus, they left on the Monday after Quasimodo, and [the viceroy] gave the title of *maese de campo* to Governor [Alvárez] Maldonado, a native of Salamanca, for having served Your Majesty loyally during the period of the rebellions. Juan Alvárez Maldonado was at the bridge [for] a month and a half, guarding it with great vigilance, having built it anew.[81] During that time, the Indians, seeing that [the Spaniards] had built [a new bridge] and realizing that [the Spaniards] must be waiting for additional people to enter Vilcabamba, believed it was wise to do everything possible to dismantle and burn it. Accordingly, 100 Indians came forward three times, as to converge at the bridge with their spears and arms, and with medallions and many feathers on their heads, as was their custom in war. In order to conceal their intent, they told [the Spaniards] to wait if they wanted to speak with Inca Cusi Titu [and] they would send word to him. [They did this] so that it would not become known that the Inca had died, or [that] the Augustine cleric who was with them in Puquiura indoctrinating them [was dead]. In this way, they would gain time so [that they could] harvest their maize and potato fields, and other fields of oca and legumes that they had planted, because if the Spaniards were to enter, [the Indians] would not be able to avail themselves of these [crops] but [rather] would have to have food brought [into the region]. [So] after harvesting them, [the Indians] kept [the crops] in secure, safe places so that they could use them in [times of] need during the war that they already surmised [was coming].

CHAPTER 79

How the Viceroy Don Francisco de Toledo sent Martín Hurtado de Mendoza de Arbieto as general against Tupac Amaru and the battle against him

After the *maese de campo*, Juan Alvárez Maldonado, had been at the bridge for a month and a half, as previously recounted, Don Antonio Pereyra, a

Portuguese gentleman [and] citizen of Cuzco, arrived with 20 soldiers.[82] Within eight days, Doctor [Gabriel de] Loarte, alcalde of the court of the [Royal] Audiencia of Lima, and Doctor Friar Pedro Gutiérrez, of the Order of Alcántara, who at that time was the judge [of the Royal Audiencia] [and] the chaplain of Viceroy Don Francisco de Toledo, and who was later [a member] of the Supreme Council of the Indies, also arrived. They brought with them 250 men, citizens and soldiers, all very distinguished and brave. These brave and gallant men came well supplied with weapons and uniforms. At the bridge, by order of the aforementioned viceroy, who had provided their supplies, they placed Martín Hurtado de Arbieto in charge, as the general and head of everyone. Don Antonio Pereyra and Martín de Meneses [were named] as infantry captains; [Francisco] Orgón[ez] de Valencia, native of Zamora, [was named] captain of artillery.[83] Captain Antón de Gatos [was named] as *sargento mayor* of the entire army. Mancio Sierra [de] Leguizamo,[84] Alonso de Mesa,[85] and Hernando Solano [were named] as advisors on affairs of war. They were citizens of Cuzco [and] were among the first conquistadors and discoverers of this kingdom. They [were] men of great fortune and valor, who had taken pleasure in serving Your Majesty on all occasions. Captain Julian de Humarán, citizen of the city of [La] Paz and permanent *regidor* [manager] of the city of Cuzco, went as quartermaster of the army in order to collect all the necessary food, weapons, and ammunition.[86]

Martín García [Oñaz] de Loyola, a Biscayan gentleman, [the] captain of the viceroy's guard, who was later [a member] of the Order of Calatrava, also went. He took with him in his squad 28 outstanding soldiers, sons of citizens and conquistadors of this kingdom, and some other principal gentlemen who wanted to serve Your Majesty on this expedition and who thus came forth to meet their obligations. Among them were Don Jerónimo Marañon[87] and Don Francisco de Mendoza, commonly called "the Paraguayan" since he was born there. He was [the] brother of Don Diego de Mendoza, whom the Viceroy Don Francisco de Toledo later beheaded at Chuquisaca.[88]

In addition, so that they could better wage war and [so] that the Indians would swoon upon seeing themselves attacked on so many fronts, the viceroy sent Gaspar Arias de Sotelo,[89] a native of Zamora, one of the most prominent gentlemen of the kingdom and a close relative of Viceroy Blasco Nuñez Vela, and who had served Your Majesty on all occasions since the rebellion of Gonzalo Pizarro. [He was] a man of great courage and conceit. Nuño de Mendoza[90] went with him as captain, along with many other citizens of Cuzco and as many as 100 soldiers. [They were] under orders that if Martín Hurtado de Arbieto were to die on the expedition, Gaspar Arias de Sotelo would become *General Supremo*. He entered through his *encomienda* by way of Cocha Caxas and Curamba,[91] which is on the Royal Road from Lima to Cuzco before arriving at Abancay. Walking through narrow mountains and tortuous trails, he arrived at Pampaconas,[92] a very cold place 12 leagues from Vilcabamba (the old), where the Incas had their seat and court. They stopped there [i.e., at Pampaconas] so that the citizens and advisors could discuss and consider what would be a suitable course of action.

The Viceroy also sent Indian war allies to help the Spaniards on the expedition. Don Francisco Cayo Topa[93] went as general of the Cuzco *orejones*. He was in charge of 1,500 Indian combatants from all the provinces surrounding Cuzco. General Don Francisco Chilche,[94] [the] *cacique* of the Yucay Valley, went [as leader of] the Cañaris[95] and *mitimaes*.[96] As mentioned above, he had been suspected of poisoning and killing Sayri Tupac, for which he was in prison in Cuzco for a year. He was in charge of 500 Indians fighters who [were] well supplied with weapons.

Crossing the bridge unimpeded, the army marched in good order until [they] were three leagues from Vitcos and Puquiura, where there is a difficult passage full of undergrowth, through a steep mountain [that was] difficult to cross, called Quinua Racay and Coyaochaca. There, because Martín García [Oñaz] de Loyola had very few people with him, they sent 30 soldiers from the three companies of Don Antonio Pereyra, Martín de Menesses, and [Francisco] Orgóñez de Valencia to join [Loyola's company of] 28 [men].

On the last day of Pentecost, the Inca captains, Colla Topa and Paucar Unya, [both] *orejones*, and Cusi Paucar Yauyo, along with other captains, gathered their forces at the abovementioned place and passage of Coyaochaca. Because the difficulty and roughness of the terrain were in their favor, they thought it was an opportune place to ruin and destroy the Spaniards. So they arranged themselves, as is their custom to fight a battle. Because of the narrow trail and the mountain, Martín García [Oñaz] de Loyola, who was in the vanguard with Don Francisco Cayo Topa and Don Francisco Chilche with 500 Indian allies, started the fight. Because the Indians had put many palm points and scattered many thorns on the ground, so that the Spaniards would fall when they came to attack, [and] many snares of creepers to entangle and trip [the Spaniards], [Loyola] divided his men into three parts.[97] Both sides fought with great resolve, and Martín García [Oñaz] de Loyola was very nearly killed. As [he was] fighting, an enemy Indian, who was so large and strong that he looked [like a] half-giant, came out and grabbed García [Oñaz] de Loyola by the shoulders such that he could not move. However, one of our Indian allies named Corrillo came to his aid with a sword. He slashed at [the enemy's] feet, knocking him down, and with a second blow he splayed his shoulders such that he fell down dead. And thus, on account of this Indian, Captain Martín García [Oñaz] de Loyola was spared from death. The courage and speed with which Corrillo took the life of the half-giant in two strokes of his sword and saved his captain was certainly a noble feat to be written in history.

The battle lasted two and a half hours, with great resolve on the part of the Indians and demonstrations of courage and bravery, but at the height of the battle, they shot an Inca captain with an harquebus, a very brave and courageous Indian named Parinango, who was the general of the Cayambis,[98] and he fell dead, along with Maras Inca, another captain, and many other spirited Indians. With this, they became discouraged and retreated, and thus the Spaniards were victorious. This victory occurred on the third day of Pentecost at three in the afternoon. The defeated Indians started retreating little by little into the hills and into the forest, and this opportunity allowed many of them to escape.

On the second day of rest after winning the victory, General Martín Hurtado de Arbieto ordered that [the Spanish army] continue looking for a path through which they could leave the mountains without endangering anyone, since there could be Indians hidden in the interior who knew the paths and trails. In the last battle, as the Indians were withdrawing, they threw boulders from a mountainside at the soldiers and killed [two] Spaniards named Gonzalo de Ribadeneira and Gonzalo Pérez. These [soldiers] were buried on the trail itself, [their graves] marked by two crosses, because they could not find a more convenient or suitable place to bury them. As the general wanted to do everything to avoid the Spaniards being killed in an ambush by the Indians, the Spanish soldiers and their Indian allies went from one place to another looking for a way out of the narrow mountains.

CHAPTER 80

A trail was discovered whereby the army entered the
Puquiura Valley, and other things that befell them

They searched for a path for three days after the aforementioned battle, when a mestizo soldier named Juanes de Cortazaga, [the] son of Juanes de Cortazaga, who was a citizen of Arequipa, found a safe place with no impediments. Greatly pleased with this, the general moved the army in an orderly fashion, and everyone left this way with the supplies. They arrived at the Puquiura Valley, where the Inca had his house and there was a church run by the Augustinian fathers, whom we have mentioned. [This was] where Cusi

Titu Yupanqui died, and [where] they had their small settled villages. They found fields of maize ready to be harvested in this valley. Since the army was short of food, the Spaniards and Indians rejoiced and were able to resupply themselves, especially as there was much native livestock, [including] rams and sheep.[99]

Having rested, the army left there for the site of Pampaconas, which, as we have said, is a very cold place where they found a great quantity of potatoes and legumes, and they [also] found 97 Castilian cows that the Incas had, as well as Castilian sheep and pigs and a salt mine.[100] From this unpleasantly [cold] place, they walked to the site at Vicos Calla, where the Incas had silver mines, as they later discovered. [These mines] were worked and continue to be worked to this day.[101] The *maestre de campo*, Juan [Alvárez] Maldonado, charged in and yelled: "*Arcay tucui nocap*" ([referring to] the livestock, food, and clothing they were bringing as plunder), which means "Take everything, for it is mine!" and [then] he fell off his horse into a swamp. The following day, they arrived at the place of Pampaconas, three leagues by trail. Because it is such rugged terrain and the mountains are densely overgrown with trees and so steep, the army stopped for 13 days, since many soldiers and Indians had fallen ill with measles. [The stop] allowed them to rest and for the ill to recover, and to gather more information and news of the road, which those of the army were not familiar with.[102]

On the eleventh day that the army was resting at that post, an Indian who had surrendered in the previous battle of Coyaochaca escaped with a cloak and dagger stolen from a soldier. This Indian was going to warn Tupac Amaru, and his uncle and nephew and their captains, about the Spaniards' situation and how they were stationed. He was caught, returned, and hanged that same day by the guards and sentinels to serve as a lesson to others who had surrendered that they [should] not attempt to escape. This Indian was named Canchari.

After 13 days, the army left from there and, with a great deal of effort on everyone's part, they passed through the forested slopes and gorges. They found sacrificed *cuyes* [guinea pigs], which are like Castilian rabbits, at three or four places along the trail. It is very common for the Indians [to make offerings] during war, and in times of hunger or pestilence, and while attempting or conducting any difficult and arduous negotiations. [This is done] in order to placate their *huacas* and to find out, through the signs revealed in the *cuyes*, what events will befall them, whether they will be prosperous or unfortunate, sad or happy and joyful.[103] They had done this in the places and areas through which the army was marching. When [the Spaniards] arrived at a passage called Chuquillusca,[104] which is a jagged cliff that runs along the edge of a voluminous river such that it was hardly possible to walk along it, the soldiers and Indian allies had to crawl or hold one another's hands, with great difficulty and risk, to get through. Upon seeing this, a Portuguese soldier, named Pascual Juárez, threw a *versete* [a small artillery piece] over his shoulder. He was able to get through this path, [even though] it was so steep that 50 Indians could not have passed with the *versete* without great danger, as already mentioned, and many [other] members of the army were [later] seen falling off [the trail]. He did a noble deed and a great service to our lord God and to Your Majesty, because they were [able to] discharge this [*versete*] and a small *culebrina* [a small canon] to put the Indians to flight and so that the Spaniards would not be endangered at such a bad pass. [This is] because the enemy was within sight of the Christians, shouting and screaming loudly, shooting arrows [and rolling] boulders. And in every difficult place that the Cañari Indian allies broke rank, leaving the company where they were protected by the Spaniards and harquebusiers, they would return with spear wounds that their enemies inflicted [when] given the chance. Although, as we know, the Cañaris were very skillful with their spears, their enemies had more practice, since there were days when they never let go of their weapons, and they were familiar with the area and knew where they could easily take advantage of our [troops]. Thus, on occasions, they were able to inflict damage.

The next day, as the army was marching to Tumichaca, an Inca captain named Puma Inca came out to [greet] the Spaniards in peace and with signs of goodwill that appeared to be sincere and true. This captain was always with the Incas Tupac Amaru and Quispe Titu, never leaving their side, and they had discussed among themselves [about] giving obedience to General [Hurtado de] Arbieto, because they wanted the war to end and have no more battles with the enemy, but instead to make peace. [This was] because on his deathbed Manco Inca, [the] father of Tupac Amaru, had ordered them [to do this] or suffer his curse if they did the contrary, since he saw clearly that they could not sustain themselves in that land if the Spaniards were to enter in numbers against them. Because the Incas had made these agreements, Curi Paucar and the other captains of the Sun, [including] Colla Topa and Paucar Unya, [both] *orejones*, had decided to kill them, since [the captains] did not want to make peace, but to continue the war and defend themselves unto death.

Some [people] say that [these captains] were the most insistent on killing the blessed Father Friar Diego Ortiz, which we have described, and that Martín Pando, a mestizo who was secretary of Cusi Titu Yupanqui, helped them. Furthermore, they say that after [Pando] helped them in that evil deed, the captains made him commit idolatry. Wicked and cowardly, or of little faith, like the Indians among whom he lived, [Pando] committed idolatry. Thus, on this occasion, the Spaniards found a very small pit in his house where he made his sacrifices that, actually, the mestizos of this kingdom generally frown upon. [Crossed out: "Some (mestizos), albeit only a few, have shown signs of virtue in their childhood and youth. On entering in ●●●● they have renounced the customs and inclinations that they inherited from their grandparents and that they suckled at the breasts of their mothers. Because in the condition and treatment, ordinarily ●● ●●●● ●●●●●●●●●●."][105] They say that as Martín Pando [crossed out: "who"] finished committing idolatry, which the Indians call a *pago* [offering], they gave him his just reward, killing this unfortunate as payback and compensation for his sin and abominable iniquity.

The day that Captain Puma Inca came out in peace, as mentioned, the army arrived with the general and other captains at Anonay, where they stopped and spent the night. They camped with great care and precaution, as they were afraid the Indians would suddenly appear, since they found many palm thorns tipped with a poisonous herb strewn on the ground, so that those who stepped on them would certainly be killed. [Puma Inca] warned of this so that they would be careful and walk cautiously. Captain Puma Inca offered obedience to General Martín Hurtado de Arbieto in the name of the Incas Tupac Amaru and Quispe Titu, stating that the Incas were asking for peace and wanted mercy. [He also stated] that the general [should] punish the rebels, [and that] they did not dare come out in person to offer obedience to the general because they were afraid that Curi Paucar and the other *orejón* captains, who were impeding [the troops], would kill them. Also [the situation] was beyond their control for the aforesaid reason, and the death of Atilano de Anaya was not at all their fault, nor had they given the order [to kill Anaya], since they were in the interior at that time. Instead, [it was] Curi Paucar and the other *orejón* captains under his authority who had done it so that the death of Cusi Titu Yupanqui, [Tupac Amaru's] brother, and [the death of] Father [Ortiz] would not become known. This Puma Inca [also] told of how the captains had built a fort, which was well supplied and fortified, called Huayna Pucará [Young Fort], and provided a sketch and [explained] the means by which it could be overtaken without putting any Spaniards or Indians in danger during the storming [of the fort]. At this time, the enemies were within sight of the army, briefly showing themselves in contempt of our [troops].

CHAPTER 81

How, through the advisement of Puma Inca, the fort
of Huayna Pucará was taken by force of arms

The following day, the army rose and marched two leagues in good order toward Huayna Pucará, where the enemy had fortified themselves.[106] They rendezvoused at a place called Panti Pampa.[107] The Spanish army stopped there to discuss how to take the fort and to prepare the things they would need for the assault, which was expected to be very difficult and dangerous. There were so many disagreements among the captains and citizens over where to station the army that they almost came to blows. Since most, if not all, of those who were there serving Your Majesty were prominent and selected, rich and powerful men, estate owners of great wealth who served at their own expense, they were losing their respect for the *maese de campo*. But then the general, who was trailing a little behind, arrived and diffused the situation, and the army settled down as best they could. Their enemies were within sight, practically within the army's camp, as they continued to approach.

The *orejón* captain, Puma Inca, who we said had come to swear obedience, the general, and the other advisors and captains who were holding counsel [discussed] the site and the place that the army, with their supplies, had to pass the next day. Through [his] plan and willingness, this captain discussed everything that he was asked and he gave very truthful and accurate advice, which was no small matter. Thus, it is well known that [it was] on account of his advice that they won the battle and took the fort.[108] [This is] because he told them that [Huayna Pucará] was very large, measuring a league and a half, reaching nearly two, and that the path along which they must walk was very narrow, like a crescent moon, across rocky [terrain] and through mountain forests, with a voluminous and wide river running beside the path. [He warned] that taking [this route], where it is impossible for two people at a time to walk or pass through, and fighting the enemy, who would be up in the heights along that league-and-a-half stretch that formed a rough knife-edge ridge, was very dangerous and foolhardy. The Indians had made a very strong fort out of stone and clay. Within the fort they had many piles of rocks to throw by hand and with slings. Also above the fort, along the entire ridge, there were very large rocks with levers. If anyone were to release them, they would send the boulders rolling down. The [natives] would have certainly done this when the Spanish army and their Indian war allies were walking in double file with all the supplies along the crescent ridge. Therefore, if God had permitted the enemy to put what they had planned and prepared into action, not a single soul of the entire army would have been left alive, neither Indian nor Spaniard, as the boulders would have killed everyone, crushing them as they came rolling down. Anyone who escaped [the boulders] with their life would have had to throw themselves into the river, where they would drown, quickly pulled under by the weight of their weaponry and clothing. And if anyone were to escape from the boulders and the river, he would also perish, because on the other side [of the river] were 500 Chuncho Indians from the Andes, archers who would leave no one alive [and] who would finish them off with arrows. So the warning of Puma Inca served the Spanish army well that day as they set out toward their desired goal, [which was] finishing the war.

The next day, Monday, all the soldiers and gentlemen of the army prepared themselves and performed all the duties that in such circumstances befit Christians; confessing, [taking] communion, and preparing their arms, because it was understood that, without a doubt, the [upcoming] combat and taking of the fort would be dangerous, given where it was situated and the precautions taken by their enemies in it. General Martín Hurtado de Arbieto went out to the army accompanied by General Gaspar Sotelo and all the citizens and captains, and from the rosters he had of the force, he started calling out the soldiers he deemed [suitable]. [When] there were about 150, he ordered them to go along a high and steep ridge a league and a half [long], along the hilltops. These soldiers then departed, as ordered. It must have been after six in the morning [when] they began climbing the hill, which was so steep and difficult that they had to crawl, holding onto one another until, finally, by the grace of God, they safely reached the summit at about one o'clock in the afternoon. Commanding the summit, they showed themselves to the enemy, who was well organized, as is customary in war. Being skillful and experienced [at fighting] in this terrain, and seeing the Spaniards above and themselves below and [thus] subject to [the Spaniards'] will, they thought it unwise to wait for them there, and so they retreated little by little to the fort of Huayna Pucará, leaving behind the boulders and rocks they had lined up to destroy the Spaniards.

The general went with the army and supplies, advancing little by little, stopping every once in a while to pass the time and to allow those taking the heights to reach the top. [He waited] until the Spaniards and Indian allies shouted from the heights, firing their harquebuses. [They] fired the artillery little by little against the fort to frighten their enemies, who were retreating there. On our part, we were doing everything possible to reach [the fort], but the rough, overgrown, and narrow trail detained [us]. But in the end, God granted [victory], with the help provided by those above [the fort] and the skillfulness of those below. As they neared, [the Spaniards] shouted

"Santiago!" [and] they attacked the fort. After discharging a good volley of harquebus fire, they took [the fort]. The Indians defended themselves for a while with courage and daring, although without endangering any of our [troops], who, as the road and the climb to the fort were so difficult and rough, were exhausted.

The next day, which was Tuesday, 13 prominent soldiers who usually were [positioned] in the heights of the bridge of Chuquichaca set out. Don Francisco Chilche, [the] *curaca* of Yucay [and] general of the Cañari, went with them. They arrived at Machu Pucará [Old Fort], where Manco Inca defeated Gonzalo Pizarro, [Francisco de] Villacastín, Captain [Rodrigo] Orgón[ez], and others. Following these prominent [soldiers] the army came to a halt, and the enemy came in numbers to attack them, with so much shouting and howling that at first it caused some confusion, such that a servant of Don Jerónimo de Figueroa, a nephew of Don Francisco de Toledo, [accidentally] set fire to a doublet he was wearing. If [Figueroa] had not thrown himself into a nearby stream, he would have undoubtedly been burned beyond salvation.

That day, the advancing army arrived at Marcanay, where they found many maize fields that had not yet been harvested, as well as bananas, chili peppers, and great quantities of yuca, cotton, and guavas. This made the forces extremely happy and they replenished themselves with the fruit and food they found, as they were starving and in need of sustenance. Because a mestizo soldier named Alonso Hernández de la Torre, [the] son of Francisco Hernández de la Torre, a man of seniority in this kingdom, broke [ranks] and took some sugarcane to eat, the *maese de campo*, Juan Alvárez Maldonado, gave him a beating in order to prevent any disobedience from the other soldiers, who were dispersing [and] breaking from their ranks for lack of discipline. [Alvárez Maldonado did this] because the Indians could be [waiting] in ambush and suddenly emerge [to attack] those who strayed from their squadron and do much damage; as we have seen on infinite occasions, an entire army can be destroyed for not remaining vigilant of the enemy.

CHAPTER 82

How General Martín Hurtado de Arbieto entered Vilcabamba and
sent [his forces] after Quispe Titu, and they apprehended him

The next morning, which was the day of Lord Saint John the Baptist, 24 June 1572, General Martín Hurtado de Arbieto ordered the entire army to be organized by their companies with their captains and Indian allies. Likewise, the generals Don Francisco Chilche and Don Francisco Cayotopa with their other [native] captains [were ordered to] march, taking the artillery and their flags in an orderly fashion. They marched into the town of Vilcabamba at 10 o'clock in the morning, everyone on foot [as] the terrain is very rough and craggy and not suited in any way for horses. They found the entire town sacked, such that if the Spaniards and Indian allies had done it, it would have been no worse because all the Indian men and women had fled into mountains, taking as much as they could with them. The rest of the maize and food was [left] in the *bohíos* [huts] and storage houses, where they typically keep them. They burned and destroyed [the city] such that it was [still] smoldering when the army arrived. The House of the Sun, where they kept their major idol, was also burned. [The Indians] believed that if the Spaniards did not find food or any sustenance quickly, they would soon turn around and leave the region rather than remain and settle it, because they had done this when Gonzalo Pizarro[109] and [Francisco de] Villacastín entered [the region]. The lack of sustenance forced [the Spaniards] to turn back and leave the land in their control. [It was] with this intention that the Indians fled, setting fire to everything they could not take.

The army rested there for one day, the soldiers relaxing in the town of Vilcabamba. The next day, which was the second day after their arrival, General [Hurtado de] Arbieto sent for Gabriel de Loarte and Pedro de Orúe, Inca de Orúe,[110] Captain Juan Balsa, [who was the] uncle of the Incas Tupac Amaru and Quispe Titu, and Pedro Bustinza, [who was] also [Tupac Amaru's] uncle, along with other outstanding friends and comrades. [Juan Balsa and Pedro Bustinza were the] sons of the two *coyas* [noblewomen] Doña Juana Marca Chimbo and Doña Beatriz Quispe Quipi, daughters of Huayna Capac. He ordered them to leave through the hills known as Ututo,[111] which is a rough mountain, in pursuit of Inca Quispe Titu, because the general had received news that he was escaping with some people toward the Pilcosuni, which is a province on the other side of the Andes, toward the Marañon River. This group left in great haste after Quispe Titu Yupanqui, and marched through the hills mentioned above, which was extremely [hard] work, as no water or food was found apart from what they had taken from Vilcabamba. At the end of six days, Captain Juan Balsa, who was in the vanguard (with Pedro de Orúe as second and Gabriel de Loarte as rear guard), came upon the place where Quispe Titu Yupanqui was with his wife, who was within days of giving birth. Also with him [were] 11 Indian men and women who served him, as the rest of [his] people had scattered. Having caught him, they turned back toward Vilcabamba. In two [days] they descended what had taken six days to walk up.

It is said that in that mountain they found a number of poisonous snakes and it pleased Divine Majesty that no one was endangered by them, because they [do] great harm. The exhaustion and hard work that they, of necessity, experienced on the road turned into flowers and happiness as a result of their good fortune. Thus, they arrived with [Quispe Titu] at Vilcabamba and handed him over to the general at the Inca's very own house.[112] There they divested [Quispe Titu and his wife] of all their clothing and baggage, such that neither he nor his wife was left with any clothes to change into, nor any of their tableware in the prison. Although it is a warm land, they suffered from cold and hunger. The temperature of the land is such that honeybees, like those in Spain, build hives under the eaves and at the rear of the *buhíos*, and maize can be harvested three times a year. The fields benefit from the good disposition of the land and from the waters with which they irrigate it at the [proper] time. Chili pepper plants grow in great abundance, [along with] coca and sugarcanes (from which honey and sugar are made), yucas, sweet potatoes, and cotton.

The town covers or, better said, used to cover an area half a league wide, similar in plan to Cuzco, and a great stretch in length, where parrots, chickens, ducks, local rabbits,[113] turkeys, pheasants, curassows, guans, macaws, and a thousand other types of birds of diverse and very beautiful plumages [lived]. The houses and *buhíos* [were] covered with good straw. There are a large number of guavas, pecans, peanuts, lucumas, papayas, pineapples, avocados, and various other wild fruit trees. The house of the Inca had upper and lower floors covered with [roof] tiles,[114] and the whole palace [was] painted with a great variety of paintings in their style, which was quite a sight to see. There was a plaza that could hold many people, where they celebrated and even raced horses. The doors of the house[s] were of very fragrant cedar, which is plentiful in that land, and the *zaquizamíes* [Arabic: gables or attic] [were made] of the same material. In this way, the Incas did not miss the pleasures, grandeur, and opulence of Cuzco in that distant land or, better said, [that] land of exile, because the Indians brought them anything they could [want to] have from the outside for their joy and pleasure; and they enjoyed themselves there.

At the time that General [Hurtado de] Arbieto sent those we have mentioned in search of Inca Cusi [*sic* Quispe] Titu Yupanqui and they brought him [in], he sent Captain Martín de Meneses in a different direction to thoroughly search for Inca Tupac Amaru. [Meneses] set out and he and his company arrived [at a place] six leagues inland, which they call Panquis and Sapacati.[115] There they found the golden idol of the Sun,[116] and much silver, gold, precious emeralds, [and] a lot of old clothing, all of which, according to rumor, would increase in value to over a million [pesos]. All of this was divided among the Spaniards and Indian allies. Even the two priests who were traveling with the army enjoyed their shares. Some theologians and learned men were of the opinion that [taking] such spoils was an injustice and that they could not take or profit from them; however the law of unbridled greed prevailed over natural and divine law. Thus, they took everything, including many silver and gold pitchers and vessels with which the Incas served themselves. Part [of this loot] had escaped the hunger of the Spaniards and the Pizarros in Cuzco at the beginning [of the conquest], and part had then been hidden away and taken out later. They had even crafted pieces in their style, in order to replace the many that they had lost and had been taken from them by the Spaniards in lawlessness and with little fear of God, as if the Incas and Indians were not lords of their estates, [but] rather, as though all rights of possession had been lost and [could be] granted to the first who could take it by force. And so everyone took whatever they could. So, in fact, their possessions [were] ill-gotten goods.

[General Hurtado de Arbieto] sent Captain Don Antonio Pereyra in a different direction in pursuit of Inca Tupac Amaru and to do everything possible to follow close behind him and the other captains who had fled with him, because [with them as] prisoners, the war would be concluded and the land peaceful and quiet. Don Antonio Pereyra set out and he showed such great skill that he caught up with and apprehended Colla Topa and Paucar Unya, [the] *orejón* captains previously mentioned, and along with them the traitor Curi Paucar fell into their hands. He was the cruelest of all the Inca captains, who had always insisted the most in sustaining the war and that peace and obedience not be granted. [Curi Paucar] had done the most harm and [was] the principal cause of Atilano de Anaya's death. [Pereyra] also caught many Indian enemies who were hidden in the mountain of Sapacatín and returned with the prisoners to Vilcabamba. On the way, a snake bit a young son of Curi Paucar, who was being carried on his [father's] shoulders. The poison was so strong that he died of the bite within 24 hours. Thus, they arrived at Vilcabamba, where [Pereyra] turned in the prisoners. Captain Don Antonio Pereyra did not take any of the spoils that were [seized] there for himself, because he was not greedy in the least. Rather, he had always served on the expedition with great valor, being the son of Captain Lope Martín, who always distinguished himself in Your Majesty's service during Pizarro's rebellion. Having gone to Spain in the company of President Pedro de la Gasca, [Lope Martín] returned to this kingdom, and in the uprising and revolution of Francisco Hernández Girón, having followed the royal standard on various occasions, and proving himself in all, was taken prisoner in the battle of the

Hoyas de Villacurin, six leagues from Ica, by Francisco Hernández [Girón], who later ordered that his head be cut off.[117] This is how he ended his days in Your Majesty's service, true and loyal. His body was later taken to Lima and buried in the main church there, where your flag was placed in the main chapel. There it remained for many years until time consumed it.

CHAPTER 83

How the general sent Captain Martín García [Oñaz]
de Loyola, who apprehended Inca Tupac Amaru

When Captain Don Antonio Pereyra returned to Vilcabamba with the prize of the abovementioned enemy captains, General [Hurtado de] Arbieto, who wanted very much to apprehend Inca Tupac Amaru because he believed that the war would not be concluded until [the Inca] was captured and that the Indians would always be restless as long as he was among them, decided to search for him again[118] Therefore, he sent General Martín García [Oñaz] de Loyola to search for [Inca Tupac Amaru] and his uncle, Huallpa Yupanqui, who had been an Inca general and was traveling with him. [Loyola] left with 40 soldiers along the Masahuay River of the Manaríes, [who are] Chuncho Indians, [in the] province of the Andes.[119] They walked 40 leagues from Vilcabamba, to where this river flows into or becomes the Marañon, and flows out into the North Sea,[120] [and where] they found six light balsa rafts, which were the ones by which the Incas and his captains and people had reached the other bank. It was there that Martín García [Oñaz] de Loyola [had previously] returned.[121]

At midday, while resting in the mountains full of huge trees and very tall mangroves, he and his soldiers saw five Chuncho Indians bathing on the other side [of the river]. The [native] who was [keeping] lookout was fishing [for] shad with his arrow. (These are very abundant in that river and the Indians kill them in the water with arrows.) Captain [Loyola] tried to [see] how they could capture some of those Indians, to obtain information and knowledge about the Inca, as no one else could know better. So he ordered six soldiers to prepare themselves. [His plan was that] as the Indians went into the mountains, [the soldiers] would get into the rafts in pairs and, crossing to the other side, attempt to capture [the Indians] any way they could because they could see smoke in the mountain. It was [coming from] a *buhío*, which was 350 fathoms long, with 20 doors, where they were cooking. Although some soldiers refused, Gabriel de Loarte finally said, "My companions and I will cross [over the river], and I am determined to bring back spoils." Thus, he [along] with

Pedro de Orúe, Captain Juan Balsa, Cristóbal Juárez (a Portuguese), [Domingo de][122] Tolosa (a Biscayan), and another got on the rafts and crossed the river in pairs. On the other side, they went into the place that he had indicated, and they were so lucky that they came upon seven Chuncho Indians, and with singular speed, they then caught five of them. The other two escaped because there were so many doors in the *buhío*. They did not [even] have time to grab their arrows, which they had in *colas de bayas* [quivers]. In the *buhío* they found cooked maize and more than 50 shads. They reassured the Chunchos with signs of great kindness. An Indian who had spent [time] with them and knew their [language] spoke to them in their language. They told them not to be afraid [and] that no harm or offense would come to them. They left the *buhío* with them and, [traveling] through the mountains, found themselves on the riverbank, where they saluted their companions, who were on the opposite bank, with their harquebusiers. When the rafts returned, Captain Martín García [Oñaz] de Loyola and his soldiers boarded them and crossed the river, where they ate in great relaxation and contentment. They were pleased with the spoils they had taken because they found 30 loads of extremely fine clothing [belonging to] the Inca, much rare velvet and rich silk, and many bundles from Rouen and Holland, cloth and basketwork [and] buskins and a lot of feathers from Spain, and, above all, an abundance of gold and silver cups and table service [belonging to] the Inca. Everyone rejoiced over [seizing] so many and such valuable spoils. It seemed to them, as there were so many of his things in the *buhío*, watched over by the Chunchos, that Tupac Amaru could not be very far from there.

Then Captain Martín García [Oñaz] de Loyola tried [to request], [speaking] with the Chunchos through an interpreter, that their *curaca* appear.[123] With [the] offerings and gifts that [García Oñaz de Loyola] gave them, their *cacique*, Ispaca, came forth to where the captain was [waiting for him] and received him very well.[124] [Ispaca] was the leader of the Chuncho Manarí Indians. [García Oñaz de Loyola] spoke with him, persuading him to tell him where Tupac Amaru was. In order to make him [feel] further obligated, he gave [Ispaca] certain garments that [belonged to] the Inca himself, and Castilian feathers, and [García Oñaz de Loyola said] that if he spoke truthfully and in good faith, [García Oñaz de Loyola] would give him much more and no harm would be done in his land or to his people. Fearful, Ispaca [crossed out, mostly unreadable: "●●●●●●●●●●●● fortune of Tupac Amaru ●●●●● ●●●●●●●●●●●●●●●●●●●●●●●●●●●● ●●●● ●●●●●●●●●●●●●●●●●"]. He said that [Tupac Amaru] had left there five days ago to travel by water in canoes[125] and to go to the Pilcosuni, [which is] another inland province. [He also said] that Tupac Amaru's wife was somber and frightened because she was days away from giving birth, and that since he loved her so much, [Tupac Amaru] himself was helping her carry her load, walking very slowly. [Ispaca] did not want to receive the gifts or the clothes of Tupac Amaru's, saying that he would be committing a great treachery against his lord. García [Oñaz] de Loyola took this *cacique* and, later that afternoon, left in search of Tupac Amaru, so that [he] would not pull ahead and escape with his general, Huallpa Yupanqui. [Loyola] left five soldiers and four Indians at the *buhío*, guarding the booty, clothes, and table service, [with instructions] to send food forward, as there was plenty of food there that the Inca had for his provisions. He took 37 soldiers with him and went into the forested mountains, following the trail that the Inca had taken. The food was [brought] after him and consisted of 10 loads of maize, five of peanuts, three of sweet potatoes, and eight of yucas for their maintenance.

García [Oñaz] de Loyola walked for 15 leagues before coming upon Tupac Amaru, who had veered from the path, along an arm of the sea, as one can refer to that large river. If García [Oñaz] de Loyola had not continued on the day that he received the news, and the following day, he would not have been able to reach [Tupac Amaru] with any amount of luck, because that day [the Inca] would have done critical things with his wife [to escape the Spaniards]. [He was] imploring her to get into the canoe so that they could travel forth by sea. But she was terrified of going so far out into open water, for more than 150 leagues, and this led to their imprisonment and death. Because if they had gotten into the canoe, it would have been impossible to catch them, as food [and provisions] had already been brought to them for [their trip] across to the opposite shore of that open water, and thus they would have been beyond reach.

The capture occurred in the following way: two mestizo soldiers who were at the forefront, named Francisco de Chávez, son of Gómez de Chávez, scribe of the Cuzco Municipal Council, and Francisco de la Peña, son of Benito de la Peña, also a public scribe of the same city, were walking at nine o'clock at night when they saw a campfire from afar. Little by little they reached the place where Inca Tupac Amaru was with his wife and General Huallpa Yupanqui, who were warming themselves.[126] Since they came upon them by surprise, they were very courteous to them, not wanting to agitate them. [The Spaniards] told [the Inca] not to be upset and that his nephew Quispe Titu was in Vilcabamba, safe and very well treated, and that he was not in any distress or being mistreated, and that his relatives, Juan Balsa and Pedro Bustinza, sons of the *coyas* Doña Juana Marca Chimbo and Doña Beatriz Quispe Quipi, his aunts, were coming for him. Because Francisco de Chávez was the first to reach the Inca, and also because he took some valuable Inca vases, he became known as "Chávez Amaru." As this was transpiring, Martín García [Oñaz] de Loyola arrived with Gabriel de Loarte and the other soldiers and apprehended the Inca. After spending a very apprehensive and cautious night, they [began their] return to Vilcabamba in the morning, where they arrived safely without any mishaps.

Tupac Amaru Inca was very affable, well mannered, modest, eloquent, and intelligent. [He was] solemn and strong and did not show concern over the quantities that he had lost, and that Loyola and all the other soldiers who had gone with him had stolen from him, except for [the loss of] a feather tied with gold thread, [made from the] tail of a macaw. He sorrowfully gave the *cacique* Ande, in person, a red blanket [so well made] that it was like fine satin from Granada, [as well as] a black velvet shirt. Because of this, Martín García [Oñaz] de Loyola became annoyed with [Tupac Amaru] and acted harshly. He shoved him, [and] it is widely said that he demanded more than one and a half million in gold, silver, Castilian clothes, silks, and many bars of silver, dishes, and bowls, as well as precious stones, jewels, and clothes. Captain [García Oñaz de] Loyola turned Tupac Amaru and his wife in to General Martín Hurtado de Arbieto, who was then granted the governorship of Vilcabamba, where he later took on the title of lord.[127]

CHAPTER 84

How Governor Arbieto ordered the body of Father Fray Diego
Ortiz removed from where the Indians had buried him

Governor Martín Hurtado de Arbieto [was] overjoyed at seeing such a fortunate end to the war, which had been deemed very difficult on account of the rough passes, grueling trails, and dense mountains found in that land where the Indians had been able to inflict much harm on the Spaniards. Having Tupac Amaru Inca, and his nephew Quispe Titu and his general and uncle Huallpa Yupanqui, [together] with Curi Paucar and the other *orejón* captains whom they had captured in his possession, [Hurtado de Arbieto] was ordered by Viceroy Don Francisco de Toledo to prevent the Spaniards from leaving, because he wanted the land settled. Therefore, [Hurtado de Arbieto] dispatched Gabriel de Loarte, Pedro de Orúe, Martín de Orúe, Juan Balsa, and Martín de Rivadeneira to the Marcanay pass,[128] where they remained on guard, without allowing any soldier to pass so that they would not return to Cuzco. [They did this because] if the Spaniards did not leave, they could settle the land better and [new] towns would be established at the most convenient places and locations.

At that time, having been told of the extremely cruel death that the Indians had brought upon the blessed father Fray Diego Ortiz, to which we have previously referred, the Governor ordered a search for the place where the Indians had buried his body, and he sent some soldiers for this purpose.[129] They finally found it, [buried] in the abovementioned way, under the roots of a large tree trunk. When they dug him out from there, they saw he had received a blow to the back of the neck from a *macana* [Taíno: club], and that he had five arrow wounds inflicted by the Indians. [When he was] removed from the pit and hole where he had been placed, the majesty of God wished to demonstrate the innocence of His servant and priest, in that after 14 months or more since he was killed by the Indians and buried in that place, they found his holy body dry, without any foul odor. He had two red roses on his face that seemed to spill blood. And [he appeared as he was] the moment after they had killed him, with no sign or trace of decay or worms, [even though] the area in which he had been buried at that time was very hot and forested, such that it always rains in the winter and summer. [In] the Ondara [*sic* Hoyara] Valley and in Chucullusca the mosquitoes disappeared until now.[130]

The soldiers put the body in a *petaca* [Nahuatl (*petlacalli*): wicker box] and took it to the town of San Francisco de la Victoria, which Vilcabamba was already called. Then, [once the body had been] placed inside a coffin, Governor Arbieto and Father Diego López de Ayala, who was vicar of that province at the time, came out with all the Spaniards who lived there at the time, in procession with their cross and a great quantity of wax, and put it on a stretcher that was being used to carry the coffin.[131] The governor, along with the most prominent [men] of the city, placed it upon their shoulders. Thus, with the greatest possible veneration, they laid him in the city church, where the vicar said mass and spoke in praise of the blessed priest and his holy zeal and intention. The governor [made] another [speech] to the Indians, denouncing the terrible and abominable deed they had committed, conveying to them the punishments that would befall them by the hand of God. When the mass was over, they put the holy body in a vault below the main altar.

But as the best proof of the blessed father's good favor before God in heaven, it would be good to tell and mention what was [included] in the reports that were written about it many years later in Vilcabamba and in the city of Cuzco.[132] Reliable witnesses state that Doña Mencia de Salcedo,[133] [a] natural daughter[134] of the aforementioned governor, went several days after [the funeral] to the coffin where the bones were kept in the vault and could be touched, since she had serious problems with her eyes and was in danger of losing them. Putting her eyes on the coffin, she prayed with great devotion to God. Divine Majesty decided to grant her mercy, whereupon she was cured of the illness that had afflicted her and [was] free of her ailment. Doña Leonor Hurtado de Ayala, [a] legitimate daughter of the governor, who mentions this in her testimony,[135] also states that because Doña Juana de Ayala [Ponce de León], her mother and the wife of the said governor, suffered from terrible pain in her molars, she would go to the coffin where the bones were kept and place her cheeks and jaw on it every time the pain got worse, whereupon the pain she felt would subside. God is powerful and knows how to honor those who serve Him in life and death. Therefore, this priest, moved by his zeal for serving God and saving souls, who in that province were in servitude and slavery to Satan, and by obedience to his prelate who sent him to enter [Vilcabamba], died in innocence. One must believe that Almighty God, [who] justly rewards the good, holds him in His glory, rewarding him for the work he had done for Him. So all of us in this kingdom who are involved in the conversion of these miserable [people's] souls must zealously do saintly [work] in order to earn God's honor. [We must] announce His Holy Name throughout these nations, leaving [behind] other vain and useless interests, which distracts from the honorable prize of the work that they themselves endure.

CHAPTER 85 (PARTIAL TRANSLATION)

How Governor Arbieto sent Tupac Amaru and the other prisoners to Cuzco, and [how] the viceroy dealt out justice to Tupac Amaru

A month after Martín Hurtado de Arbieto had captured the Indians Tupac Amaru, Huallpa Yupanqui, and Quispe Titu, an order arrived from Viceroy Don Francisco de Toledo. [It stated] that those who wished to leave for Cuzco could leave, since the land was peaceful and calm and there was no reason to fear, as the Incas who could rebel were now not able to do so. Therefore, he sent them to prison in the city of Cuzco, and Paucar Unya and Colla Topa, [Tupac Amaru's] captains, and other important prisoners also went with them. The viceroy ordered that they be brought to him so that he could see them and carry out his plans, because he was deeply hurt by the death of his ambassador, Atilano de Anaya.

On the way to Cuzco, Huallpa Yupanqui, [the] uncle of the Incas, fell ill with bleeding in his stomach. The disease became worse and he died a league before reaching Cuzco. Consequently, he did not see the pain and sadness that would befall his nephew, Tupac Amaru, within a few days.

Everyone entered the city of Cuzco in formation with the prisoners. Captain Martín García [Oñaz] de Loyola, who was the one that had captured Tupac Amaru, led him with a gold chain fastened around his neck, and his nephew, Quispe Titu, had one of silver (figure 3.3). All the captains and soldiers marched along with him according to their rank as the viceroy had ordered: the prisoners of greater and lesser status and the captains and principal *orejones* with them. Viceroy Don Francisco de Toledo was in residence in his mansion, which belonged to Diego de Silva,[136] [a] citizen of Cuzco, [who was] native of Ciudad Rodrigo [and a] gentleman of high station. [Toledo] watched from a window as the people entered. Fray García de Toledo, his uncle and member of the Order of Santo Domingo, was with him, and behind him was his chaplain, Fray Pedro Gutiérrez, who later was [a member] of the Royal Council of the Indies. When the Indians reached the window from which the viceroy was [watching], Captain [García Oñaz de] Loyola ordered them to take off their *llautos* [headbands], and Tupac Amaru [to remove] the tassel he wore as royal insignia; [however], they refused. Instead, they simply touched the *llautos* with their hands [and] bowed their heads toward the viceroy. Some people say that when Captain [García Oñaz de] Loyola told him to remove his tassel, Tupac Amaru said that he did not want to, because who was the viceroy but the King's *yanacona*, which means "servant of the king." In his anger, Loyola dropped the gold chain he was carrying, with which Tupac Amaru was being led as prisoner, and struck him twice, thinking that he was doing Your Majesty a service and pleasing the viceroy. Be that as it may, everyone present deemed it to be an undignified [act] for a nobleman. Tupac Amaru and his nephew, Quispe Titu Yupanqui, were put in prison in the house of Don Carlos Inca, [the] son of Paullu Topa, which the viceroy had turned into a fortress.[137]

[The Spaniards] conferred and discussed the case of the Incas at great length, [debating] over how to administer justice to them. Many people spoke and pleaded with the viceroy to temper his anger against them, but [their entreaties] were of no avail. Many theologians said that the Incas did not deserve death because they had not been baptized or initiated into the community of the Holy Roman Catholic Church, [and because] they had always striven for peace and acknowledged and given obedience to His Majesty, our King Felipe. [They asked] that [the Incas] be allowed to remain in their land and live in peace, and that they receive the faith and holy baptism.[138] Thus, [the theologians] presented many arguments on [the Incas'] behalf, to which the viceroy turned a deaf ear, determined to publicly mete out justice to Tupac Amaru, decapitating him in front of their eyes to remove any [possibility] of an insurrection once and for all. And to convey to the Inca Indians and the

FIGURE 3.3. *Tupac Amaru, in chains, being led by Captain Martín García Oñaz de Loyola. Drawing by Guaman Poma de Ayala; in Murúa ([ca. 1590] 2004: 50v).*

other provinces that King Felipe, our lord, was their only king and that they must obey him without looking to anyone else in the kingdom.

Thus, [the viceroy] ordered that the sentence against the Inca captains Collao Topa and Paucar Unya be carried out. Their hands were cut off. Curi Paucar Yauyo, who had opposed the Spaniards on every occasion and played the primary role in the death of Atilano de Anaya, was hanged in the plaza on the gallows of the city of Cuzco, putting an end to him and his evil deeds.

To execute Tupac Amaru, they built a scaffold covered in black in the middle of the public plaza of Cuzco. When he learned what was to become of him, [Tupac Amaru] pleaded emotionally with the viceroy to spare him, as he had committed no offense, nor would his death be of any value. [He asked] to be sent to His Majesty to be his *yanacona*, which means servant, but [Toledo] did not take advantage of the offer, nor was the hard heart of the obstinate viceroy moved to compassion or pity. Nor [was he moved] when Don Fray Agustín de la Coruña, bishop of Popayán, threw himself at the viceroy's feet in tears, pleading for [Tupac Amaru's] life because he was innocent and did not deserve the death that was planned for him, and [requesting] that he be sent to His Majesty in Spain [instead].[139] [Coruña was] an ecclesiastic [who led] an exemplary life, as is widely known in this kingdom, and had nobly granted the unfortunate Tupac Amaru his request to be baptized while [he] was in the houses of Don Carlos Inca. [However,] the viceroy resolutely refused him and closed the door on his requests and appeals in this case.

The city of Cuzco had never been seen in all its [prior] hardships or [at the time of Manco Inca's] siege, so on the verge of being lost, as it was on the day that the sentence was ordered to be carried out. An infinite [number] of Indians came out, [including] Incas and *orejones* from other provinces, to see [the Spaniards] bring out the unfortunate Tupac Amaru to be decapitated. Dressed in mourning cloth, weeping, he was escorted by Viceroy Don Francisco de Toledo's guard and halberdiers. It was such that one could not walk through the streets, and the balconies were full of people, important lords and ladies who [were] moved by compassion, weeping together at seeing a young man taken to die before his time. Thus, it can truly be said that no one, of neither high nor low status, did not grieve his death. The viceroy was widely cursed, as were all who counseled him [to rule] against the sad Amaru. [The Inca] stepped up onto the scaffold, where Bishop Don Fray Agustín de la Coruña, who had washed him the day before with the water of holy baptism, publicly confirmed [the Inca] before all, giving him strength through the grace of that Holy Sacrament instituted by Christ into the Catholic faith.

They say that a notable and wondrous event [then occurred].[140] As the plaza was completely full with a multitude of Indians watching the sad and deplorable spectacle and [knowing] that their lord Inca was going to die, the skies thundered and resounded with their shouts and screams. His relatives, who were close by, marked this sad tragedy with weeping and tears. Those who were on the scaffold at the execution ordered the people to be quiet, upon which the poor Tupac Amaru, lifting his hand, clapped, at which everyone fell silent, as though there were not a living soul in the plaza, and not a voice or a sob was to be heard. This was a demonstration and a clear sign of the obedience, fear, and respect that the Indians had for their Incas and lords. So [Tupac Amaru], who most had never seen, as he was always secluded in Vilcabamba since he was a child, was able to suppress weeping and tears that come from the heart, which are so difficult to conceal and hide, with a single clap. Then the executioner blindfolded him and, holding him on the platform, cut off his head with a cutlass, and thus the sad and broken young man ended his days and the male line descending from Manco Inca ceased (figure 3.4).[141]

His nephew, Quispe Titu, was banished to Lima by Viceroy Don Francisco de Toledo. Because the climate there was so hot and different from that of the mountains, where the young man had been raised, he ended his days prematurely.[142] [Toledo also assigned] some [of his] sisters and aunts to the houses of the citizens of that city, [but as a result] of their work and misfortunes and lack of shelter, they went from one place to another, with much compassion and pity.

They brought Manco Inca's body from Vilcabamba, where he was murdered by Diego Méndez, a mestizo, [together] with Briceño y Escalante and others who escaped from the battle of Chupas, Huamanga, as previously mentioned. Having brought [his body], Viceroy Don Francisco de Toledo ordered that it be burned in the heights of the old fortress, named Quíspiguaman.[143] He gave this order so that the Indians who knew where he was buried would not secretly remove him and worship him.[144]

As I have stated, there remained a legitimate daughter of Sayri Tupac and granddaughter of Manco Inca, great-granddaughter of Huayna Capac, universal lord of these kingdoms, named Doña Beatriz Clara Coya de Mendoza, whose marriage to Captain Martín García [Oñaz] de Loyola, captain of his guard, was arranged by the viceroy.[145] Regarding the marriage, since Cristóbal Maldonado, native of Salamanca, claimed to have married her first, there were great disagreements and lawsuits between them, which lasted for many years.[146] The bishop of Cuzco and archbishop of Lima issued rulings on these, all of which were concluded by the ruling of the *maestro* Fray Juan de Almares, ecclesiastic of the Order of Saint Augustine. [He] was an erudite professor

FIGURE 3.4. *The execution of Tupac Amaru. Drawing by Guaman Poma de Ayala; in Murúa ([ca. 1590] 2004: 51v).*

of literature and apostolic judge at the Royal University of Lima. [As a result, García Oñaz de Loyola was able to] remain with her.

Captain Martín García [Oñaz] de Loyola, who was [later] sent by the governor of the kingdom to Chile, where he went with his wife, was killed in an unfortunate event along with 700 other men by the Indians at the end of the year 1598.[147] Therefore, his wife went to Lima, where she died within a year of her husband's death. She was survived by one legitimate daughter,[148] who was taken to Spain, having inherited the *encomienda* of Indians that belonged to her mother, which comes out to about 10,000 assayed pesos in rent, and so this branch of the Inca lineage was destroyed and put to an end.

There are many other descendants of Huayna Capac in the city of Cuzco, especially, as already mentioned, [the son of] Paullu Topa,[149] whose baptismal name was Don Cristóbal Paullu Topa and who served Your Majesty so [well]. He had many sons and daughters with various women, but the most important was Don Carlos Inca, [who was] legitimate [and] married a noble Spanish lady, named Doña María de Escobar. Because of certain suspicions against him, Viceroy Don Francisco de Toledo kept this one [i.e., Carlos Inca] in prison for a long time and took away a certain income that he had; as a result he became very poor.[150] Some say that when a son was born to him, whom he named Don Melchor Inquill Topa, who is also called Don Melchor Carlos Inca, [Carlos Inca] crowned [his son as Inca] in front of many Incas and *curacas* who were at that time in Cuzco.[151] Even if this had been so, it would have been more out of frivolity and ignorance than an intention to rise up against Your Majesty. After Don Carlos died, [Melchor Carlos Inca], being of marrying age, made a marriage agreement with Doña Leonor Carrasco, [the] legitimate daughter of Pedro Alonso Carrasco, a Knight of the Order of Santiago. Because [Pedro Alonso Carrasco] was a man of spirit and courage, in the year 1601, he was in prison for the month of May in Cuzco. [This was] on the orders of Juan Fernández de Recalde, a judge of the Royal Audiencia of Lima, for which reason, at that time, Don García de Solis Portocarrero, a Knight of the Order of Christ and a corregidor, also went to prison, for trying, as it was rumored, to rebel against Royal service. It was said that he had an agreement with Don Melchor Carlos Inca. But, in the end, Don García [de Solis Portocarrero][152] was decapitated by [order of] licentiate Francisco Coello, alcalde of the court of Lima [and] judge of the commission who was sent [to investigate] this matter by Viceroy Don Luis de Velasco, [a] Knight of the Order of Santiago, who was governor of the kingdom of [Peru] at this time.

According to the Royal Audiencia and the investigations that were conducted with great care and diligence in this case, Don Melchor Carlos Inca was not found to have made any agreement, or to have known what [the conspiracy] entailed or participated in this. So he was set free and most honorably declared [innocent]. [This] was publicized and made known throughout the kingdom. In that same year, by order of Your Majesty, he went to the kingdom of Spain, having been given, to this end, great aid to cover the expenses. Several days after arriving at the court where Your Majesty resides, he was granted the favor of 7,000 ducats in income. He was ordered to give up his holdings in Peru and to remain in Spain forever, where he is presently, and to bring his wife there.[153]

NOTES

1. Many of the illustrations in Murúa's ([ca. 1590] 2004; [ca. 1616] 2008) works appear to be by Guaman Poma de Ayala. There is also some overlap in the information presented by these two authors in their separate manuscripts. The nature of their relationship is, however, not well understood.

2. In 1591 and then again in 1596, Murúa presented an early version of his work to the local lords of Cuzco for their approval (Ossio 2008b: 116).

3. Murúa's earliest work briefly describes the execution of Tupac Amaru, but it provides very little information on the Vilcabamba region. That is because he did not have access to the Ortiz documents at that time (see document 5, this volume).

4. For additional information on the censorship of Murúa, see Adorno (2008).

5. More commonly known as Paullu Inca or simply Paullu.

6. The first raid into Vilcabamba occurred in 1537 under the leadership of Rodrigo Ordóñez and Rui Díaz (Pizarro [1571] 1921: 365). Soon afterward, Ordóñez was captured by Pizarro's forces during the battle of Las Salina and then executed.

7. This raid into the Vilcabamba region occurred in 1539.

8. Francisco de Villacastín, having sided with Gonzalo Pizarro in the civil war, died in prison in Cuzco soon after the battle of Jaquijahuana (1548). Coincidentally, he was the stepfather of Juan Balsa, the younger, who was among the troops that entered Vilcabamba in 1572.

9. Pedro de Oñate may have also entered the Vilcabamba region in 1537 along with Ordóñez. Titu Cusi Yupanqui and two of his sisters were captured during this raid and sent to live with Oñate in Cuzco (Titu Cusi Yupanqui [1570] 2005: 118). Within two years, however, Titu Cusi Yupanqui returned to Vilcabamba and was there to witness the 1539 raid of Gonzalo Pizarro. Oñate died in 1542 during the failed revolt of Diego de Almagro (the younger).

10. Since Juan Balsa (the elder) was a follower of Almagro, he may have entered the Vilcabamba region with Ordóñez in 1537. His son, Juan Balsa (the younger), who was a cousin of Tupac Amaru, entered the Vilcabamba region in the raid of 1572.

11. Inquill and Huaipar were both sons of Huayna Capac, although they held a lower status than Manco Inca. Both are mentioned by Titu Cusi Yupanqui ([1570] 2005: 108) as fighting on the side of the Spaniards in the 1536 siege of Cuzco. Titu Cusi Yupanqui ([1570] 2005: 123) also indicates that both of these brothers were captured and killed during the 1539 raid into Vilcabamba. In this way, the war between Cuzco and Vilcabamba was a continuation of the civil wars that had divided the Inca Empire at the time of the European invasion. In other words, the various factions that were created with the death of Huayna Capac continued to fight against one another well into the colonial period.

12. This battle appears to have taken place at Huayna Pucará (see Pizarro [1571] 1921: 397–404).

13. This was Cura Ocllo.

14. Here and elsewhere we have selected to translate "Ciudad de los Reyes" as Lima.

15. We have not translated chapter 71 because it does not contain information on Vilcabamba.

16. That is to say, from the west rather than from the east.

17. Much of the rest of this chapter overlaps with information provided in Cobo ([1653] 1979: 173–176). It appears that both Murúa and Cobo extracted their information from the same, or very similar, texts.

18. The fighting that is described here appears to be the 1538 battle of Oncoy, which took place in the province of Andahuaylas.

19. Francisco de Cháves was one of the most powerful Spaniards in Peru at this time.

20. Vaca de Castro was already en route to Peru when he learned of the death of Francisco Pizarro.

21. Francisco de Carvajal was an aging but highly effective military leader. He fought on the king's side in the Almagro uprising but a few years later turned against the king and fought with Gonzalo Pizarro.

22. Cotomarca is located along the Abancay-Limatambo road, near the community of Mollepata. It is about three days' walk from Vitcos.

23. A tossing game played with balls tied together with string.

24. Titu Cusi Yupanqui, the son of Manco Inca, was by his father's side during this attack and barely escaped with his life.

25. Pizarro ([1571] 1921: 438) also states that the Inca captains returned on the day that Manco Inca was killed.

26. For additional information on the mummification of the Inca rulers, see Bauer and Coello Rodríguez (2007).

27. Fray Bartolomé de Las Casas (1474–1566), the bishop of Chiapas, fought against the exploitative practices of the Spaniards in the New World and lobbied the crown to institute measures to protect the indigenous peoples.

28. This is a reference to Las Casas's *Brevísima relación de la destrucción de las Indias*.

29. In 1542 King Charles V of Spain instituted what are generally called the New Laws, a detailed reassessment of the *encomienda* system in use in the Americas.

30. Antonio de Mendoza was the first viceroy of Mexico (1535–1550) and the second viceroy of Peru (1551–1552).

31. Sebastián de Castilla rebelled in 1553.

32. Francisco Hernández Girón rebelled in 1553 and was defeated the following year.

33. By the time that Murúa wrote, there had been several different books written on the various uprisings that had occurred in Peru.

34. Also known as Beatriz Huayllas Ñusta.

35. Juan Sierra was the son of Beatriz Quispe Quipi Coya and Juan Sierra de Leguizamo. He is believed to have held a critical role in gaining Sayri Tupac's trust (see Garcilaso de la Vega [1609] 1970: 1435–1436). In this journey he traveled with his stepfather, Diego Hernández.

36. Alonso Juárez would later play an important role in the conquest and occupation of the Vilcabamba region.

37. The royal tassel (*mascapaicha*), the insignia of the royal Incas, was worn in the middle of the forehead.

38. Sayri Tupac arrived in Lima on 5 January 1558 (Hemming 1970: 294).

39. Francisco Hernández Girón's holdings included the *repartimientos* of Jaquijahuana, Pucará, Quipa, and Guayla. Sayri Tupac's new holdings also included the wealthy *repartimiento* of Yucay, which encompassed the former country estate of his grandfather Huayna Capac. Originally, the Yucay *encomienda* was taken by Francisco Pizarro after the conquest and was later passed to his two sons.

40. Garcilaso de la Vega ([1609] 1970: 1443) states that Miguel Astete gave Sayri Tupac the very fringe that was worn by Atahualpa when he was captured in Cajamarca.

41. Garcilaso de la Vega, who was in Cuzco and witnessed the baptism, indicates that Sayri Tupac took the name Diego after the patron saint of the conquistadors Santiago. The name de Mendoza came from the viceroy Antonio Hurtado de Mendoza.

42. If papal dispensation was granted, it seems more likely that it was under Pope Paul IV (1555–1559) or Pope Pius IV (1559–1565) than Pope Julius III (1550–1555).

43. This crossed-out section is difficult to read. We believe it reads: "para su validación por haber muchos doctores teólogos antiguos y más de nos que tienen por cierto ser prohibido el tal matrimonio por derecho natural. P●●● ●●● ●● ●●● ●●●●●●●●●● lo● anteponer de su voluntad sin faltas ni violencias algunas ●● del matrimonios." This crossed-out section and the accompanying margin note most likely reflect a censor's concerns over the discussion of brother-sister marriage among the royal Incas.

44. After the death of her father, Sayri Tupac, Beatriz Clara Coya's inheritance rights became the focus of the Acobamba treaty negotiations between Titu Cusi Yupanqui and the Spaniards (Nowack 2004; Guillén Guillén 1977a, 1977b).

45. Sayri Tupac died in 1560 or 1561.

46. Murúa writes this Inca's name as Cusi Titu Yupanqui rather than Titu Cusi Yupanqui. This unusual name order (Cusi Titu) is also found in the 1595 and 1599 depositions concerning Ortiz's death (Bauer et al. 2014).

47. This last sentence was added after the chapter was completed. Presumably it was written by Murúa once he had finished chapter 93, which discusses the decedents of Sayri Tupac.

48. Most of this chapter is based directly on information provided by Juana Guerrero in the town of Socospata in 1595 (see document 5, this volume). At that time, she was being interviewed concerning the death Diego Ortiz. Said to be in her fifties, Juana Guerrero had been the wife of Martín Pando at the time of Ortiz's death. She ratified her statement in another interview, held in 1599 (Bauer et al. 2014).

49. Lope García de Castro, Count of Nieva, was interim viceroy of Peru (1564–1569).

50. Marcos García entered Vilcabamba in 1568 for the baptism of Titu Cusi Yupanqui.

51. Diego Ortiz entered Vilcabamba in September 1569 (Titu Cusi Yupanqui [1570] 2005: 134).

52. The mention of Diego Ortiz brings with it a complex history. As will be described by Murúa, Ortiz was killed following the sudden death of Titu Cusi Yupanqui in about 1571. The Augustinians, starting as early as 1582, began to collect information on the death of Ortiz (Levillier 1935: 344; Hemming 1970: 476). Their efforts increased in 1595 and in 1599–1600 as they began an effort to nominate Ortiz for sainthood. Interviews were conducted in the Vilcabamba region as well as in the city of Cuzco (see document 5, this volume). Both Murúa ([ca. 1616] 1987) and Calancha ([1638] 1981) had access to these investigations while writing their chronicles.

53. Here Murúa is confused; Titu Cusi's son was baptized Felipe Quispe Titu in the town of Carco on 20 July 1567 by the Augustinian prior Antonio de Vera. Titu Cusi Yupanqui was baptized Diego de Castro Titu Cusi Yupanqui in late August 1568 by Juan de Vivero (Titu Cusi Yupanqui [1570] 2005: 133).

54. It was during this visit that Titu Cusi Yupanqui ([1570] 2005) dictated his famous letter to Lope García de Castro in which he told of his father's life and that of this own. The account was recorded by Martín Pando and signed by both Marcos García and Diego Ortiz on 6 February 1570 in the Inca town of Vilcabamba. It is believed that the two clerics returned to Puquiura soon afterward.

55. In her 1595 testimony, on which most of this chapter is based, Juana Guerrero (Bauer et al. 2014: 81) describes "a white rock above a spring" (una piedra blanca encima

de un manantial de agua). The phrase 'white rock' is correctly copied by Calancha ([1638] 1981), but Murúa altered the description and wrote "large and rough stone above a spring" (una piedra grande y basta encima de un manantial de agua).

56. In 1911 Bingham correctly inferred that the modern site of Ñusta España (also called Yurak Rumi) was the ancient shrine that Murúa calls Chuquipalta. This shrine and its connection with the former Inca city of Vitcos became the focus of a series of preliminary reports that were published in the following year (Bingham 1912a, 1912b, 1912c, 1912d). The destruction of this shrine by burning was confirmed by excavations in 2008 and 2009 (Bauer, Aráoz Silva, and Burr 2012; Bauer, Fonseca Santa Cruz, and Aráoz Silva 2015).

57. Titu Cusi Yupanqui subsequently banished Marcos García from Vilcabamba, an event that is not mentioned by Murúa.

58. María Cusi Huarcay was the sister and wife of Sayri Tupac and mother to Beatriz Clara Coya. She left Vilcabamba with Sayri Tupac in 1557 and remained in Cuzco until her death. In 1586 she wrote to Viceroy Torres y Portugal (Hemming 1970: 476–477; Levillier 1925: 54–55, 229–236). In the letter, Cusi Huarcay, who had lived in the Vilcabamba region for many years with Sayri Tupac, revealed the names and approximate locations of various mines, and she requested permission to return to the Vilcabamba region to reopen them. While denying the request, the viceroy wrote enthusiastically to the king in 1587 and 1588 suggesting that the wealth of the region was large and that he would investigate the matter.

59. Much of the information presented this chapter is taken from the 1595 testimonies of Alonso de la Cueva and Juana Guerrero (Bauer et al. 2014: 80–89) concerning the death of Ortiz. As noted earlier, Juana Guerrero had been the wife of Martín Pando at the time of Pando's and Ortiz's death, but at the time of the testimonies she was married to de la Cueva. Alonso de la Cueva was among the Spanish soldiers who entered Vilcabamba in 1572, and he witnessed the exhumation of Ortiz's body several months later. He is mentioned in numerous Vilcabamba-related documents (see Maúrtua 1906).

60. Angelina Polan Quilaco, one of Titu Cusi Yupanqui wives, was baptized by Marcos García at the same time as the Inca in 1568 (Hemming 1970: 321). A resident of Lucma, she was around fifty years old when she was interviewed on 25 January 1595 by Antonio de Monroy Portocarrero concerning the death of Ortiz. In an unusually short statement she indicated that she knew nothing on the matter (Bauer et al. 2014: 68). However, several other people interviewed suggested that she had added to the panic following the death of Titu Cusi Yupanqui (see document 5, this volume).

61. Variations of these names appear in several 1595 testimonies (Bauer et al. 2014).

62. The settlement of Marcanay was located on the Inca road between Pampaconas and the town of Vilcabamba. Its exact location is not known with certainty, but it was likely near the homestead now called Concevidayoc (see Lee 2000).

63. The story of Juan Quispe is often repeated by writers interested in the death of Ortiz. Juan Quispe himself testified in the town of San Francisco de la Victoria de Vilcabamba at least two times, once in 1595 and again in 1599 (Bauer et al. 2014). Surprisingly, his withered arm is not mentioned during either of these depositions.

64. Testimonies dating to 1599 suggest that the final blow came from a native named Manacotaba (Bauer et al. 2014).

65. Walking on a fallen enemy was a common Inca practice (see Sarmiento de Gamboa [1572] 2007: 110–111).

66. Here Murúa interjects his own voice within information taken from Alonso de la Cueva's testimony.

67. The text reads "ninieron" (with the *ni* crossed out).

68. The Divine Office, also known as the Liturgy of the Hours, is a series of prayers made throughout the day.

69. The making of *chuspas* from Ortiz's clothes is mentioned in several testimonies describing the death of Ortiz (Bauer et al. 2014).

70. Here again Murúa interjects his voice within information provided in the Ortiz testimonies.

71. Murúa is referring to the 29 December 1599 testimony of Angelina Llacsa Chuqui, in which she described the deaths of many of the Inca captains who participated in the killing of Ortiz (Bauer et al. 2014: 137–138).

72. Diego Aucalli is said to have been the personal servant of Titu Cusi Yupanqui and to have overseen the Inca's mummification. His conversion is described by Alonso de la Cueva (Bauer et al. 2014: 85–90).

73. Here Murúa makes a direct reference the testimonies that he had access to concerning the death of Ortiz collected by the Augustinians (see Bauer et al. 2014).

74. Chapter 84 describes the reburial of Ortiz in the town of San Francisco de la Victoria de Vilcabamba and several miracles that occurred afterward (see Bauer et al. 2014). This information was taken from the Ortiz testimonies (see document 5, this volume).

75. All three of these captains were later captured by Antonio Pereyra and Martín García Oñaz de Loyola in the town of Panquis soon after the fall of Vilcabamba.

76. In 1565 Titu Cusi Yupanqui agreed to leave Vilcabamba sometime in the future, after he received the tribute from the Yucay *encomienda*. It is logical that Atilano might have been carrying those funds since he was the guardian of Beatriz Clara Coya, who had inherited the Yucay *encomienda*.

77. After the fall of Vilcabamba, Diego López de Ayala became the first vicar of the region.

78. This is the first Sunday after Easter, also called Low Sunday.

79. Sarmiento de Gamboa, who was among the Spaniards sent with Alvárez Maldonado, states that these troops left Cuzco on Thursday, 15 April 1572.

80. Coya Doña Marca Chimbo was the daughter of Huayna Capac and thus a sister of Manco Inca.

81. The raid into Vilcabamba was delayed until the beginning of the dry season.

82. During the Vilcabamba raid, Antonio Pereyra captured several leading Inca nobles. Years later, in 1589, he was asked by the viceroy to investigate Martín Hurtado de Arbieto's administration of the Vilcabamba region, and Pereyra filed a damning report of widespread corruption (Maúrtua 1906: 181–192).

83. As described near the end of this chapter, Francisco Orgóñez de Valencia played a critical role in the conquest of Vilcabamba when, armed with an harquebus, he killed an Inca loyalist named Parinango, a general of the Cayambis.

84. Mancio Sierra de Leguizamo was an elderly veteran, who on his deathbed famously repented his role in the conquest of Peru (see Stirling 1999).

85. Alonso de Mesa was an elderly veteran, who, like Mancio Sierra de Leguizamo, was with Pizarro at Cajamarca.

86. Soon after the fall of Vilcabamba, Julian de Humarán became sick and was replaced by his second in charge, Francisco Pérez Fonseca (Maúrtua 1906: 140–169).

87. Later, in 1578, Jerónimo Marañon testified on behalf of Francisco Valencia concerning events that occurred during the Vilcabamba campaign (Maúrtua 1906: 106).

88. Diego de Mendoza was the governor of the Mojos region. He rebelled against the crown (1573–1575) but was defeated and killed by royalist forces.

89. At this time, Gaspar Arias de Sotelo was the *encomendero* of Abancay, so it is logical that he chose to enter Vilcabamba via this route. Gaspar Arias de Sotelo had been a member of a 1565 convoy to Vilcabamba that, led by Matienzo, had attempted to negotiate with the Inca (Lohmann Villena 1941).

90. Nuño de Mendoza was the *encomendero* of Curamba (Toledo [1573] 1975: 207), which boarders on the Vilcabamba region and Abancay. Titu Cusi Yupanqui ([1570] 2005) writes that several Andeans tried to escape his oppressive oversight and fled into the Vilcabamba region.

91. Cocha Caxas was a way station and Curabamba was a major Inca settlement. Both of these installations are on the road between Abancay and the Andahuaylas (Bauer, Kellett, and Aráoz Silva 2010: 96–100).

92. The forces of Gaspar Arias de Sotelo and those of Martín Hurtado de Arbieto met in Pampaconas.

93. Francisco Cayo Topa is frequently mentioned by Murúa; however, little else is known of this individual.

94. The leader of the Cañaris in the Cuzco region, Francisco Chilche, appears to have been a witness to or held a major role in several important events that directly benefited him, including the death of Sayri Tupac and the capture of Tupac Amaru.

95. During the time of Huayna Capac and his father Tupa Inca Yupanqui, a large number of Cañaris had been taken from their homeland in central Ecuador and resettled into the Cuzco region. They became close allies of the Spaniards.

96. Beside the Cañaris, individuals from many other ethnic groups had been moved by the Inca into the Yucay region.

97. Various other writers describe the battle of Coyaochaca. For example, Sarmiento de Gamboa, testifying in 1578, also notes that Loyola divided his troop into three groups and that the height of the battle was marked by Francisco Orgóñez de Valencia's killing an Inca captain with a shot from an harquebus (Maúrtua 1906: 111).

98. The Cayambis are an ethnic group from central Ecuador.

99. This is to say, llamas and alpacas.

100. The salt mine of Qollpacasa and the remains of an Inca platform can still be seen at Pampaconas.

101. The possible mineral wealth of the Vilcabamba region was of great interest to the Spaniards, and the existence of mines is frequently mentioned in early descriptions of the region.

102. While the forces of Martín Hurtado de Arbieto were resting at Pampaconas, they were met by the troops of Gaspar Arias de Sotelo, who had entered the Vilcabamba region by way of Curamba.

103. This refers to the Andean practice of killing a selected animal and then examining the internal organs for indications of future events.

104. Gonzalo Pizarro and his forces conducted a raid into the Vilcabamba region between April and July of 1539. In that raid a major battle took place at Chuquillusca, where between thirteen and thirty-six Spaniards were killed with boulders that were rolled down the steep mountain slope.

105. At the time of Murúa's writing, there was a major concern that mestizos entering the priesthood would teach the Andean peoples a false Christianity since they would be influenced by their own traditions (Hyland 2003). Perhaps this view influenced the censor to strike these lines.

106. The battle for Huayna Pucará was a key event in the 1572 raid into Vilcabamba. The location of Huayna Pucará, now called Tambo, was first identified by Lee (2000).

107. Panti Pampa is between Pampaconas and the area of Tambo.

108. A battle had taken place in this same location in 1537 as Spanish troops pushed deep into the Vilcabamba region. After taking heavy loses, the Spaniards took the heights above the fort and the Inca retreated (see Pizarro [1571] 1921: 396–404). In 1572,

however, the Spaniards avoided casualties since they were forewarned of the fortification by Puma Inca.

109. Here it seems that Murúa suggests that Gonzalo Pizarro reached the city of Vilcabamba, while other sources suggest that Pizarro withdrew after running out of supplies and meeting indigenous resistance before arriving at the town of Vilcabamba.

110. Like Juan Balsa and Pedro Bustinza, Pedro de Orúe (the younger) was a mestizo and closely related to the ruling Incas in Vilcabamba.

111. Ututo is located along the Inca road between Pampaconas and the Inca city of Vilcabamba.

112. We can presume that both Tupac Amaru and Quispe Titu met resistance in the town of Vilcabamba.

113. That is to say, guinea pigs.

114. Both Bingham (1914: 196–197) and Savoy (1970: 97–98) noted the remains of Spanish tiles in the ruins of the site of Espíritu Pampa. Hemming (1970) later used the presence of these tiles, as well as this passage by Murúa, in his identification of Espíritu Pampa as the Inca town of Vilcabamba.

115. Elsewhere written as Sapacatín.

116. Toledo later sent this idol to Spain (see Nowack and Julien 1999; Toledo [1575] 1899d: 126).

117. Lope Martín was captured and killed in 1554 by Hernández Girón. His death is described in detail by Pizarro ([1571] 1921: 480–481).

118. Details concerning the final hunt for Tupac Amaru can be found in the various petitions sent by Martín García Oñaz de Loyola to the king of Spain, asking for rewards for his actions, as well as in the eyewitness testimonies of many of the men who accompanied him (see Maúrtua 1906: 3–70).

119. Here Murúa is attempting to describe lands unknown to him, and he is not sure of the relationship between the major rivers downstream from Vilcabamba. Tupac Amaru certainly reached as far as the Pichu River and may have arrived at the Mantaro-Urubamba confluence before attempting to flee on foot eastward into Pilcosuni territory.

120. That is to say, the Atlantic Ocean.

121. This is a reference to García Oñaz de Loyola's first attempt to capture Tupac Amaru while he was a member of Antonio Pereyra's forces.

122. The first name of this Spaniard is not known with certainty; however, a Domingo de Tolosa did testify on behalf of García Oñaz de Loyola in 1572 (Maúrtua 1906: 52).

123. Here Murúa compresses two different events that occurred during the Spaniards' hunt for Tupac Amaru. The encounter between the native lord, Ispaca, and García Oñaz de Loyola occurred near the town of Momorí, many leagues and many days

downriver from where the Spaniards found the large stash of Inca goods (see Maúrtua 1906: 3–70).

124. Several individuals who were with García Oñaz de Loyola and who later testified on his behalf also mention the leader Ispaca (Maúrtua 1906: 33, 40, 49).

125. We have chosen to translate "para entrarse en la mar en canoas" as "to travel by water in canoes."

126. Murúa is mistaken; the Inca general Huallpa Yupanqui was captured one or two days before Tupac Amaru.

127. Murúa is mistaken; Viceroy Toledo granted Martín Hurtado de Arbieto the governorship of Vilcabamba, while García Oñaz de Loyola was given a bounty for capturing Tupac Amaru and Huallpa Yupanqui and was also granted permission to marry Beatriz Clara Coya.

128. This is most likely the pass between Espíritu Pampa and the settlement of Concevidayoc.

129. One of the soldiers who found the body was Alonso de la Cueva. Antón Álvarez may also have been present (Bauer et al. 2014).

130. This passing reference to the absence of mosquitoes in the Vilcabamba region following the death of Ortiz betrays Murúa's knowledge of a series of odd events that followed the reburial of Ortiz. The body of Ortiz was reburied in the village church in Hoyara (a.k.a. San Francisco de la Victoria de Vilcabamba). Some twenty-two years later, in 1595, the bones of Ortiz were stolen by Fray Pedro de Aguiar as he completed an Augustinian effort to investigate the death of Ortiz. It is worth noting that although Murúa describes the death of Ortiz in great detail, he does not cover the theft of Ortiz's remains by the Augustinians.

131. This information is taken from the 11 March 1595 testimony of Alfonso de la Cueva.

132. During their 1595 and 1599–1600 investigations, the Augustinians record several miracles associated with Ortiz: the remarkable preservation of his body, the disappearance and reappearance of mosquitoes in the region, and various healings (Bauer et al. 2014).

133. Francisco de Mariaca married Mencia de Salcedo Hurtado de Arbieto in 1582. He was killed a year later during a failed expedition to the Pilcosuni region under the leadership of Martín Hurtado de Arbieto. The miraculous healing of Mencia is mentioned in various testimonies taken in 1595 and 1599, particularly those given by Martín Hurtado de Arbieto's wife and his other daughters.

134. That is to say, illegitimate.

135. Here Murúa again makes a direct reference to the 1595 and 1599 investigations into Ortiz's death (Bauer et al. 2014). Witnesses included, in 1595, Juana de Ayala Ponce de León, the wife of Martín Hurtado de Arbieto, as well as two of his

daughters, Leonor Hurtado de Mendoza and Mariana Hurtado de Mendoza; and, in 1599, another daughter, Francisca de Arbieto.

136. Diego de Silva was the godfather of Garcilaso de la Vega. His house is described by Ocampo as one of the largest and most prominent houses of the city. Its location is described by Garcilaso de la Vega ([1609] 1970: 429).

137. Tupac Amaru was imprisoned in the former palace of the Incas, Colcampata, on the slope between Cuzco and Sacsayhuaman. Soon after the death of Tupac Amaru, Toledo seized the palace. Years later, after Carlos Inca's son, Melchor Carlos Inca, had sued the state, it was returned to the family.

138. Ocampo Conejeros ([1611] 2013) provides additional information on the pleas offered to the viceroy to spare Tupac Amaru's life.

139. Augustine of Coruña was one of the first Augustinians to enter Mexico in 1533 and was ordained as bishop of Popayán, Colombia, in 1564. He was a longtime supporter of native rights. He is also mentioned by Ocampo Conejeros ([1611] 2013) as pleading for Tupac Amaru's life.

140. Ocampo Conejeros ([1611] 2013) also tells of this event in similar but not identical words. This suggests that Murúa and Ocampo may have shared the same informant. If this is the case, it may have been Father Friar Nicolás de los Ríos, who Ocampo indicates was one of his main sources.

141. Guaman Poma de Ayala provides very similar drawings for the death of Atahualpa in 1532 by Pizarro and the death of Tupac Amaru in 1572. While the actual details of the two executions differed greatly, for Guaman Poma de Ayala they were almost identical events.

142. Quispe Titu died in Lima in 1578.

143. "Quíspiguaman" should read "Sacsayhuaman."

144. In early colonial times it was not unknown for indigenous people to exhume the mummified bodies of their ancestors that the Spaniards had confiscated and buried.

145. The marriage between Captain Martín García Oñaz de Loyola and Beatriz Clara Coya de Mendoza was arranged on the very day that Tupac Amaru was put to death (Maúrtua 1906: 65–67).

146. In a failed attempt to gain control over her estate in Yucay, Cristóbal Maldonado kidnapped and raped Beatriz Clara Coya de Mendoza in 1566.

147. García Oñaz de Loyola was killed, along with about fifty Spaniards, near the end of December in 1598 while he attempted to put down a revolt of the Mapuches in Chile.

148. Ana María Lorenza de Loyola.

149. More commonly known as Paullu.

150. Carlos Inca eventual won his release from prison and regained some of his confiscated property. He died in Cuzco in 1582.

151. Melchor Carlos Inca was born before Toledo arrived in Cuzco. The infant's father, Carlos Inca, asked the viceroy to participate in the baptism, which was held on 6 January 1572. This royal patronage and the creation of the ceremonial *compadre* relation between Carlos Inca and Toledo, as well as a *ahijado* relationship between Melchor Carlos Inca and Toledo, did the indigenous Cuzco line little good. Once Tupac Amaru was captured, Toledo immediately turned on Carlos Inca and his infant son. Melchor Carlos Inca inherited his father's reduced wealth in 1582. Leading an opulent lifestyle, he was in constant conflict with local and crown authorities. In the wake of the conspiracy charges against García de Solis Portocarrero, Melchor Carlos Inca was banished from Peru and ordered to live in Spain (see Hemming [1970] for a detailed account of Melchor Carlo Inca's life).

152. García de Solís Portocarrero was executed in the town of Ayacucho in September 1601.

153. Melchor Carlos Inca died in Spain in 1610.

Document 2

*Baltasar de Ocampo
Conejeros and the
Province of Vilcabamba*

Little is known concerning the life of Baltasar de
Ocampo Conejeros. Apparently a man of limited means
and few political connections, he emerges from virtual
obscurity in 1611 as an elderly, impoverished Spaniard
living in Lima, Peru. Having fallen on hard times,
Ocampo writes a history of the Vilcabamba region for
Viceroy Juan de Mendoza y Luna in the hope that this
act, combined with his long service to the crown, will
merit royal support in his final years.[1] While it is not
known if the history persuaded the viceroy to grant
Ocampo any favors, his efforts have provided future
generations with an important account of the early
colonial period of Peru and the final years of independent Inca kingship in the Andes.

Ocampo's report for the viceroy is titled *Descripción
de la provincia de Sant Francisco de la Victoria de Villcapampa*. It is held in the British Library (Add. 17585:
0001–00073). Written in a clear, clean script with
wide margins, it is easy to read. The first transcription of Ocampo's manuscript was produced by Victor
M. Maúrtua (1906) as part of a major work containing many important documents on the Vilcabamba
region. The following year, an English translation was
published by Clements Markham (1907). Markham
also produced a Spanish edition in 1923. Nevertheless,
Ocampo's account remains one of the least studied
documents describing the ultimate decades of Inca
resistance in the Vilcabamba area.

DOI: 10.5876/9781607324263.c004

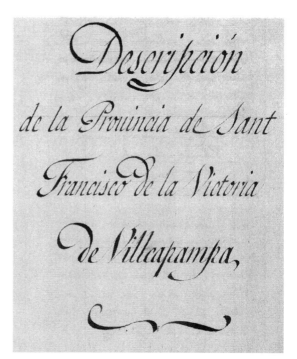

FIGURE 4.1. *The title page of Ocampo's report to Viceroy Juan de Mendoza y Luna concerning the history of Vilcabamba. Courtesy British Library Add 17585: fol. 2.*

OVERVIEW OF OCAMPO'S ACCOUNT

Ocampo's description of Vilcabamba begins with a formal title page followed by a three-page cover letter addressed to Juan de Mendoza y Luna, Marquis of Montes Claros (figure 4.1). In this letter Ocampo notes that he had served Philip II and Philip III for more than forty-four years, suggesting that he arrived in Peru around 1567. The cover letter is signed by Ocampo but not dated.

The account that follows the cover letter is titled "Description of the Province of San Francisco de la Victoria de Vilcabamba: How It Came to Our Knowledge and Its Discovery and the Defeat of the Inca Tupac Amaru and of His Death and Tragic Events" (Descripción de la Provincia de Sant Francisco de la Victoria de Vilca Pampa: cómo se tuvo noticia della, y su descubrimiento y el vencimiento del Inca Tupac Amaru, y de su muerte, y otros acaecimientos lastimosos). The document, totaling sixty-three pages, is complete, ending with "May [Your Excellency] have joy for ever and ever. Amen" (Que goce [Vuestra Excelencia] en los siglos de los siglos Amen). The account is not signed, nor is it dated; however, it is written in the same hand as the cover letter (figure 4.2). It is believed that the document dates to around 1611, since near the end of his work Ocampo refers to an event which occurred "in the year [15]71, which was forty years ago."

Ocampo begins his account of Vilcabamba with the arrival of Viceroy Francisco de Toledo in Cuzco (1569) and the baptism of Melchor Carlos Inca. Ocampo then jumps back approximately a decade in time to tell of the prolonged negotiations that occurred between Titu Cusi Yupanqui and the Spaniards. These negotiations ended with the sudden death of Titu Cusi Yupanqui and the subsequent killing of Fray Diego Ortiz by Inca loyalists (ca. 1571). As a longtime citizen of the Vilcabamba region, Ocampo had heard many people speak of Titu Cusi Yupanqui's death and the murder of Ortiz. He had personally talked to some of the eyewitnesses of the event and had conversations with others who believed that several miracles occurred related to Ortiz's remains.[2]

Ocampo's narrative then turns to the Spanish raid, led by Martín Hurtado de Arbieto, into the Vilcabamba region in 1572 and the subsequent capture and execution of Tupac Amaru. During his long residency in the Vilcabamba region, Ocampo lived among many of the soldiers who had participated in the raid. There is no doubt that those monumental events were recounted over and over, and Ocampo is able to provide details that are not recorded in other accounts.

Nearly all writers of the European-Andean contact period end their description of the Vilcabamba region with the execution Tupac Amaru. However, Ocampo carries the narrative further, discussing the subsequent settlement of the region by the Spaniards and many other events that occurred over the next thirty years. From Ocampo as well as a set of lengthy court cases (Maúrtua 1906), we know that Viceroy Toledo granted Martín Hurtado de Arbieto the governorship of the Vilcabamba region for two lifetimes as a reward for the successful defeat of the Inca loyalists. Hurtado de Arbieto quickly founded a new settlement called San Francisco de la Victoria de Vilcabamba, near the modern-day town of Hoyara, and encouraged other Spaniards to occupy the region. More than 1,500 indigenous people were then reduced into this city, and various soldiers who were involved in the 1572 Vilcabamba raid elected to remain in the area.

During the twenty-six years that Hurtado de Arbieto held power in Vilcabamba (1572–1598) he led a number of additional raids against different Amazonian groups in the surrounding territories. Most of the raids yielded limited results and were military and financial disasters. Ocampo provides detailed information on the two largest misadventures. They occurred in 1582 and 1583 as Hurtado de Arbieto attempted a conquest of the Pilcosuni, a

Descripción

de la Prouincia de Sant Frascisco
de la Victoria de Vilca Pampa, como
se tuuo noticia della, y su descubrimiento: y el vencimiento del Inga
Topa amaro, y de su muerte, y otros
acaecimientos lastimoso &.

Quisiera Exc.mo principe acertar à dar el
punto que es necessario al gusto sabroso
el paladar de V. Exc.a y que fuesse de tanta
suauidad como lo pide la razon y mis
viuos desseos en historia tan verdadera
mas si en alguna cossa faltare à lo que
digo, no será por no querer satisfacer al
pie de la letra, sino por no alcanzar mas
mi corto entendimiento, como en mi Epis-
tola tengo hecha la salua à V. Exc.a, y assi
digo, que estando el Señor Visrey Don
Fran.co de Toledo en la Ciudad el Cuzco,
por los principios el año de setenta y uno,
Don Carlos Ynga vecino de aquella Ciudad,
hijo lexitimo de D.n Christoval Paullo Cacicopa
Ynga, y de doña Catalina Ocsica Coya su

large tribal group that lived downriver from Vilcabamba. These raids mark the beginning of events actually witnessed by Ocampo since he entered the Vilcabamba region in 1582, having been recruited by Hurtado de Arbieto to participate in them.

The first incursion was poorly timed, since the Spanish forces, supported by indigenous allies, headed down the Urubamba River in early August at the beginning of the rainy season. Ocampo notes that in just a few days of setting out from Quillabamba, Hurtado de Arbieto's troops had lost much of their supplies, and many of their boats were destroyed. Furthermore, several individuals had drowned in the rapids. Hurtado de Arbieto then ordered the troops to abandon the river and to continue on foot, cutting their way through the forest. Weeks later, exhausted by the terrain and fearing that they would all soon die, the beleaguered troops petitioned Hurtado de Arbieto to end the journey and return to Vilcabamba. Surely disheartened, Hurtado de Arbieto agreed to end the expedition and to return to the town of Vilcabamba.

Within a year of his return to Vilcabamba, Hurtado de Arbieto organized a second expedition against the Pilcosuni. Having failed to reach their territory by traveling down the Urubamba River, the 1583 expedition journeyed down the Apurímac River. This time the Spaniards reached the territory of the Pilcosuni and established a settlement. After a year, however, tensions grew and the Pilcosuni attacked the town and the Spaniards were forced to return to the highlands. In his report to Mendoza y Luna, Ocampo suggests that he was also a member of the 1583 expedition. However, while testifying in 1590 on the merits of Hurtado de Arbieto, Ocampo makes it clear that he had remained in Vilcabamba and only learned of the events that occurred downriver through messages sent back from the governor.[3]

Ocampo also offers information on the resources of Vilcabamba, especially the mineral wealth, in his report to the viceroy. The mines of the region were of great interest to the Spaniards, and for a time the crown ordered that *mita* laborers be diverted from the infamous Huancavelica mercury mine and sent to work the Vilcabamba silver mines. Ocampo supported the use of indigenous labor in the mines, and in his report he strongly recommends that Mendoza y Luna reintroduce *mita* labor to the Vilcabamba region. He also provides the only known description of a slave revolt that occurred in the Vilcabamba region around 1608. Led by a Pilcosuni, Francisco Chichima, the revolt lasted over a month, and the Spaniards of the area were forced to remain in a blockhouse. The revolt was put down only with the arrival of a large number of well-armed Spaniards and native allies. In the concluding pages of his account, Ocampo describes the first Mercedarians to arrive in the region and their departure some fifteen years later. He ends his narrative with a detailed description of the massive celebration that was held in Cuzco upon the arrival of Viceroy Toledo.[4]

Ocampo indicates that he has done his utmost to present a fair and unbiased history of the Vilcabamba region. Nevertheless, he wrote his account when he was at an advanced age, and readers familiar with the final years of the Inca will note many mistakes. Ocampo truncates many events, skips over important facts, and combines similar events. He also confuses names, dates, and the sequence of some events all within a rambling narrative. We have attempted to address some of Ocampo's shortcomings through the inclusion of numerous footnotes.

ADDITIONAL DOCUMENTS BY OCAMPO

During our research into Ocampo's life, we found four additional documents that were signed by him and were produced during some of the very events described in his history of Vilcabamba. These include what we call *El testimonio de Baltasar de Ocampo Conejeros en apoyo de Martín Hurtado de Arbieto y Miguel de Otaça de Mondragón* (San Francisco de la Victoria de Vilcabamba, 23 October 1601); *El testimonio sobre la muerte de Fray Diego Ortiz* (Cuzco, 20 February 1600); *El testimonio de Baltasar de Ocampo Conejeros en apoyo de Martín Hurtado de Arbieto* (San Francisco de la Victoria de Vilcabamba, 4 December 1590); and *La petición de los soldados para volver a Vilcabamba* (Puerto del Rio Simoponte, 18 September 1582). We have published these documents in Spanish (Bauer and Halac-Higashimori 2013: 71–84). There is also a short land sale document in the Archivo Regional de Cuzco indicating that on 12 February 1604 Ocampo sold 172 *fanegas* of land near Puquiura, called Guayavilca and Guayobamba, to Cristóbal de Albornoz (ARC. Gaspar de Prado. Prot. 277. 1603–1608; Jesús Galiano Blanco, personal communication).

OCAMPO'S LETTER TO JUAN DE MENDOZA Y LUNA

To the most excellent Lord Don Juan de Mendoza y Luna, Marquis of Montes Claros, representative of the King, our lord, Viceroy, Governor, and Captain General in these kingdoms and provinces of Peru and Chile, etc.[5] Captain Baltasar de Ocampo [Conejeros], your servant, wishes you eternal happiness.

Although my age and white hair do not require that I continue to write of past [times] and bloody histories, but instead occupy my time finding and acquiring a peaceful repose with which to bring closure and finality to my tired life, I will continue in the service of the royal person of Felipe II,[6] our lord and natural King, and [his] original, true, and rightful [successor], Felipe III.[7] I have served these [kings] for more than 44 years on all the occasions that time and events have offered. I have tried to be among the first to serve my King and lord as a loyal vassal, with my own person, arms, horses, and servants at my own expense and will, without having been rewarded or remunerated for these [expenses].

And although it has been more than two years since I came to this Court to inform Your Excellency of my condition and to communicate my great needs (having been dispossessed of my property, using it as I have [just] described), I now present, as I have done before, my memorials and proofs to Your Excellency's person.

Finding myself exhausted, and destitute, and without a hope of any remedy, I dared to kiss Your Excellency's hands, and to verbally give an account of the city and province of San Francisco de la Victoria de Vilcabamba, and its origin and foundation, and how [we] learned of it, and in general [what has occurred] since the time of its discovery.

Having received some pleasure from my narration, Your Excellency ordered me to write it down. Believing that this would provide a pleasurable service to Your Excellency, I focused my memory on the notable events of those former golden years; above all, I made every effort to offer the most truthful history, according to what I could remember. For it is just that a prince (such as Your Excellency) should receive the unvarnished truth without the appearance or evidence to the contrary.[8]

Receive this, Your Excellency (with benign, calm, and mild affect, since you are a most Christian prince), from your servant who, in all things, hopes to succeed, serve, and please. And judge me not, Your Excellency, by my simple style and rustic language, but instead by the sincere spirit, pure and clean, with which I recount [this history]. So that when I die of hunger (more than what I am already suffering) and I ask of those friends that I have, by God, and do not receive any other reward beyond His beneficence and acceptance, I will [die] well paid, and I will understand that I deserve nothing [more] from God, His Majesty, Your Excellency, and mankind.

This being the case, do me the courtesy, Your Excellency, of looking over this document and description of that land; with luck, it will resound like an agreeable and sweet harmony to the appreciative ear of Your Excellency. [May] the Majesty of God Almighty protect [you] for many long and prosperous years, during which may you derive happiness from your lands and titles, as Your Excellency deserves. As your servant, I desire this for you.

Most Excellent Lord,
Your Excellency's servant, who kisses your hands and feet
BALTASAR DE OCAMPO CONEJEROS

DESCRIPTION OF THE PROVINCE OF SAN FRANCISCO DE LA VICTORIA DE VILCABAMBA

How it came to our knowledge and its discovery and the defeat of the Inca Tupac Amaru and of his death and tragic events

I hope, Excellent Prince, my [description] will be suitable to Your Excellency's good taste, and that it is as smooth an account as is needed, as it is my expressed sincere desire to provide a true history. What is more, if I fail to do so, it will not be for lack of desire to provide a complete and exact account, but rather because my limited knowledge does not allow me to provide more [information], true to the oath I made to Your Excellency in my letter.

And so I begin: when the Lord Viceroy Don Francisco de Toledo was in the city of Cuzco, at the beginning of the year of [15]71, Don Carlos Inca, citizen of that city, [the] legitimate son of Don Cristóbal Paullu Cusi Topa Inca[9] and his wife Doña Catalina Ussica Coya, was living a married life (as he always had) with Doña Maria de Esquivel, his legitimate wife, [who was] native to Trujillo of Estremadura in the kingdoms of Spain. Having become pregnant, she carried to term and gave birth to a boy in the fortress of the city of Cuzco.[10] This caused great rejoicing and happiness in the city, because they had been married a long time and they had never had children or offspring.

As the Inca Don Carlos was a high-ranking person, being the grandson of Huayna Capac, who was (in his time) the universal lord of that land, the parents searched within the city for [an appropriate person] to baptize the infant and to be godparent of the newborn. They asked and entreated the Lord Viceroy Don Francisco de Toledo to provide such a noble grace and favor as to honor them with his most excellent presence and authority in bringing their son to the [baptismal] font, and to be his godfather and their *compadre*; and that he allow that Doctor Fray Pedro Gutiérrez Flores, his chaplain and confessor, of the Order of Alcántara ([who is the] brother of the Lord Don Pedro Orgóñez y Flores, who has been an Apostolic Inquisitor in these kingdoms and who is currently the Archbishop of the New Kingdom of Granada) baptize him in the parish church of the Lord San Cristóbal de Colcampata, which is adjacent to the said fortress.[11] And the Lord Viceroy enthusiastically agreed to be the boy's godfather and the *compadre* of the parents.

On the day of the baptism (which was the Day of the Epiphany), the sixth of January of the same year, [15]71, [the boy] was given the name Melchor[12]; there were large parties, celebrations, bullfights, jousting, and fanciful dances, which are very costly and newly invented (of which they are inclined to do in Cuzco on such occasions). People gathered for these [festivals] from areas located more than 40 leagues' distance from [the city]. For this celebration, all the Inca gathered at the arranged time from the parishes of Pacariqtambo, Araypallpa, Colcha, Cucharipampa, Pampacuchu, Pacopata, Accha, Pilpinto, Pacoray, Huayhuacunca, Parcos, Quiquijana, Urcos, Andahuaylas la Chica, Oropesa, San Jerónimo de Corama, San Sebastián, Anta, Puquyura, Conchacalla, Jaquijahuana, Marco, Equequo, Zurite, Limactambo, Maras, [Ollantay]tambo, Urubamba, Chinchero, Yucay, Urcos, Palpas, Pisaq, and San Salvador. All these towns are inhabited by Incas. Also [attending were representatives] of the Canas, Canches, and Collas,[13] and from as many other nations that could come together (figure 4.3). Among all those who came to the baptism celebrations were Titu Cusi Yupanqui Inca and his younger brother, Tupac Amaru Inca, who came from the province of Vilcabamba.[14] (They were infidel idolaters who worshipped the Sun, saying that it was the creator of all things, and they had made a gold idol and sanctuary [for the sun]).

When these last two Incas saw the grandeur, majesty, and sumptuousness of the Christians, and that the divine worship was celebrated with such grandeur, and saw the brotherhood of Christianity in the churches, as men of good understanding they were easily convinced of the sanctity and goodness of Christian law. It [therefore] seemed appropriate to Titu Cusi Yupanqui to join the society of the Holy Mother Church [and] to convert to our Holy Catholic Faith. And [Titu Cusi Yupanqui] was impressed with the lordly way that the Lord Viceroy was treated, respected, and revered by all his subjects, and he saw the loyalty [that the viceroy's] persona called forth from his royal guards. So that [the Spaniards] would know [Titu Cusi Yupanqui's] majesty and greatness and so that they would know he was a lord and esteemed in his land, [Titu Cusi] resolved in his heart to become Christian.

At the end of festivities, which lasted many days in Cuzco, he retired with his brother, Tupac Amaru Inca, to his land and region of Vilcabamba. Being a crafty man, filled with ambitions, which is a common trait among tyrants, he put his younger brother in the House of the Sun with the acllas[15] and mamaconas, an ancient rite [practiced] in all the towns of all the nations of these Kingdoms before the arrival of the Spaniards. [Tupac Amaru Inca] was the natural and legitimate lord of that land, and was a grandson of Huayna Capac. [However,] because [Tupac Amaru Inca] was an inexperienced youth, [Titu Cusi Yupanqui], with his ingenuity and scheming, held him [in the House of the Sun] secluded and imprisoned, usurping his position as lord and leader.

Titu Cusi Yupanqui [then] sent his ambassadors to the city of Cuzco to the Lord Viceroy, telling him that he was eager to become a Christian, having seen the grandeur and majesty that the Christians used in their acts of public worship and in the Christian religion. He [wanted] to let [the viceroy] know

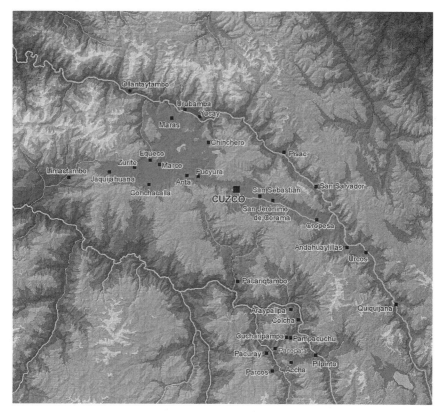

FIGURE 4.3. *Locations of towns listed by Ocampo as sending representatives to the baptism of Melchor Carlos Inca (redrawn from Covey 2006).*

what kind of person the Inca, [being] universal lord of that land, was, and that [he] hoped His Excellency would grant him the kindness of sending ministers of God to instruct and catechize him in the ways of our Holy Catholic Faith, and [that he would also send] some people to teach and advise him on the ways of urbanity and courtesy, so that after being instructed and taught he would go to the city of Cuzco to give obedience to His Majesty and to Your Excellency in his royal name.

The Lord Don Francisco de Toledo, full of joy and delight, gathered the prelates of the [monastic] orders, the Council of the Cathedral, and the Chief Magistrate, and [other] city officials; and with words that expressed his joy, [the viceroy] related (being a prudent lord) the new message that Inca Titu Cusi Yupanqui had sent with his ambassadors.[16] [Toledo said] that he would like to send some clerics and priests to teach and catechize the Inca, as well as some other secular persons who would accompany the priests. In this way, they could instruct the Inca in the ways of the Court, so that he could be instructed in all matters that would serve his official position as the Inca.

Each of the prelates of the religious orders offered to provide one or two clerics from their convents, and in the end it was determined that Father Fray Juan de Vivero, who at that time was the prior of the convent of the Lord Saint Augustine, and Fray Diego Ortiz, who was later martyred,[17] would go to do this good work. The Lord Viceroy sent Atilano de Anaya[18] as his ambassador. [Anaya was a] citizen of Cuzco and a serious man of a pleasant manner and well versed in the language of the Indians. [He also sent] Diego Rodríguez de Figueroa as High Constable [of Vilcabamba], whom the Lord Viceroy rewarded with that commission for life, which he served. Francisco de las Veredas,[19] a very discrete and courteous [individual], [was sent] as royal scribe in order to oversee and instruct Titu Cusi Yupanqui in what was beneficial to him and to be like a tutor and steward in his home. [The viceroy also sent] Pedro [i.e., Martín] Pando,[20] a mestizo and native of Cuzco, who was a great speaker of that language. [This occurred] in the year 1571[21] after the said baptismal festivities of Don Melchior Carlos Inca, [who was] the son of Don Carlos Inca and Doña Maria de Esquivel, his wife (may God bless [her]), to whom His Majesty, the King, our lord, has granted many favors, such as the robes of [the Order of] Santiago[22] and 10,000 ducats of rent in Spain.

Once the aforementioned [individuals] had been sent on their way, Lord Don Francisco de Toledo sent [the Inca] many gifts, [including] velvets, brocades, and linen, for his personal adornment and house as well as vats of wine, raisins, figs, and almonds, along with other valuable objects. All [of these] were received with great joy by Titu Cusi Yupanqui. He showed the highest officials of his Kingdom the favor and gifts that the Lord Viceroy had sent to him with his ambassadors, and he ordered all his vassals to respect and regale those who had brought the gifts, as persons sent by a great prince. Pedro Pando, the interpreter, explained the need of showing the two priests respect, honor, and veneration because they were ministers of another, higher prince than he who had sent the ambassadors, who was God of Heaven and His earthly representative, His Holiness the Roman Pontiff. [Pando also explained] that [the priests] had come at the request of the Viceroy, and in the service of God, our lord, to catechize, instruct, and baptize him. [The priests were also] to say mass and preach publically the evangelical law to him, and to convert him to the ways of our Holy Catholic Faith. Because until then [Titu Cusi Yupanqui] had been a slave of the devil, worshipping the sun, [which] is a creation of God and not [the] creator; rather, [it was] created for the benefit of mankind. [Pando] explained to [Titu Cusi Yupanqui] that the idolatrous were those who adored [the sun] as well as the mountains, *huacas*, and *apachitas* [cairns], which are piles of rocks made by the Indians on some of the large rocks or cliffs. They superstitiously throw coca, which they hold in great esteem, on top of these piles. [The Indians] carry it in their mouths with the sole purpose of offering it to the *apachitas*, with which they say they leave behind all the exhaustion of the journey, and others leave *ojotas* [sandals], which in our vernacular means shoes. [Pando also told Titu Cusi Yupanqui] that the aforementioned fathers and the others in Christendom were respected, revered, esteemed, and highly venerated by the kings and the great lords for being Ministers of God, and that they did not occupy themselves with any other matters except those that were sacred and dedicated to the King of Heaven. And that they were people who were held in such esteem, that all the princes and sovereigns of the earth would kneel in their presence and kiss their hands. They were so infused with the power of God that when they are at the altar they could summon Him to descend from heaven into their hands, which are consecrated with holy oil. For communicating so familiarly with the lord of the heavens and earth, which neither the emperors nor any other monarchs of the world could do, [their hands] were kissed by all because they blessed the people. And in the name of God Almighty, through the authority that they have, [they] pardon, absolve, and cleanse the sins of men, confessing them, as to representatives of Jesus Christ, [the] lord and creator of all things of the universe.

And as I have said, in the year [15]71,[23] which was 40 years ago, the same Titu Cusi Yupanqui, through God's will, discovered this province and he sent his ambassadors [to Cuzco] after having seized the lordship and rule from his brother, Tupac Amaru Inca, [the] natural and legitimate lord of that land. Titu Cusi Yupanqui, his older brother, who was a bastard, was clever; he rose up and usurped the empire and rule from the real lord, Tupac Amaru; for which he had no pretense or right to do. [He succeeded because] Tupac Amaru Inca, his brother, was a young man without governance or experience. And to this end, Titu Cusi Yupanqui, his bastard brother, kept him oppressed and imprisoned with the *acllas* and *mamaconas* in the House of the Sun, where he was when the Lord Viceroy Don Francisco de Toledo sent [his representatives to] the aforementioned Titu Cusi Yupanqui. [They] persuaded him, with loving words and many gifts, to leave the Vilcabamba province and to come to the city of Cuzco to give his obedience to His Majesty and Your Excellency in his royal name, as the Inca had communicated through his ambassadors. He resolved to do so, [but] having become somewhat stubborn, he delayed leaving for some time, one day to the next.

Father Fray Juan de Vivero, recognizing that the Inca was acting stubbornly, left for Cuzco with Atilano de Anaya, Diego Rodríguez de Figueroa, Chief Magistrate, and Francisco de las Veredas. [They] left Father Fray Diego Ortiz and Pedro Pando with the Inca and sent word to Your Excellency about what had occurred. [As Your Excellency was] already angry and it appeared to him that the Inca was belittling your person and authority, he once again sent Father Fray Juan de Vivero and Diego Rodríguez de Figueroa, under the auspices[24] of Royal Justice, so that, as Chief Magistrates, they would overcome all the difficulties and bring [Titu Cusi Yupanqui] back along the road [to Cuzco] under their care and service. He also sent Atilano de Anaya so that he would administer [the Inca's] property and person.

In the midst of all these comings and goings, Titu Cusi Yupanqui became ill and was near death. As the Indians saw his danger and peril, they spoke to Father Fray Diego Ortiz, as he was a Minister of God, [asking] him to pray [to God] to cure Titu Cusi Yupanqui Inca of his sickness. [Father Ortiz] told them that he did that every day, and that if it pleased God, [the Inca's] health would be [restored], and if not, everyone would have to accept God's will, because His Majesty knows what is best for each person's soul. Your Excellency should know that the Inca had been baptized at his own request by Father Fray Juan de Vivero, in the province of Vilcabamba, and he was given the name Don Felipe Titu Cusi Yupanqui.[25] As he was baptized and catechized as a Christian, the two Fathers said mass for him every day.[26] Their chapel was next to my houses and on my own land, in the settlement of Puquiura, next to the metal ore processing mill of Don Cristóbal de Albornoz, who was [formerly] the Precentor of the Cuzco Cathedral.[27]

And while things were in this state, the Inca died. The high-ranking men in the province and captains were aware that the Inca Don Felipe Titu Cusi Yupanqui had died, not having benefited from the personal and public prayers, or the sacrifices that Father Fray Diego Ortiz made.[28] An Indian named Quispe, who is alive today, came before the Father and asked him: "why his God had not cured the Inca, when [Ortiz] claimed he was so powerful?" And without giving him [time] to respond, the Indian Quispe hit him. For this, our lord caused his right arm, from his hand to his shoulder, to wither.[29] It remains withered to this day, indicating to the Indian that he had committed a sin. The cleric knelt, offering the other cheek so that they would be equal[ly affected], and being a barbarian [Quispe hit him again]. [A group of Indians] then tied [his] hands behind him and dragged him. They cut him with a knife that the Indians call a *tumi*, from below the beard up through the mouth. They then threaded him with a rope and dragged him around the area. They martyred him with unheard-of cruelty. The blessed Father went smiling, directing his eyes toward heaven. He was 33 years old, having led an exceptional life and [achieved great] fame, as [his remains] performed great miracles in the province [of Vilcabamba] for women, children, and other people. His fragrant body [was laid] in a cedar box lined with crimson satin. It is presently in a tabernacle in the convent of Saint Augustine in the city of Cuzco, on the gospel side[30] of the principal chapel, next to the cross.

That same day, they killed Pedro Pando, his interpreter, with unheard-of cruelty in an atrocious death, as barbarian people with neither law nor faith [would do]. Afterward, they performed certain ceremonies [for Titu Cusi Yupanqui] that the Incas customarily [conduct] at burials of the lords of this land and at the end of the year. They are called *purucaya* in their language, which means honors, and they are performed exclusively for the Inca. [They] parade through the streets with the royal insignias. These consist of the *tumi*, a battle-axe, the *chuqui*, which is a lance, the *chilpana*, which is an armlet for the left arm, the *llauto*, which is a crown, the *jacolla*, which is a cape, the *uncuy*, which is a shirt that they wear as a tunic, the *huallcanca*, which is a gorget made of silver or feathers, the *ojotas*, which are their shoes, the *duho*, which is the royal chair, and the [*mascapaicha*, which is a] tassel that adorns the crown, the *huantuy*, which are their litters or carriage[s], the *achihua*, which is a marvelously crafted parasol of various colored feathers. [They marched with] muffled drums, with great groans and sobs. Each insignia was carried one by one by their important lords who were dressed in mourning. This ceremony is still, to my knowledge, practiced today. They went to the House of the Sun, its sanctuary, where the Inca Tupac Amaru, [the] true and legitimate lord, [the] brother of the recently deceased Titu Cusi Yupanqui, resided as a boy, with the *acllas* and *mamaconas*. The *acllas* were women chosen for the Sun, and the *mamaconas* were matrons who protect the chosen women, who were very beautiful, as well as Inca Tupac Amaru. [Tupac Amaru] was in the fort of Pitcos [Vitcos[31]], which was on a very high hill, from where [the Inca] ruled over a large part of the province of Vilcabamba.[32] [In Vitcos] there was a flat plaza of supreme grandeur, with sumptuous and majestic buildings, made with great skill and craftsmanship. All the lintels of the doors, the principal as well as the lesser, were made of famously worked marble.[33] They brought forth the Inca Tupac Amaru from this place, and they pledged their obedience to him as their natural lord.

And with regard to what happened to Father Fray Diego Ortiz and Pedro Pando, if there is anything more, I could not tell Your Excellency.

Following this, [the Inca] received reports from the *chapas* or *cabmihuas*, meaning spies, which they typically have, that people were coming from Cuzco. [He sent] seven captains along the road that leads to Cuzco; one of them was called Curi Paucar, and another [was a] Huanca, an especially bellicose [group of] Indians from the province of Jauja. I do not remember the names of the other five. They waited at the Chuquichaca Bridge, over the large [Urubamba] River, which is the entrance and key to the province of Vilcabamba, for Ambassador Atilano de Anaya, Father Fray Juan de Vivero, and Diego Rodríguez de Figueroa, who were traveling as an envoy for the second time to the province to [meet with the] Inca, Titu Cusi Yupanqui, [who had] died. When Father Fray Juan de Vivero and Diego Rodríguez de Figueroa were in the town of [Ollantay]tambo, which is along the road that leads to [Vilcabamba], they received certain news that caused them to remain [in Ollantaytambo].[34] They did not want to enter [Vilcabamba] with the ambassador, and they ordered him not to enter until they understood what was occurring inside there.

But Atilano de Anaya, a sincere and affable man, who was well liked by the Indians, could not abandon the task he was sent to do by the Lord Viceroy. He arrived at the bridge of Chuquichaca, [where he intended] to spend the night because there was a house for him to stay in and grass for his horses. After putting in order all the presents and refreshments he had brought for the Inca, he saw the [Inca] captains come toward him with determination and armed for war. Before they arrived, it seems that an Indian appeared, who advised him of what had happened inside [Vilcabamba]. And not trusting [the Inca captains], he called one of his African [servants] and sent him to saddle a good mule, and [Anaya] gave him a gold token so that he would travel quickly back to the city of Cuzco and give it to Doña Juana Machucha, his wife, as a sign that they would never see each other again, which he knew from the warning he was given by that Indian who had disappeared. It is now understood that the [Indian] was an angel sent from heaven.

After the African left, the captains arrived where the ambassador was. He gave them something to drink and eat, and received them caringly, willingly giving them all that he could. After receiving this good deed, they repaid [Anaya] by killing him; he preferred to suffer death rather than to fail to complete the task his prince had sent him to do, because he could have left with his African but he did not.

Three days later, the African [reached Cuzco] with the painful news of the death of the ambassador, and what had been done to the blessed martyr

Fray Diego Ortiz and Pedro Pando, and notified the Lord Viceroy. Then His Excellency brought together the city officials of Cuzco, in the palace where he lived, and told the magistrate, mayor, and aldermen the sad news that he had received of the death of the priest and the others. [The viceroy] left determined to form an army to send to punish [the Incas] for having precipitated the events I have described in my narrative.

After consulting with the town council, he left determined to gather [together] soldiers, captains, and officials. The Lord Viceroy nominated as general Martín Hurtado de Arbieto, a citizen and magistrate of the city, a leading knight and conqueror; Juan Alvárez Maldonado,[35] citizen of Cuzco and Governor of the province of the Chunchos, was named *maese de campo*; Don Jerónimo de Figueroa, [the] nephew of the Lord Viceroy, [was named] assistant to the council of war. As captains, [he named] Martín García Oñaz de Loyola, [who was the] Captain of the Lord Viceroy's Guard [and] Knight of the Order of Calatrava, and Captain Ordoñez de Valencia, a citizen of Lima, who was [the] Captain of Artillery; Captain Juan Ponce de León, a citizen of the city of Huamanga, [the] brother-in-law of the said General,[36] was named to the position of Military Officer of the Army. [Others included] Captain Don Luis Palomino and Captain Don Gómez de Tordoya,[37] Captain Don Antonio Pereyra,[38] Captain Mancio Sierra de Leguizamo, Captain Alonso de Mesa, [now] lord of the town of Piedrabuena [in Spain],[39] Captain Martín de Olmos, Knight of the Order of Santiago, Captain Martín de Meneses, [and] Captain Julian de Umarán.

With their army organized, these captains and general left from Cuzco through the Yucay Valley and [Ollantay]tambo, [traveling] straight to the province of Vilcabamba and bridge of Chuquichaca. [Meanwhile,] Captain Gaspar Arias de Sotelo, uncle of Lord Don Diego de Portugal, President of the Charcas, a leading knight [and a] native of Zamora, and Captain Nuño de Mendoza, a distinguished knight, [both] citizens of Cuzco, entered [by way of] the Curahuasi Valley and Abancay with their companies, to block that route in case, by luck, the Inca chose to flee by that route to the province of Andahuayllas, where he could find an escape to the Mayomarca Valley, [which is] very close to the province of the Pilcosoni, [a group of] warring Indians [who had yet] to be conquered. It is a very large province, which will be mentioned later.

The army that departed from Cuzco through the Yucay Valley arrived safely at the bridge of Chuquichaca, where they encountered Tupac Amaru Inca, who had already been taken out of the House of the Sun, with his army organized. There our [army] had a confrontation with him and his people.

Four volleys of light artillery and the soldiers' harquebuses were shot from across the river; [this] routed the Inca and his army, forcing them to retreat. Our forces won the bridge, which was not inconsequential for the royal army, because, like barbarians, [the Inca loyalists] had not remembered to burn or destroy the bridge. This act was attributable to God, given the large [amount of] work that it would have taken the Spaniards to [re]build it, since it lay over a large and raging river.

Leaving our guards and a garrison there [to await] the arrival of provisions and the other necessities, the Spanish army departed in pursuit, attempting to overtake [the Inca] and his people, since the Inca army had been routed. The road was narrow going up, covered with forested mountains on the right and a steep and deep ravine of varying depths on the left. This prevented the soldiers from marching as a formed squadron, marching two by two instead. Captain Martín García Oñaz de Loyola, who was in the vanguard, went armed [and] alone, like a good captain, when out of nowhere and without being seen by anyone, a captain of the Inca named Huallpa came out from the mountainside and grabbed [García Oñaz de Loyola], pinning his arms and preventing their use in such a way that he could not draw his weapons. He intended to push [García Oñaz de Loyola] into the ravine below, where his body would be dashed to pieces and fall into the river. One of Captain [García Oñaz de Loyola]'s *yanacona* Indians, named Corillo, who is alive today [among the] Indians of his *encomienda* in the Yucay Valley,[40] who was with him, drew the sword from Captain [García Oñaz de] Loyola's scabbard, and with great dexterity and courage [Corillo] killed the Indian Huallpa, who had pinned his master. In this manner he prevented [Huallpa] from carrying out his evil plan. To this day the place where this occurred is [still] called Loyola's Leap.

Continuing their pursuit, [the army] arrived at the place of Oncoy,[41] which holds extensive and fertile plains. They found herds of livestock there, [including] cattle as well as llamas with their lambs. This made the captains and the soldiers very content and happy because [the herds] would provide food for the army. Thus pursuing the enemy, they took many enemy captives, both Indians and captains. Pressured to disclose the route the Inca had taken, they told [the Spaniards] that [the Inca] had gone inland toward the Simaponte Valley,[42] fleeing to the province of the Manarís, who were warring Indians and friends of [the Inca], where there were rafts and canoes ready so they could save themselves by [continuing downriver]. With this news, a war council was held [and] Captain Martín García Oñaz de Loyola was chosen to follow [the Inca]. He accepted and left with 50 soldiers and reached [the Inca] at Vilcabamba (the old),[43] capturing him along with many other captains and Indians. None was able to escape because the army had divided up into smaller companies, which went everywhere, and captured them without leaving any[one] behind. Only two Spanish soldiers were killed, one of whom was called Ribadeneira and the other's name is not known.

After capturing the Inca and his captains and Indians, taking them well guarded and in an orderly manner, [the Spanish army] returned to the Hoyara Valley. There they settled the Indians in a large town and they founded a Spanish city [that they] named San Francisco de la Victoria de Vilcabamba. [This name was selected] to pay respects due to San Francisco for two holy and just reasons: the first was because victory was won on the day of Lord San Francisco, on the fourth of October of [15]71,[44] and the second was because this was the saint's name of the Lord Viceroy [Francisco de Toledo], to whom the victory was attributed. Large celebrations were carried out in the city of Cuzco when they heard news of the victory.

This city was founded on a very large plain with a marvelous climate, next to a river, [from] where they dug canals for the service of the city. The water from the river is particularly sweet because it passes through gold ore. In consideration of the rich silver mines that were discovered in the hills of Huamani and Huamanate, this city was [later] relocated from where it was [originally founded] to the small town of Villa Rica de Argete[45] in order to be close to the mines. [This town] had been founded by order of Lord Don García Hurtado de Mendoza y Manrique,[46] Marquis of Cañete and Viceroy of these Kingdoms. With the consent of an open council,[47] which was held in the city of San Francisco de la Victoria, four priests were allowed to join. One of them was Don Cristóbal de Albornoz, Precentor of the Cathedral of Cuzco and the most illustrious [man] of the city. And in accordance with the [regional] governor's wishes, it was decided that the city would move to the site and place where the Villa Rica de Argete was founded. This was in the place of Oncoy, where the Spanish who discovered this land found cattle and llamas as described above.

In this council meeting it was decided that they would send a Procurator General to ask for permission and consent from Lord Don Luis de Velasco, who was viceroy of the kingdom at the time.[48] For this negotiation, I, Baltasar de Ocampo, was named as the Procurator, and I came to this city[49] and I met with the Lord Viceroy. [Changing the location of the town] appeared to be an action beneficial to the service of our lord God and His Majesty, raising the royal taxes,[50] and advantageous for the citizens and inhabitants of the city. Having examined, addressed, and consulted the stipulations and justification provided for moving it, the Lord Don Luis de Velasco gave his approval and authorization [for the city to] move to the place where it is now.[51] He ordered that [the new settlement] should be given the [same] title and name of the original settlement, San Francisco de la Victoria de Vilcabamba.

In this move, I, Baltasar de Ocampo, did a great service to God, our lord, and to His Majesty because, as a result of my labor, requests, and care, a very good, large church was built with a main chapel and large doors. [This was necessary] because there was [only] one small chapel in the whole town, where one could not fit more than just the citizens and miners.[52] The *mita* Indians had to stand outside [exposed to] the sun and water when it rained. The sacrament of the Holy Eucharist is now conducted at the main altar. Because of these acts of divine worship, God granted that things be ordered for the common good and prosperity, and that the royal fifths be increased with large quantities of gold (as will later be mentioned). Before our victory, idolatry and devil worship were everywhere, which was an offense to the majesty of God. The martyr Father Fray Diego Ortiz burned many sanctuaries and visibly exorcised the devil from them.[53] [The devil was] unable to resist the Father's prayers, exorcisms, and incantations, [or] the fumigations with which he tormented and afflicted them.

After General Martín Hurtado de Arbieto delineated the limits of the [new] city and began building the foundations for the city, he named the citizens who would be *encomenderos*. He distributed among these more than 1,500 Indians for personal service until Lord Don Francisco de Toledo intervened. [Hurtado de Arbieto] left the city well defended, leaving more than 50 soldiers guarding the city, and he marched back to Cuzco with all the prisoners, including Inca Tupac Amaru and his captains.[54]

Arriving at the Arch of Carmenca,[55] which was the entry to the city of Cuzco coming from [Vilcabamba], the army organized themselves. Governor Juan Alvárez Maldonado, as the *maese de campo*, led the Inca captains, who were chained together. Tupac Amaru Inca walked, unshackled, last of all. He was dressed in crimson velvet robes and shirts, his *ojotas* [were made from] a kind of fleece of local [i.e., alpaca] wool of various colors, his *llauto* included a tassel in the middle of his forehead, that in his language was called *mascapaicha*, which is the insignia of the royal Incas, like the crowns that kings wear. Celebrating their victory, [the army marched] straight to the palace where Lord Don Francisco de Toledo lived, which was [in] the houses of Don Tristan de Silva y Guzman, and of Juan Pancorvo Celiorigo, citizens of the city of Cuzco. These are the largest and most prominent houses of the city, as the Lord Doctor Alonso Pérez Marchán, President of Guadalajara, who lived in one of them, can testify for Your Excellency. [Thus] the general and his captains triumphantly entered [Cuzco], marching in formal military formation, and they presented their prisoners to the Lord Viceroy.

After rejoicing over the defeat of [the Inca], [Toledo] ordered Inca Tupac Amaru and his captains to be taken to the fort, which is in the Parish of San Cristóbal de Colcampata, to the home of the castle warden Don Luis de Toledo [Pimental],[56] the uncle of the Lord Viceroy. This fort [included] the large, majestic houses of Don Cristóbal Paullu Inca, a citizen of Cuzco, the father of Don Carlos Inca, and the grandfather of Don Melchor Carlos Inca, who was born there. They seized [these houses] from Don Carlos Inca to make a royal fort and garrison house, to guard the city, because he had hidden Titu Cusi Yupanqui and Tupac Amaru Inca, his first cousins, in this house during the baptism and did not tell anyone. [These houses] dominate the city of Cuzco and its six parishes, and more than four leagues of the valley up to the *tambo* [waystation] of Quispicancha [on] the road to Potosí. This fort belonged to His Majesty for many years, but because of a lawsuit filed by Don Melchor Carlos Inca regarding Your Royal Person's houses, it was mandated that [the houses] be returned to Don Melchor Carlos Inca, and they were, in fact, returned.

Returning to our story, a few days after the triumph, having studied the events leading to the deaths of the Father Fray Diego Ortiz, Pedro Pando, and Ambassador Atilano de Anaya, Doctor Gabriel de Loarte, the Justice of the Peace of this court, who was the corregidor of the city of Cuzco at the time,[57] sentenced the murderous captains to be hung and Tupac Amaru Inca to be beheaded. The sentence [against the captains] was executed [immediately]. They were taken through the city streets to [the site where they would] be brought to justice while the voice of a town crier declared their crimes, which have been described above. The three died in the common streets, [only] two [of them] at the place of execution, because [while] in the prison they had [contracted the disease] *chapetonada*, and they were [already] near death. However, despite their sickness, they were carried out in blankets to comply with the sentence for being murderers. The other two, Curi Paucar and the Huanca, paid for all, being hung on the gallows.

Two or three days passed while Tupac Amaru Inca was instructed, catechized, and baptized. He was taught by two clerics of our Lady of Mercy. One was Fray Gabriel Álvarez de la Carrera, who was the first creole to be born after the siege of Cuzco. [He was the] son of a knight, one of the first conquerors, who [participated] in the siege. [The other was] Fray Melchor Fernández. [Both] were skilled linguists who excelled in speaking with the Incas, especially Father Fray Gabriel Álvarez de la Carrera. He was unmatched in speaking [Quechua], because until now no one else has been found who can speak it with such grace and eloquence.

In short, the Inca was instructed by the [two] clerics, who performed the duties of their holy office so expertly it was as if they were feeding it to the Inca with a spoon. He was taken from the fort through the public streets of the city, guarded by more than 400 Cañari Indians,[58] who were great enemies of the Incas, wielding lances in their hands. The Inca, dressed in white cotton, held a crucifix in his hands, rode on a mule adorned for mourning. [He was] accompanied on either side by the two clerics [i.e., Fray Melchor Fernández and Fray Gabriel Álvarez de la Carrera], as well as by Father Alonso de Barzana,[59] of the Order of Jesuits, and Father [Cristóbal de] Molina, [a] cleric who preached to the natives, who had the Parish of the Hospital of Our Lady of the Remedies.[60] All were instructing and speaking words to comfort [Tupac Amaru's] soul. They brought [Tupac Amaru] to a scaffold that was [built] up high in the middle of the plaza, next to the Cathedral. The Fathers ascended with him, giving religious counsel and comforting his soul with holy preparations.

The roofs, plazas, and windows of the parishes of Carmenca and San Cristóbal were so full of people, that if you threw an orange, it would have been impossible for it to reach the ground, because the people were so packed and pressed together. When the executioner, who was a Cañari Indian, raised the sharp knife to cut off the head of Tupac Amaru Inca, a marvelous thing happened; all the native people raised such a great outcry and clamor that it seemed like Judgment Day. None of the Spaniards hid their feelings, publicly weeping; their tears falling with pain and sorrow. When the Inca heard this great outcry, he did nothing more than lift his right hand in the air and let it fall. As he remained serene with a lordly air, all of the outcries passed to a deep silence and not a living soul moved, neither those furthest away nor those who were in the plaza. [Tupac Amaru] then spoke the following with composure, not like someone who would soon die: that his reign had ended and that he deserved this death. He begged, pleaded, and charged everyone present who had children, that [when] their children misbehaved, they should not curse them, but instead punish them, because when he was a child, his mother had put a curse on him; that he would rather be beheaded than die a natural death. Since he was now going to die, he realized that the curse had been fulfilled. Because of this, he was reprehended by the priests, Fray Gabriel Álvarez de la Carrera and Fray Melchor Fernández, who told him that this was the will of God and not the curse of his mother. As the said Fathers were such skilled orators, they preached [as effectively as] Saint Paul (if this can be said).[61] They subdued him with ease and he repented what he had said. [The Inca then] asked them all to forgive him and that they tell the Lord Viceroy and Mayor of the Court to pray to God for him.

This being the state of affairs, they took him through the public streets. Many clerics kneeled and asked the Lord Viceroy to grant mercy and allow the Inca to live; among them were the Revered Don Fray Agustín de la Coruña, Bishop of Popayán, who was one of the famed 12 members of the Order of Saint Augustine who entered Mexico,[62] preaching the Evangelical law and its principles; and the Father *Presentado* Fray Gonzalo de Mendoza, who was Provincial of the Order of Our Lady of Mercy; and the Father Fray Francisco Corral, Prior of Saint Augustine of [Cuzco]; the Father Fray Gabriel de Oviedo,[63] Prior of Santo Domingo; the Father Fray Francisco Vélez, Guardian of San Francisco; the Father Fray Jerónimo de Villa Carrillo, Provincial of San Francisco; the Father Fray Gonzalo Ballestero, Prefect and Provincial Vicar of the [Order of Our Lady of] Mercy; and Father Luis López, Rector of the Jesuits. Dropping to their knees, they beseeched that [Tupac Amaru] be sent to Spain to the King. But none of these entreaties was powerful enough to [persuade] the Lord Viceroy. [Then] Juan de Soto, Chief Constable of the Court and servant of His Excellency, galloping furiously on horseback and brandishing a staff in his hand, opened a path through the crowd, trampling many people as he rode through. On behalf of the Lord Viceroy, he ordered the beheading of the Inca in compliance with the sentence. The Inca was consoled by the Fathers who were at his side. Bidding farewell to all, [Tupac Amaru] placed his head on the block like a lamb. The executioner then came forward. He grabbed [the Inca's hair] with his left hand and with the sharp knife in his right, he severed [the Inca's head] with a single blow and raised [it] high so all could see. At the moment that [Tupac Amaru was beheaded], the bells of the Cathedral started to ring, followed by those of all the monasteries and parishes of the city, which caused everyone great sadness and tears. They took the body to the house of Doña María Cusi Huarcay, who was both his mother and aunt, since in their infidelity brother and sister were married. The marriage was later ratified by the Papal Bull of Paul III,[64] which was [carried out] by the Lord Don Fray Jerónimo de Loayza,[65] who was the first archbishop of this archbishopric of Lima [during the period when] the Lord Don Andrés Hurtado de Mendoza, Marquis of Cañete and Head Guard of Cuenca, was viceroy.

The next day, at the hour of mass, the body of the Inca was buried in the high chapel of the cathedral by officials of the church. The Lord Bishop Don Fray Agustín de la Coruña said the Pontifical Mass. The gospel [was read by] the Canon Esteban de Villalón and the Epistle [by] the Canon Juan de Vera. [Clerics from] all the religious orders attended the burial, and each one said their vigils and sang masses for the laid-out corpse, expressing the great sentiment and sorrow that they felt for the Inca. Although they were greatly comforted [by the fact] that he was baptized just before being brought to justice by beheading. Throughout the nine days [of mourning], they sang mass, with organ accompaniment, for him, as was fit for a lord and Inca. Likewise, they honored him on the ninth day; all the religious orders each [held] their vigils and said their mass, without prompting.

From this it is inferred that God, our lord, was pleased, because as soon as they cut off his head, it was put on a spike in the pillory that was in the plaza next to where they made the scaffold. Each day [the head] became more beautiful, although in life the Inca had been ugly. The Indians arrived at night to worship the head of their Inca, until one morning Juan Sierra Surujano looked out the window and saw the idolatry the Indians were committing. He reported this to Lord Don Francisco de Toledo, who ordered the head removed and buried with the body. This was done with no less solemnity than that carried out for his burial. Thus, the Indians' troublesome adoration of the head was ended. And in this city a cleric of our Lady of Mercy, named Father Fray Nicolás de los Ríos, heard and saw all of the events that I have recounted until now.[66] He touched [the burial site] with his hands and walked upon it with his feet. [He is] a faithful cleric, and very familiar with the land of Cuzco, from whom Your Excellency could gain valuable information because he has a good memory and is a great authority, having been an eyewitness to all of these events.

Returning to the original topic, which is to provide Your Excellency with a clear description of the land under governorship within the province of Vilcabamba, I say, Excellent Lord, that this land is more than 300 leagues in size with many fertile plains. In the places they have discovered and conquered, they have planted many sugarcane fields along the valleys, which annually yield a large amount of money. One citizen of the city, named Toribio de Bustamante,[67] has alone collected sufficient [income] in rent, that, after his expenses, he saves more than 10,000 pesos each year. He has built two houses in Cuzco for God and his servants, a grandiose [act] for which he is held in high esteem. Of these, one is a monastery of barefoot Franciscans, flawlessly finished with embellishments and everything necessary for divine worship. The finest achievement of his efforts is all the [elaborate] woodwork of the church: doors, windows, and chapels [are] made from the finest cedar brought from the province of Vilcabamba. He is currently building a monastery for the Dominican nuns that is called Our Lady of the Remedies, which, when completed, will be flawlessly finished. It will be a work of no less perfection and rarity than that of the barefoot [Franciscans].

[Bustamante's] heroic acts are worthy of worldwide praise. When he arrived in [the Americas] he was a very poor soldier. Yet many Castilian lords and nobles could not match the spirit of generosity that this soldier has shown. He was held alone, captured and imprisoned, on the island of Dominica for more than two years by those barbarian Indians. There his life was put on the line an infinite number of times, in particular, when the Indians [were] in a drunken state. [He was held] until God granted the arrival of a Spanish fleet. When some small boats came ashore to replenish the fresh water of the ships, he fled, running toward the Spaniards, shouting, naked, covered only with *bibao* [?] and banana leaves. This was how he escaped and he went on to complete such lofty works that they are worthy [of] eternal memory. All this good fortune came to him for being a citizen of San Francisco de la Victoria de Vilcabamba.

In addition to this soldier, there are many others who have very impressive and productive [sugar mills], because of both the size of the land as well as its great fertility. It should be understood that this is the reason why the Incas selected this land, it being the richest and most opulent in all of Peru.

[Within the province] there are *chacras* [fields] of coca, wheat, maize, barley, potatoes, yuca [cassava], and, finally, [fields] for all type of foods. There are also many hills containing silver deposits, not counting those that are [already] discovered, which are the hills of Huamani and Huamanape, which have rendered great wealth. They have been mined since the time of our lords Marquis Don García Hurtado de Mendoza and Lord Don Luis de Velasco. This great quantity of silver has greatly augmented His Majesty's royal fifths. There have been various years that the Royal Treasury has received more than 30,000 pesos *ensayados,* produced by only 300 *mita* Indians.[68] This is the largest [number of Indians] that has been made available [at any one time] to provide labor in the mines, refine the metals, work in the crushing mills, collect firewood and carbon, and other works. The Indian [*mita*] labor was drawn from different provinces: 200 [came] from the province of Andahuaylas la Grande,[69] owned by the Royal Crown, and 100 [came from] the province of the Chumbivilcas, from the *encomienda* of Don Diego de Vargas Carvajal.

Of these [workers], as Your Excellency well should know, the 200 from Andahuaylas were reassigned to labor in the mercury mines of Huancavelica. This [reallocation of labor] was ordered by the Lord Count of Monterrey,[70] who was not well informed of the great damage that would result to the royal fifths and to the citizens and owners of the mines of that province.[71] [This occurred] because [the Count of Monterrey] did not obtain reports from the magistrate of the region nor from the royal officials of Cuzco, [who] collect the royal fifth by order of the Lord Viceroys. They report on the royal fifths paid to Your Excellency each year, [and] they have reported great losses [as a] result [of the reassignment of labor]. So that Your Excellency has assurance that this is the truth, it will be necessary for the Official Royal Judges from Cuzco to send an account of the fifths of each year. This will show I am correct.

There has been a report, most excellent lord, of the great treasure in a *huaca* of the Inca, which is in this province. There are many clues that it will be discovered, our lord being served, next to a ravine of gold. The ravine is called Purumata, and the Spaniards have [already] extracted great quantities of very fine gold of all grades. A gold nugget was found there, perhaps four years [ago], the size of a chicken egg. The *maese de campo,* Diego García de Paredes, as Magistrate, took a bag of fine gold nuggets, including the one I just described, to Spain to show His Majesty. They have not yet discovered [the source of] this treasure because there are few available Indians. I hope there will be a way, through your support and help, [if] Your Excellency would do us the favor [of sending] some Indians, that these riches will be discovered during Your Excellency's reign. This would be the greatest discovery of wealth that has been made in this kingdom, such that all the Indies and our Spain would return to the opulence and grandeur that existed when these provinces of Peru were first discovered. [At that time] men made powerful by this wealth traveled to Spain rich in possessions and estates. They acted with great generosity and largesse. When needy gentlemen arrived to request alms, they did not worry about whether they or their children would later find themselves in need. These great men gave 3,000 or 4,000 pesos to the needy as if it were nothing. Today that [amount] is [equal to] the wealth of a well-off man who could never be mistaken for poor.

There were feats worthy of being exalted. For example, one was [carried out by] a distinguished citizen of Cuzco, named Don Luis Palomino.[72] When a soldier gave a handsome and rare clavichord as a gift to his unmarried sister, Doña Mayor Palomino, this gentleman [Palomino] gave [the soldier] 2,000 baskets of coca in return. When the coca sold in Potosí, where [it was worth] 12 to 14 pesos per basket, the soldier emerged from poverty for the rest of his life, returning to Spain very rich and powerful. And the same gentleman, being the municipal magistrate of the city, performed another magnificent public act in the plaza. Once, while on horseback, a soldier arrived to ask him to order a constable to return his sword, which had been taken from him the night before. [The soldier] had offered a mark[73] for the return of his sword, but [the constable] was unwilling to do it. So the good gentleman said to the soldier that these were the prerogatives of constables, and he took the sword from his belt, being decorated with gold, pearls, and shell, all inlaid in silver, and gave it to the soldier, to avoid denying the constable his gains since [Palomino's] sword was worth a silver bar. Seeing the splendid example of the municipal magistrate [i.e., Palomino], the Minister of Justice was pleased to return the [original] sword to its owner without an ulterior motive, [and] the soldier, [in turn], returned the opulent sword to its owner.

[These] events are worthy of being written into history so that they will live on in eternal memory; because there is nothing so splendorous as the generous spirit of one who does good deeds. Because, as the theologians say, good deeds affect those who carry them out in four ways: the first is making [the person] as good as the good of the deed. The second is curing him of the vices that are harmful to him [and] expelling them from his home. The third and greatest is earning grace and glory. The fourth is preparing him for the pain that he will endure in this world or in Purgatory. The citizens of this kingdom have carried out many other prodigious acts worthy of retelling to Your Excellency, but for brevity I will leave them out.

The province of the Manarí Indians is, most Excellent Prince, of Indians allied with our Spanish Nation. They are good-natured and fair-skinned, gentle. The men as well as women are very good-looking; they all dress well and have a dignified manner. Their lands are pleasant and very fertile, [including] expansive plains suitable for the cultivation of all types of fruit and grains. [These lands are also] famous for their sugarcane fields, delightful freshwater rivers, and abundant pastures of great length and breadth for all kinds of livestock. It seems to me [we can engage] with these people without needing to shed even a drop of blood or engage in skirmishes or prolonged conflict. Instead we could enter with a group of affable, kind, and charitable soldiers, who, although perceivably bearing arms, would not commit atrocities, murder, or cruelty, as was customary in the past. [These people] would then give [in to us] without any resistance, and would make great contributions toward the expansion of the royal patrimony and its kingdoms.

The reason that I am moved to say this is that after the province of Vilcabamba was pacified, and the city was founded and populated with Indians, and when everything [had become] peaceful and calm, I witnessed two captains with only two soldiers, who were Captain Antón de Álvarez,[74] Captain Alonso Juárez,[75] Pedro Gudiño (a Portuguese), and another soldier, whose name I do not remember, go further inland into the Manarí province.[76] The Indians received them with great affection and willingness. They gave [the Spaniards] much food: tapirs, peccaries (whose navels are on their backs), turkeys, ducks, and other game and a great quantity of river fish (i.e., shad), [as well as] yuca, peanuts, toasted and boiled corn, and many delicious fruits of these lands, especially [fruit] from their many orchards, including avocados, guavas, pacays, and a great quantity of almonds, much larger and better than those of Castile, and cacao.

The Indians showed themselves to be so affable and friendly that the four Spaniards brought an image of Our Lady painted on a canvas. To entrust themselves to God, the soldiers instructed the Indians to construct a small chapel, which they built, where they hung her image.[77] [They also erected] a large cross outside of the chapel on a stone pedestal and other small crosses inside the chapel. [The Spaniards] went to pray there each morning and [pledged] to commend themselves to God. They did the same in the afternoons. Seeing this devotion, the Indians went to the chapel to pray; kneeling and raising their hands toward the sky; they [then] struck their chests. With this the Spaniards rejoiced; seeing them so friendly and desirous of being Christian.

When these four soldiers left the province for Vilcabamba, their most important lords, which they call Apu, which is a way of saying lord or governor, begged [the soldiers] to entrust them to an *encomendero*. [The Manarí also told them] that if [the Spaniards] wished to enter the province of the Pilcosuni with armed men, they could easily do so as it was nearby. [The Manarí] gave their word to serve [the Spaniards] in that journey against the bellicose [Pilcosuni] Indians. They were moved to do so for two reasons. The first was so that they would know and understand the law of God and become Christians. The other was to avenge the damage inflicted upon [the Manarí] by the Pilcosuni.

After more than eight years, the governor [i.e., Hurtado de Arbieto] wrote with this news to Lord Don Martín Enríquez [de Almanza],[78] who was at the time viceroy of these Kingdoms, [requesting that the viceroy] grant him permission and license to go in person to discover the province of the Pilcosuni and Asháninka. The Manarí had advised Captains Antón de Álvarez and Alonso Juárez that they were located nearby and that [the Manarí] could provide warriors. [The viceroy] did so, recapitulating certain reasons why this would benefit His Majesty.

Up to one hundred soldiers were raised from the city of Cuzco and its surrounding valley districts, not [counting] the mestizos, mulattos, and freed Africans.[79] The Spaniards were able to enter [the province] with this [force], because the Spaniards were skilled soldiers. We departed on our journey from the Quillapampa Valley; [there we embarked] downriver in the rafts and canoes, [which] we had laboriously made with great expense, such that we looked like an armed flotilla.[80] After having navigated for four or five days, we became wrecked on the boulders and outcrops of the hills that we passed through, in some rapids and sharp turns in the rivers.[81] We landed on a beach after several Spaniards, Indians and mulattos, and Captain [Miguel de] Andueza drowned. We also lost the governor's chest and many of the soldiers' things, as well as the vestments of the [three] Fathers: Pedro de Cartagena of the Jesuits, brother of Don Fernando de Cartagena, a citizen of the city of Cuzco; Doctor Montoya Romano, [also] a Jesuit; and brother Madrid, who is alive today.[82] We convened a war council and it was agreed that we would make a path through the mountains using our axes and machetes. [We] suffered from great hunger, exposure and cold, getting stuck on tree branches that shredded our clothing. We were left without any covering and in need of food, as this is an uninhabited land without paths to travel along.[83] If our friends, the one hundred Manarí Indians from the province, had not accompanied us, giving advice to Governor [Hurtado de Arbieto] about how [to go about] conquering the Pilcosuni, we would have all perished. [The Manarí] came looking for us, and we were seen by two *cacique* leaders who led us out of grave danger. They showed us the Inca roads to the land of the Pilcosuni, providing us with supplies that they scavenged and brought.

If it would be beneficial to Your Excellency during this period of your government to conquer all of this land, at low cost to His Majesty, Your Excellency [need only] name [the] General, *maese de campo*, and officials, [and] I, at my advanced age, with all my white hair, would take up the order to join that expedition. [With] the virile spirit that God has given me, [and] my diligence and experience in the region, which is more than I had [during the original expedition], and since the paths and areas close to the jurisdiction of the city of Huamanga are now open, it would be easy to conquer [the region].

Returning to the Pilcosuni,[84] I say, most excellent lord, that we were informed by a Pilcosuni Indian, who called himself Opa,[85] when we were close. However, he eventually double-crossed us, fleeing one night from where we had bivouacked. A very good fort was made in a convenient place with many trenches, fortified towers on the corners, and embrasures whence to discharge the harquebuses. [The Pilcosuni] returned there, making grandiose gestures and signs of peace, feigning profound humility and bringing the royal [troops] much food. He pledged obedience to the governor [Hurtado de Arbieto] and embraced him with great laughter and happiness, and made similar gestures to me, as the head constable and *maese de campo* (a title that in this kingdom is customary to give to leading and worthy soldiers, given that there are few of them in the militia).[86] One day when they thought they saw us with our guard down, at about two in the afternoon, they showered us with a volley of arrows and spears, badly wounding various soldiers, including the governor, who guarded the door of the fort. This spirited gentleman fought valiantly with [the Pilcosuni], coming to resemble Saint Sebastian,[87] given all the arrows that stuck in his *escaupil* (which are vests made from cotton cloth, loosely quilted with cotton thread, stronger than steel). Being an older man, [he fought] holding a large battle-axe. He did more [damage to the Pilcosuni] than Mucius Scaevola,[88] wounding and killing with great valor and noble spirit and in a knightly manner. [That day] he clearly proved himself to be [both] a Hurtado and Mendoza, committing heroic acts worthy of eternal remembrance.

We were advised by the Manarí that, on account of the shipwrecks we had in that great river, the loss of property and supplies, the deaths of soldiers, [our clothes] being torn by the forests, the lack of provisions and necessities for corporal sustenance, that we were at great risk if we stayed. [Moreover,] we were so few and were in such bad shape, and our enemies in only one Pilcosuni town, named Hatun Pilcosuni, were innumerous. Being bellicose, both the young and old among them took arms and alerted the rest of the province. [Therefore,] for our own good, we raised the royal [banner] and left, at a furious pace, along the Inca road, guided by the Manarís. Leaving the [Pilcosuni] land and province behind, we returned to ours, more than anything so that the Jesuit Fathers would not perish than out of fear for our own lives. If we had not lost such great [quantities] of gunpowder, shields, mortars, and guns to the river, we no doubt would have conquered the [Pilcosuni], even if they were more bellicose.

According to the news we received, and given the evidence we saw of their farmsteads, fields, flocks, and numerous herds, and given the lay of the land, they appeared to be mountain people. [We saw] hills with much silver ore of great value; there were also *yunga* people there and marvelous lands well suited for grains and sugarcane. There was an abundance of streams and a great river that girded and irrigated everything. [The river had] a great quantity of fish, among them shad, gilthead, and catfish, although we do not know the quality of the water or its freshness. And a great number of people [lived there]. And returning to our royal [army], most excellent lord, if our [Indian] friends had not advised us, no man would have remained alive from the destruction done to us by the immense [army of] our enemies. They would have dealt us a cruel death without leaving anyone alive. God, our lord, liberated us from that difficult situation. His Majesty knows the reason.

Eight years have passed,[89] Your Excellency, [since we witnessed] one of the greatest and strongest [ordeals] that we could have suffered, as if the hardships and misfortune that the citizens of the city and of all the region had been through in relocating the city and mines, as I have mentioned earlier, were not enough. In that province there are numerous mills and they are all supported by African slaves. The land is suited to their constitution and they are naturally soulless, without God, and without a conscience. We found ourselves, six Spaniards and one cleric priest, [the] nephew of the Chantre Don Cristóbal de Albornoz, in [the middle of] a great conflict. There was a terrible escalation [of tensions], precipitated by a group of African slaves conspiring to revolt from all the mills in the valleys of Quillabamba, Hoyara, Amaibamba, and Huayobamba. Working in concert with the African [slaves] of Cuzco, Arequipa, and Huamanga, [they planned] to invade the [Vilcabamba] region and convert it into another Vallano,[90] which Your Excellency will have heard of.

As leader of the Holy Brotherhood,[91] the position which I then held and have held over the past 14 years until now, [in compliance with] the orders of the Lord Viceroys, the Marquis de Cañete and Don Luis de Velasco, whom I have already mentioned, I learned the following information. According to my instructions, a *ladina* African, [the] wife of an African thief, and another Indian woman were arrested in a cane field and [in] the mountains [respectively] and on my orders were imprisoned. These women's husbands had killed two Indians and a free mulatto, while robbing them to get the clothes and food that they had in their fields. They killed them there. The murderers were an Indian named Francisco Chichima, a Pilcosuni native, and an African slave of the widow of Melchior del Peso, who has a mill there. I had the women in stocks and threatened to quarter them the next day if they did not tell me where their husbands were. That same night, Captain Ormachea, who had a large hacienda, was with me. Fearing death and having seen me mete out justice to others that same night, the African [woman] called him over and asked him to beg me not to quarter her. She [promised] to reveal the truth to me [and said what she could tell me would] save the life of all the mill owners and those of their foremen and many other merchants.

Listening closely, I walked over to where the prisoners were, and asked Captain Ormachea what the African [woman] had told him, although I had heard. The captain responded that the African woman was a drunk and a liar and she did not know what she was saying. To verify this, I gently asked her to tell me the truth, and [I told her] that I would not only let her go but I would give her freedom in the name of His Majesty. She revealed to me how that night, at midnight, all the Africans of [Nicolás de] Ormachea and Toribio de Bustamante,[92] and those of the widow of Melchior del Peso, and of other mills that were in the valley, and all the Africans of the mills of the valleys of Hoyara, Amaibamba, [and] Huayobamba, had conspired with all the Africans of the cities of Cuzco, Arequipa, and Huamanga. They had decided to revolt that night and burn, as actually they did, the houses and sugar mills of Torribio de Bustamante. That night they killed 24 Indians and a *curaca* [chief] who had come to extinguish the fire. From there, they were supposed to kill Toribio de Bustamante and four Spaniards and a priest who were with him. Then, after setting out again, at midnight, they were supposed to attack Captain Ormachea and all those who were with him. [When I asked] how she knew this, she gave her sworn declaration that on Sundays and holidays when all the Africans got together to drink, [she had heard them] talking in their native tongue, and they were [amassing] arms and supplies. They had collected corn, peanuts, and ocas[93] that they stored in their granaries built in the mountains.

I diligently sent word to Magistrate Diego de Aguilar y de Cardona at Vilcabamba, with two Indians whom we sent well paid, and another two Africans born-to-house.[94] The Africans did not reappear, because the [rebels] killed them and threw them in the river, but the Indians, who were born in that area, took a route that allowed them to warn Vilcabamba quickly. In the meantime, while help arrived, we constructed a fort out of wood to protect ourselves and in which we assembled a number of Indians native to the area. We also sent sentries out, so that the Africans would not find us without fore-warning. We were enclosed for 30 days, defending ourselves with guns and other arms, with the Indians [positioned to] fire over the top of the fort without exposing their faces.[95] We were arranged like this when 50 soldiers sent by the Magistrate Diego de Aguilar y de Cardona arrived. They were well armed and visibly well equipped with guns, ammunitions, gunpowder, and rope and a large supply of cheese, biscuits, beef jerky, maize, and other things. They were accompanied by a number of Indian allies with their bows and arrows, who assisted us in breaking the siege and putting down the revolt.

Because of certain concessions they made for Toribio de Bustamante, who was building the monastery of the Barefoot [Augustinians] of Cuzco and [who needed] the Africans to cut cedar and other woods for his work; no more than eight or 10 captains were brought to justice in addition to Francisco Chichima, a Pilcosuni Indian, who was one of the murderers and the most bellicose Indian of the many that have lived in our times. The Africans themselves selected him as their captain since he was so brave, and they obeyed his orders and wishes, even though generally the Indians were subservient to the Africans, being mistreated in word and in deed. The Indians called the Africans "lords" and the Africans called the Indians "dogs," as Your Excellency can confirm. As the only Indian, Francisco Chichima was outnumbered by Africans; nevertheless, he was so courageous that they named him captain and obeyed him as they would a chief since they feared him as they feared death.

When the city of Vilcabamba was first settled, the fathers of Our Lady of Mercy entered and founded a convent. They were given a parcel of land for their monastery and land for their cemeteries. There they built a church and a residence, where they said mass. They settled there for more than 15 years. The prefects of the monastery were the fathers: Fray Juan de Ribas, Fray Francisco Guerrero, Fray Nicolás Gomez, and Fray Gonzalo de Toro Caballero.[96] Because they did not have *yanacona* or *mita* to work the lands, [or] anyone to bring them a jar of water, their council made the decision to leave the site and lands. They left the sacred vestments, chalices, bells, and images under the protection of a secular [priest], and they left that province for Cuzco. The church remains [in Vilcabamba] to date. On four or five occasions they have attempted to resettle there, because the populace of the city felt such great devotion toward the fathers, as they were the first clerics to settle there. They served Our Lady and were the first to introduce the [Catholic] faith and spread the Evangelical law in all these Kingdoms of Peru, Chile, Tucumán, Paraguay, and Santa Cruz de la Sierra. [However,] because they did not have [Indians for] personal service, they were so wary that they do not dare [to return for fear of] dying of hunger.

[Other clerics] saw the Fathers of Our Lady of Mercy and saw them leave [the town] of their own free will. No other [clerics] have wanted to settle there, so as not to face the extreme needs experienced by the fathers. And so the city of Vilcabamba has only a parish church, and the citizens cannot go to hear mass early in order to attend to their needs as they see fit. Their [only option] is to attend [the mass] in the parish church whenever it is given. This is intolerable and demands to be remedied. They should return and rebuild the monastery of Our Lady of Mercy, as this would make the lives of the citizens of the town easier. [They would return] if Your Excellency would allow [the clerics] to have *yanaconas* and *mitayos*, who would loyally and steadfastly serve them.[97]

All that which I have told you until now, most excellent prince, is, to the best of my abilities, what my weak memory allows me to recall of events [that took place] so long ago. Understand that I summarized the events as they occurred and have tried in my writing to capture the essence of the most pleasant things that I could describe well, [including] the parades, battle reenactments, and other preparations for war that occurred in the city of Cuzco before departing for the expedition. I will paint [a picture] for Your Excellency [of] the great and renowned festivals that they held. [The festivities] included bull[fights], jousting, and reenactments of battles with Moorish castles. In the plaza of Cuzco they constructed [panoramas] of mountainous jungles with tall trees that appeared to reach to the sky. Tethered within them were tigers, lions, bears, tapirs, large and small monkeys, squirrels, ferrets, peacocks, ducks with many different-colored feathers, guacamayos, which are large parrots with red, green, blue, purple, and yellow [feathers], talking parrots of different kinds, parakeets, large and small birds of many and varied colors. These were subtly tied to the trees and together they produced a pleasant birdsong that everyone fell in love with. [They built] a fountain there [and acted out how] when the mountain girls and other peoples went to collect water, the Moors came out of their castles and captured them. After the tournaments, all the [Christian] knights appeared and held a skirmish against the Moors, whom they captured and arrested, and the Christian captives were set free. [These events] entertained and pleased everyone who watched them from windows and balconies, as well as those who were in the plaza.

The Lord Don Francisco de Toledo jousted that day, adding to the overall enjoyment and happiness [of the festival], which celebrated [the day of] Lord Saint John the Baptist.[98] No expense was spared to pay for the livery, [which was] made of expensive fabric, adorned with silver and gold; harnesses [were] richly adorned with shell, pearls, and stones of great worth. The lances were adorned with strips of silver wound around them. Forty-eight gentlemen mounted on horseback emerged, among the greatest leaders and most distinguished of the kingdom. Eight teams of three each [emerged from each side of the plaza]. The Lord Viceroy rode the most beautiful horse. It was a horse of great spirit and speed, yet the most assuredly gentle and loyal of horses that has been born of a mare. His horse was so good that they called it the "fool with silver feet," because it had dark chestnut hair except for white patches from its knees down, and a strip of white hair down its forehead that enhanced its beauty, and the bushiest mane and tail that had ever been seen on a horse.

Among the participants were the Factor Juan de Salas de Valdés (the brother of the most illustrious Cardinal Don Fernando Valdés, Archbishop of Seville), Don Jerónimo de Figueroa, [the viceroy's] nephew, and Francisco de Barrasa, [the viceroy's] steward, who were captains of the first team of 24 [gentlemen] who entered from above.[99] General Jerónimo Castilla, a man of the Order of Santiago, and Captain Juan de Pancorvo, both citizens of [Cuzco], as well as Don Jerónimo Marañón, a gentleman of great esteem and High Constable of the city, were captains leading the team of [24 who entered] from below.

[Among] the players were Captain Lope de Suazo; Governor Juan Alvárez Maldonado; Don Luis Palomino; Treasurer Miguel Sánchez; Gonzalo

Hernándes de Valencia [and] his son, Pablo de Carvajal; Captain Julian de [H]umarán; Captain Nuño de Mendoza; Captain Don Antonio Pereyra; Pedro Alonso Carrasco, who today belongs to the Order of Santiago; Captain Francisco de Grado; Captain Jerónimo Pacheco; Captain Juan de Quirós; Captain Rodrigo de Esquivel; Don Gómez de Tordoya; Francisco de Valverde of the Order of Santiago; Governor Melchior Vasques Dávila; Captain Martín Dolmos of the Order of Santiago; Captain Martín de Meneses; Pedro Núñez Manuel; Don Juan de Silva of the Order of Santiago; General Jerónimo de Frías; Captain Diego Barrantes de Loayza; Juan de Sotomayor of the Order of Santiago; Captain Alonso de Loayza, first cousin of Lord Archbishop Don Jerónimo de Loayza; Pedro Costilla de Nocedo, Juan de Berrio, Miguel de Berrio, and Sancho de Orozco, his brothers; Gonzalo Mejía de Ayala, second son of the Count Gomera (the elder); and other very important gentlemen, whose names my fading memory prevents me from recalling, all of which were citizens of Cuzco, and other meritorious servants of the lord viceroy and greatly esteemed officials of other cities. And then six riders, wearing ferocious devil costumes, emerged onto the street entering the plaza. They had other demons, made from plaster, on the haunches of their beautiful horses. They rode in their saddles with high stirrups, as if they had been born there, riding shoulder to shoulder. They also jousted and used the [plaster] devils as shields. Following them was a 12-year-old boy, dressed in a fine brocade with a bishop's miter, made of silver fabric [woven] solely for this purpose. He wore city gloves and many rings of gold and emeralds on the fingers of his hands. He went about giving blessings, riding on a mule, facing backward. Behind him [were] six choir boys on horse[back] in red choir robes with songbooks in their hands. They sang, lowering and raising the song as those who were in charge of this saw fit. Then, further back, a group of satyrs on horseback emerged, I do not know how many. They were clothed as well-dressed gentlemen. And at the back came a [man dressed as a] *hirco* [a male mountain goat], covered in crimson, with his jacket and a black cape of cut velvet. He wore a velvet belt and hat, and a gilded plaster crown, an alchemy chain, and a gilded sword. He was followed by many servants. And after having made their rounds in the street along the perimeter of the plaza, they reordered themselves to make their entrances and divided in half.

The game began, with the lord viceroy being the first. He only jousted three rounds, and afterward he got down from his horse and climbed up to the viewing gallery of Diego de los Rios, a citizen and very important gentleman, from where [the viceroy] watched the jousting tournament. After that ended, they released a ferocious bull, the most aggressive that I have seen, who ran around for a long time entertaining [the crowd] in the plaza. In the end, he entered the forest, where he saw the wild beasts and charged the tiger[100] with great impetus and fury. Since [the tiger] was tightly bound, he could not use his claws or take advantage of his agility, [but] he sufficiently defended himself, and he also attacked until the injured bull was so tired and exhausted that he left and entered the plaza area, where he charged the knights in the bullring. Nightfall put an end to the festivities and celebration of the victory. For a long time, no one could talk of anything else.

I would like, most excellent lord, to write with the eloquence of that orator Cicero and to have the wisdom of the most knowledgeable Solomon, to describe this history in an honest style with polished language, so that everyone would enjoy it. What is more, I would be satisfied if I knew that Your Excellency would accept this with benign prudence and excuse the mistakes, which are many, that I may have made. I ask as earnestly as I can, if I have been [excessively] lengthy in my narration, that you will pardon me, as it could not be shorter [and tell] the history of events in this Kingdom. As I am certain that this is the essence of the truth, I have been so bold [as] to tell [of these events]. And in this city, as I have said earlier, there is an elder cleric of the order of Our Lady of Mercy who saw all these things with his eyes, and heard them as they occurred and touched them with his hands, and personally walked in [these same lands]. Your Excellency could obtain information from him, and with luck, being younger than I, and his memory being better, he will able to recall other details, since it is impossible for me to know them all. Of those that I have remembered, I have done my duty, without adding anything that could thwart or diverge from the truth, because I typically shun fabulous tales, so as not to lose credibility as an honest man, because it is advantageous to be one, although the sinful multitude may say otherwise.

Given my proper conduct, I seek recourse from Your Excellency, hoping that you will be merciful to me in every way. By recognizing my [lifelong] service, in addition to having served their majesties, the kings, your lords, Your Excellency will carry out one of the most worthy acts of compassion of the innumerable [acts of mercy] you have exercised in this lifetime. I gave the flower of my youth to my kings and lords until these last years, in which I have found myself, in my tired life and old age, suffering the hardships of poverty. In return for your mercy may God, our lord, grant Your Excellency the utmost happiness in this life, and eternal rest in that to come, [and] glory for which you were raised. May Your Excellency have joy for ever and ever. Amen.

NOTES

1. Ocampo had come to the court of Mendoza y Luna two years earlier, and, having impressed the viceroy with his knowledge of Vilcabamba, the viceroy requested that Ocampo set his memories to paper. Ocampo includes a brief apology for the long delay in writing his history in the opening pages of the account.

2. Ocampo was interviewed on 20 February 1600 to find out what he knew about Ortiz's death (Aparicio López 1989: 288–290; Romero and Urteaga 1916, 2:143–145; Bauer et al. 2014: 143–144).

3. Ocampo testified in support of Martín Hurtado de Arbieto on 4 December 1590 (Bauer and Halac-Higashimori 2013: 73–78).

4. These celebrations are also briefly mentioned by Salazar (see document 4, this volume).

5. Juan de Mendoza y Luna served as viceroy of Peru from December 1607 to December 1615.

6. The Spanish crown passed from Felipe II to his son Felipe III in 1598.

7. We have chosen to translate "Tercero deste nombre" (the third of this name) as simply "Felipe III."

8. Despite his best intentions, Ocampo confuses the timing of many events and often compresses a series of different events together.

9. Cristóbal Paullu Cusi Topa Inca died in 1549. His son, Carlos Inca, immediately took over the role of the Spanish-supported Inca in Cuzco.

10. At that time the Cuzco nobility were living in the former Inca palace called Colcampata, just below the fort of Sacsayhuaman. Part of this structure can still be seen today.

11. The parish church of San Cristóbal stands on the flanks of Sacsayhuaman, adjacent to Colcampata.

12. The name Melchor was selected since the event took place on the Epiphany, the day when the Three Magi arrived to see the infant Jesus.

13. These ethnic groups are located between Cuzco and Lake Titicaca.

14. Given that Titu Cusi Yupanqui died ca. 1571 and after his death Vilcabamba was isolated from Cuzco for more than a year, it seems most unlikely that these two Incas attended the baptism of Melchor Carlos Inca.

15. *Acllas* were preadolescent girls; *mamaconas* were specially selected women who served the state.

16. Intense contact between Titu Cusi Yupanqui and the Spaniards of Cuzco most likely began in 1560 following the death of Sayri Tupac. They increased during the interim viceroyalty of Lope García de Castro (1564–1569). Unfortunately, Ocampo has confused the names of the individuals who attended different meetings as well as the dates of the meetings themselves. Many of the encounters that Ocampo suggests took

place under Toledo occurred during the earlier rule of Lope García de Castro. See Hemming (1970), Guillén Guillén (1979, [1977] 2005), and Nowack (2004) for detailed retellings of the events that occurred during this time period.

17. Diego Ortiz entered Vilcabamba in 1569 and was killed in ca. 1571.

18. Atilano de Anaya was the caretaker of Beatriz Clara Coya, Sayri Tupac's daughter, whose inheritance rights were at the center of the Acobamba treaty negotiations between Titu Cusi Yupanqui and the Spaniards (Guillén Guillén 1977b; Nowack 2004). Anaya was killed several years later, in March of 1572, while attempting to enter Vilcabamba on a mission for Toledo. Following his death, Toledo declared outright war against the Incas of Vilcabamba and launched a massive campaign into the region that concluded with the capture of Tupac Amaru.

19. Francisco de las Veredas was a priest, who, along with Antonio de Vera, entered the Vilcabamba region in July 1567 to baptize Felipe Quispe Titu, the son of Titu Cusi Yupanqui.

20. Martín Pando spent many years in the Vilcabamba region working as the interpreter and secretary of Titu Cusi Yupanqui. He was killed in ca. 1571 after the death of Titi Cusi Yupanqui by Inca loyalists. After the fall of Vilcabamba, Pando's wife, Juana Guerrero, provided information on the events that occurred in Vilcabamba during Titu Cusi Yupanqui's rule (Aparicio López 1989; Bauer et al. 2014).

21. As noted above, the meetings between Titu Cusi Yupanqui and the Spaniards began in 1566, during the rule of Lope García de Castro, and ended with the Inca's death in ca. 1571. Ocampo has truncated and confused much of this timeline.

22. King Felipe III inducted Melchor Carlos Inca into the Order of Santiago when Melchor was in Spain around 1607 (Hemming 1970: 465–466).

23. This statement suggests that Ocampo wrote his document in 1611.

24. Here we have translated *vara* (literally, the staff of office) as "auspices."

25. The Inca actually took the name Diego de Castro Titu Cusi Yupanqui. His son, Quispe Titu, had taken the name Felipe at the time of his own baptism about a year earlier.

26. Titu Cusi Yupanqui was baptized two times: once as a youth in Cuzco and a second time in 1568 by Juan de Vivero. The second baptism and Titu Cusi Yupanqui's conversion to Christianity were conditions written into the Treaty of Acobamba in 1566.

27. In his own writings Albornoz ([ca. 1582] 1984) notes that he had a gold ore processing mill near Puquiura. Also see Albornoz's letter to the king of Spain, in which he states that he will soon be entering the Vilcabamba region to build a mill (Millones 1990: 307–308).

28. Ocampo was interviewed in Cuzco on 20 February 1600, when he gave a sworn testimony concerning what he had heard concerning Ortiz's death (Bauer et al. 2014).

29. Ocampo also tells the story of Juan Quispe in his 20 August 1600 deposition (Romero and Urteaga 1916: 144–145; Aparicio López 1989: 288–290; Bauer et al. 2014). The story is often repeated by writers interested in the death of Diego Ortiz (see Murúa [ca. 1616] 1987 and Calancha [1638] 1981). Juan Quispe testified in the town of San Francisco de la Victoria de Vilcabamba at least two times, once in 1595 and then in 1599 (Bauer et al. 2014); however, the beating of Ortiz is not mentioned during the depositions.

30. That is to say, on the left-hand side facing the altar.

31. The ruins of the city of Vitcos, now called Rosaspata, still stand near the town of Puquiura (Bauer, Fonseca Santa Cruz, and Aráoz Silva 2015).

32. While Ocampo provides a good description of Vitcos, which he no doubt visited during his long stay in the Vilcabamba region, he is incorrect in suggesting that Tupac Amaru was in Vitcos at the time of Ortiz's death. The Inca was in the town of Vilcabamba, and because of that, Ortiz was dragged from Vitcos to near Vilcabamba before being killed.

33. The lintels of Vitcos are made of white granite.

34. The town of Ollantaytambo is located two or three days' walk up the Urubamba River from the bridge of Chuquichaca.

35. Juan Alvárez Maldonado was a seasoned explorer of the eastern slopes of the Andes. He was with Gonzalo Pizarro in the 1539 campaign into Vilcabamba, and in 1567 he led an expedition into the Madre de Dios area.

36. Martín Hurtado de Arbieto was married to Juana de Ayala Ponce de León. Years after the Vilcabamba raid, in 1583, Juan Ponce de León helped rescue his brother-in-law during his failed attempt to conquer the Pilcosuni (Maúrtua 1906: 242).

37. A rival of Juan Alvárez Maldonado, Gómez de Tordoya, had also been a leader of an earlier expedition into the eastern Andes.

38. In 1588 Antonio Pereyra led an inquiry into Hurtado de Arbieto's rule of Vilcabamba (Maúrtua 1906: 181–191).

39. Here Ocampo confuses Alonso de Messa (the younger), who became the lord of Piedrabuena, with his father, Alonso de Messa (the elder), who entered Vilcabamba in 1572.

40. As part of the reward for capturing Tupac Amaru, Martín García Oñaz de Loyola was allowed to marry Sayri Tupac's only child, Beatriz Clara Coya. In this way he gained control of her vast holdings in the Yucay Valley.

41. The plain of Oncoy was located where the colonial town of San Francisco de la Victoria de Vilcabamba was later resettled.

42. Part of the lower Urubamba River Valley, below modern Quillabamba, appears to have been called the Simaponte Valley.

43. Here Ocampo presents a very compact version of the fall of the Inca city of Vilcabamba and the capture of Tupac Amaru.

44. Ocampo is incorrect on this point. The Inca city of Vilcabamba was taken on 24 June 1572.

45. References to Villa Rica de Argete can be found in other colonial documents (e.g., Maúrtua 1906: 226; Bauer et al. 2014).

46. García Hurtado de Mendoza was viceroy of Peru from 1590 to 1596.

47. *Cabildo abierto* (open council) was a public meeting that the prominent citizens of a town, who did not have seats in the *cabildo* (town council), were invited to attend.

48. Luis de Velasco was viceroy of Peru from 1596 to 1604.

49. This is most likely a reference to Lima.

50. It reads "*sus reales quintos*" or "your royal fifths" since the king received 20 percent of all income produced in his colonies.

51. San Francisco de la Victoria de Vilcabamba remains a small town today.

52. On 16 August 1590 the viceroy granted Antonio Luis de Cabrera permission to build a Meridian church in Villa Rica de Argete and to set aside agricultural land to support the associated priests (Barriga 1942: 280–281).

53. This is a reference to Ortiz's burning of the Yurak Rumi shrine (Bauer, Aráoz Silva, and Burr 2012) which is described in the 1595 testimony of Juana Guerrero (Bauer et al. 2014).

54. This is incorrect. Hurtado de Arbieto remained in the newly established town of San Francisco de la Victoria de Vilcabamba while Martín García Oñaz de Loyola returned to Cuzco with the captives and the loot from the campaign.

55. Carménca is the sector of Cuzco now called Santa Ana.

56. Luis de Toledo Pimental played a minor role in the Vilcabamba campaign by occupying the Osambre area to prevent the Inca from fleeing down the Apurímac River.

57. Gabriel de Loarte was with Viceroy Toledo when he arrived in Cuzco and played important roles in the 1572 Vilcabamba campaign as well as the viceroyalty in general.

58. The Cañari were traditionally from Ecuador, although the Incas had relocated a large number of them, one or two generations before the arrival of the Spaniards, to the Cuzco region. They played a major role in the Spanish-led conquest of the Vilcabamba region.

59. Alonso de Barzana was a skilled linguist who preached mostly in the area that is now Bolivia, northwest Argentina, and Paraguay.

60. Cristóbal de Molina was an excellent Quechua speaker and wrote two accounts on the Inca. His first, dated around 1572, told of the history of the Incas and is now lost. His second, titled *Account of the Fables and Rites of the Incas*, was written around 1575 and has survived (Molina 2011).

61. Saint Paul was said to have spoken Greek and Aramaic, which helped him to spread Christianity.

62. Agustín de la Coruña entered Mexico in 1533 and was ordained as bishop of Popayán, Colombia, in 1564. He was a longtime supporter of native rights. He is also mentioned in Murúa's description of Tupac Amaru's execution.

63. Gabriel de Oviedo wrote his own eyewitness report on the death of Tupac Amaru (see Markham 1907).

64. This appears to be incorrect since the papacy of Paul III ran between 1534 and 1549. If a papal bull was issued for the brother-sister marriage of Sayri Tupac and Cusi Huarcay, it seems more likely that it was arranged by Paul IV (1555–1559) or perhaps Pius IV (1559–1565).

65. Jerónimo de Loayza was archbishop of Lima from 1546 to 1575.

66. Ocampo is frequently cited as an eyewitness to the execution of Tupac Amaru. However, he may not actually have seen it, but instead relied on the account of Nicolás de los Ríos.

67. Toribio de Bustamante is mentioned by Ocampo further on in this document. He also gave a number of testimonies concerning the actions of others in the Vilcabamba region (Maúrtua 1906: 240–246).

68. As in many regions in the Andes under Spanish control, the exploitation of the Vilcabamba mines was largely dependent on a system of forced labor called the *mita*. The system, misnamed after the rotational labor system of the Incas (*mit'a* = turn), demanded that each community provide a specific number of individuals to work in the mines each year. Later in his document Ocampo returns to the topic of *mita* labor in Vilcabamba.

69. The area of Andahuaylas came under crown control in 1579 after the death of Francisca de Guzman, the widow of Diego Maldonado (Bauer, Kellett, and Aráoz Silva 2010: 36). As noted by Ocampo, the inhabitants of this region were generally assigned to work in the Huancavelica mines.

70. Gaspar de Zúñiga Acevedo y Fonseca, fifth count of Monterrey, was viceroy of Peru from 1604 to 1606.

71. The mines of Vilcabamba proved not to be especially productive, and over the course of twenty years (ca. 1590–1610) the *mita* labor was stopped and started several times.

72. Luis Palomino, the son of Juan Alonso Palomino, held many *repartimentos*, including Pacariqtambo, Puquiura (Cuzco), Cabina, Cuchua, Pitomarca, Chunchos, Pampallacta, Saylla, Pocomarca, and part of Challabamba (Toledo [1573] 1975).

73. An eight-ounce coin.

74. Antón de Álvarez participated in the 1572 Vilcabamba campaign. He was later appointed as the lieutenant governor of Vilcabamba (see Maúrtua 1906).

75. Alonso Juárez and Pedro Gudiño participated in the 1572 Vilcabamba campaign and are mentioned in numerous other documents concerning the Vilcabamba region (see Maúrtua 1906).

76. Much of the information provided below is also offered in Ocampo's 4 December 1590 testimony (Bauer and Halac-Higashimori 2013: 73–78; Bauer et al. 2014).

77. The construction of these churches is mentioned in other documents related to the Vilcabamba region (Maúrtua 1906: 125, 268).

78. Martín Enríquez de Almanza was viceroy of Peru from 1581 until 1583.

79. According to his 20 February 1600 testimony, Ocampo first entered Vilcabamba to participate in this campaign (Bauer and Halac-Higashimori 2013: 67–69; Bauer et al. 2014: 143–144).

80. Hurtado de Arbieto led two major raids into the Pilcosuni region: the first in 1582 and the second in 1583. While Ocampo presents clear descriptions of the two different raids in his testimony of 4 December 1590, in this description of the Vilcabamba region he compresses the two raids into one. The rendering of the two raids as a single campaign is adventitious to Ocampo, since he participated only in the 1582 raid.

81. A fuller account of the disastrous events that took place during the 1582 raid can be extracted from various Vilcabamba-related documents (Maúrtua 1906: 195–290).

82. The names of these fathers are confirmed in a document that is also signed by Ocampo (e.g., Maúrtua 1906: 287–288).

83. The 1582 expedition into the Pilcosuni region ended after the soldiers petitioned Hurtado de Arbieto to end the journey.

84. Here Ocampo jumps from events that occurred in 1582 to those that occurred during 1583.

85. Several other Spaniards also speak of a Pilcosuni named Opa (or Oparo) who visited Cuzco sometime before 1579 (Maúrtua 1906: 269, 273, 278).

86. This fortified community was called Ciudad de Jesús. It is well documented that Hurtado de Arbieto was wounded in 1583 when the town of Jesús came under attack by Pilcosuni (Maúrtua 1906: 195–296). In a testimony dating to 4 December 1590 (Bauer and Halac-Higashimori 2013: 73–78), Ocampo clearly states that he was not a member of the expedition at this time but learned of the events afterwards.

87. A Christian saint martyred with arrows.

88. A legendary hero of early Rome.

89. If this passage is correct, then the slave revolt that is described by Ocampo occurred in 1603.

90. The settlement of Vallano was founded in the region Nombre de Dios (Panama) by escaped African slaves.

91. The Holy Brotherhood represented a self-selecting police force in many medieval towns of Spain. Ocampo also mentions that he was the leader of this group in his 20 February 1600 testimony (Bauer and Halac-Higashimori 2013: 143–144).

92. Toribio de Bustamante was a veteran of the 1572 Vilcabamba campaign as well as the 1582 and 1583 raids into Pilcosuni territory. He testified on behalf of Martín

Hurtado de Arbieto in Lucma in 1590 (Maúrtua 1906: 240–246) and in Cuzco in 1601 (Bauer and Halac-Higashimori 2013: 59–63).

93. A tuber native to the Andes.

94. This is to say, these men were born into slavery as domestic servants. The assumption here is that these kinds of messengers would be loyal to the Spaniards.

95. We are uncertain about how to translate this sentence fragment; it reads: "...y estuvimos cercados treinta días defendiéndonos con escopetería y otras armas que los indios mostraban por encima del fuerte, sin que les fuesen vistas las caras ..."

96. In 1590 Fray Gonzalo de Toro Caballero, then the head of the Mercedarian order in Vilcabamba, petitioned for additional agricultural lands to support their work in the region (Barriga 1942: 278–279).

97. Several royal decrees prohibited priests from having Indians for personal service.

98. Here Ocampo suggests that this large celebration took place on 24 June 1571.

99. Most of the men listed here participated in the 1572 Vilcabamba campaign.

100. Most likely a puma.

Document 3

*Diego Rodríguez de
Figueroa's Journey
into Vilcabamba*

In 1565 Juan de Matienzo, who was then the chief judge
of the Audiencia de Charcas, sent Diego Rodríguez
de Figueroa into Vilcabamba to meet with Titu Cusi
Yupanqui with hopes of starting peace negotiations. The
mission was necessitated by the death of Sayri Tupac
Inca, some five years before, and the ascension of Titu
Cusi Yupanqui to a position of power in Vilcabamba.
Titu Cusi Yupanqui had launched several raids into
Spanish-controlled regions, and the leaders of Cuzco
wanted him to leave Vilcabamba and to settle in the
Yucay *encomienda*, as his brother had done years earlier.

Rodríguez de Figueroa left Cuzco on 8 April and
entered Vilcabamba via the Chuquichaca Bridge. After
making contact with soldiers of the Inca, he traveled
under their protection into the region. Through messengers, it was established that Titu Cusi Yupanqui
would meet Rodríguez de Figueroa at the village of
Pampaconas, about halfway between the towns of
Vitcos and Vilcabamba. Both sides were true to their
agreement, and Rodríguez de Figueroa and the Inca
arrived in Pampaconas a few days later.

While Rodríguez de Figueroa was in Pampaconas
meeting with Titu Cusi Yupanqui, three messengers
arrived from Lope García de Castro, the interim viceroy
of Peru (1564–1569), and García de Melo, the royal treasurer in Cuzco. Melo had made a trip into Vilcabamba a
month or two earlier to also negotiate a possible settlement with Titu Cusi Yupanqui.[1] Although Rodríguez
de Figueroa's mission, which was ordered by Juan de

DOI: 10.5876/9781607324263.c005

Matienzo, and García de Melo's earlier mission, which was ordered by García de Castro, were independent of each other, their goals merged with the fortunate arrival of the viceroy's communiqué while Rodríguez de Figueroa was in Pampaconas. Titu Cusi Yupanqui found the terms, which were not unlike those offered to Sayri Tupac Inca, agreeable.

At the end of their meeting in Pampaconas, which lasted three days, Rodríguez de Figueroa volunteered to remain with Titu Cusi Yupanqui as a hostage if Titu Cusi Yupanqui sent representatives to Cuzco to meet with the Spanish authorities. Titu Cusi Yupanqui's delegation was well received in Cuzco, and the two sides then agreed on a face-to-face meeting at the Chuquichaca Bridge. As a result, Rodríguez de Figueroa left Pampaconas with Titu Cusi Yupanqui in late May, and they traveled to the bridge to meet a delegation from Cuzco led by Juan de Matienzo and García de Melo.

The Chuquichaca meeting proved to be highly successful, and the basic terms of a peace treaty were laid out. The most important points included the following:

1. The Inca would accept the authority of the king and allow a Spanish overseer to be appointed for the province of Vilcabamba.
2. Priests would be allowed to enter into the province.
3. Titu Cusi Yupanqui and his son, Quispe Titu, would be baptized.
4. Quispe Titu would be allowed to marry his cousin, Beatriz Clara Coya, who was the only child of Sayri Tupac.
5. The future of finances of Titu Cusi Yupanqui would be assured through income produced by several *encomiendas*, including that of Yucay, which was held by his niece.

Although these terms were agreed upon at the Chuquichaca Bridge, it took over a year for the final document to be drafted and approved. During this period, Rodríguez de Figueroa returned to Vilcabamba on several occasions. The final signing of the peace treaty took place in the town of Acobamba on the edge of Vilcabamba in late August of 1566. At that time, Rodríguez de Figueroa was named corregidor of Vilcabamba. After the conquest of Vilcabamba in 1572, he was granted an *encomienda* in the region with 100 Indians. However, after just four years, Rodríguez de Figueroa left Vilcabamba for Potosí because of tension with Martín Hurtado de Arbieto (Rodríguez de Figueroa 1965: 68).

The following is an English translation of Diego Rodríguez de Figueroa's report on his 1565 meeting with Titu Cusi Yupanqui. This report is of exceptional importance, as it describes the pomp and circumstance of a royal encounter in the waning days of the Inca Empire. It was written on the eve of Rodríguez de Figueroa's return to Cuzco after having helped arrange the peace negotiations at Chuquichaca. As such, it is a unique and essential document, providing us with a glance into the inner workings of the Inca realm and insights into one of its least-known rulers.[2]

Account of the route and journey made by Diego Rodríguez [de Figueroa] from the city of Cuzco to the land of war of Manco Inca, who is in the Andes rebelling against the service of Your Majesty, and of the things that he discussed with him in a peaceful manner, and also so that he would receive the evangelical doctrine of our lord Jesus Christ, which is the [subject of] the following account

I left the city of Cuzco on the 8th of April [1565] after having received letters from Judge [Juan de] Matienzo for the Inca Titu Cusi Yupanqui and permission to be able to enter, after having volunteered to go by that route. I spent the night at [Ollantay]tambo, where they gave me seven Indian porters so that they could show me the way. Three of them from that town agreed to enter with me, after the *cacique* had told them that if the Inca asked them where they were from, they [should] say they were from somewhere else and not from [Ollantay]tambo. This is because [Ollantytambo] is [along] the frontier with the Inca and a garrison, and he would kill them [if] they said they were from there.

On April 9th, I crossed to the other side of the mountain range, passed [through] the snowy wilderness, and slept in Yanamanchi, which is [a group of] large caves. There I learned how the Inca runners had reached Chuquichaca, which is adjacent to the land of peace, and that they had come to cross over it to attack this side of the river, which belongs to the Spaniards. I encouraged the Indians not to be afraid and [told them] that I would go with them to see what [kind of] people they were and what they wanted, but they would not hear of it. So that night my seven Indian porters who were carrying some presents for the Inca, bought with my own money and at my expense, fled. And, having seen one thing and the other, I would have returned if I had not been concerned about being embarrassed and for other secret reasons.

I hid the loads under some straw and advanced five leagues to a valley of Amaibamba, three leagues from the land of the Inca, where there is much coca and there are always many Indians during the harvest. [However,] it was deserted, because they were all hiding in the mountains. Since there was no one to show me the ford in a river, which is nearby, I crossed there with the horse. Thanks to God, I and the horse beneath me were miraculously protected, as [the river] was more than 300 *estados* wide.

There, on the 10th of April, some of the Indians who had fled from me, as well as the runners, returned. I encouraged them and told them I would go to the bridge to see what there was. I also [told them] that [the Inca's men] were infidels and that they were not Christians and that [just] one [Christian] was enough to fight all of [the Inca's men] because they were infidels and [our men] were Christians. They responded to this [by telling me] that they had been robbed more than 10 or 15 times, and that some of them had their wives and sons and daughters there, and that [the Inca's men] were not men but devils, and that they did not fear God. [They also told me] that after having robbed them of all that they had, [the Inca's men] would burn their houses, and out of contempt for the Christians they burned their churches and they had broken their images. Also that [the Inca's men] had burned and cooked a sheep with the cross that was placed in front of the church. This is true, as I saw the burned church and they showed me burned pieces of wood that surely must have been from [the] cross. I told them, God permitted [these actions] because of our sins, and that God would send great punishment upon [the Inca's men]. [I also told them] that I would go [and] speak with the Inca on behalf of the President of the Cabildo of Cuzco and the Royal Audiencia of the city of La Plata and to tell them to accept our Holy Catholic faith and obedience to His Majesty, and if they did not do so, war would be waged against them. [I instructed them] that while I was there, they were to guard the bridge well, until [we could] see when the runners would arrive so that I could speak with them. They said that they did not dare to do this and they also advised me not to go there, because I would be killed and fed to the Andes Indians.

On seeing the Indians' lack of courage, I sent them to retrieve the cargo where I had hidden it, and as the path is very rough I left the horse there at Amaibamba. In some places one cannot even go on foot but rather crawl. I arrived at the bridge, which is between two high mountain ranges, on April 11th. I made a large fire on the other side of the river to see if any of the Inca's runners would come, and I put a flag [made] of a handkerchief on a tree as a sign of peace and a very large cross at the entrance of the bridge so they would understand that a Spaniard and a Christian was there. Then two runners from Yucay, which is from the land of peace, arrived. They told me that my cargo had already arrived, and that it was in Amaibamba, and that the Indians who had fled to the forest were already [gathered] together in the town, and that they were not afraid because I was at the bridge, and because it seemed to them that if I was there, they would be safe, and that the Inca and his captains had returned [to Vilcabamba].

On the 11th of that month, [the Inca's men] lit large fires and we saw a lot of smoke on the other side of the bridge, about two leagues [away]. That night the two Indian runners who were with me fled to the hills, as they did not dare to sleep where I was sleeping, which was next to the entrance of the bridge. There I suffered more from the many mosquitoes, which were biting me all day and night, than from fear of the Inca's men. Thus, [we,] myself and the two runners, were making smoke on our side of the river and they from the other, without being even able to see a runner or person from the land of the Inca.[3] This being the case, I decided to return to Amaibamba and to leave those runners [at the bridge], which is three leagues from there, so that if they saw anything, they would come tell me, because my feet and hands had swollen from the mosquito bites and I had suddenly come down with a fever.

On the 20th of April, Good Friday, in the small hours of the morning a runner came and told me that six of the Inca's men had arrived at the bridge and that he thought there were more to come. [He said] that he did not know what their intention was, beyond that they had left [in place] the flag and cross that I had left there. All of the Indians armed themselves and some fled to the forest in fear. I then left for the bridge, commending myself to our lord, along a very bad trail and at night, where I fell many times and found myself in great hardship. I took two Indians with me against their will, with some bread, coca, and things to eat. When I arrived at the bridge, which was around three in the morning, I started to shout and lit a fire. The runners then came to the bridge, and by the light of straw torches, we spoke with one another. I told them that I came in peace to speak with the Inca and I had letters for him from the Cabildo [of Cuzco] and Judges of the city of La Plata. [I also asked them] to deliver a letter from me and another I brought from Judge Matienzo [to the Inca] so that he would grant me permission to enter and speak to him. They said they were pleased. So with a sling I threw the letters to them from the other side of the river, and with a rope [we] sent them coca and bread to eat. I requested that they leave one or two Indians until a response arrived from the Inca, and they did so.

On the 28th of April the Inca replied in a very brief letter, telling me that he appreciated the effort I had made, and that, as for the rest, he did not want any Spaniard to enter, neither in peace nor in war, because they were [surely] coming as spies or to deceive him. [He stated that] I should not enter because his captains would kill me. Apart from that, [he stated] that he kissed the hands of Judge Matienzo and of all the others who had written to him, and [that] he did not respond because he was ill. [He said] that I should return with this reply and do him the favor of sending him the letters that I said I was carrying to hand him. Having seen that day the determination of the Inca, and [knowing] that, if I returned, they would say in Cuzco that I was trying to circumvent [my duties] out of fear and looking for an excuse not to enter to

[see] the Inca, I decided to give the letters to the runners and at the same time some items I was taking as gifts, such as raisins, sweets, figs, quince jam, three handkerchiefs, three pairs of scissors, four knives with sheaths, some needles, and other things. I wrote to him to consider me a friend and to understand that I did not come to deceive him, but rather to tell him what would be in his interest, and that if he still wanted to grant me permission, I would enter there to meet him in person and, given the opportunity to serve him, I would do it. So that he would know this to be true, I sent him a decree of the Defender of all the Indians of this kingdom from the Count of Nieva.

On the 6th, I mean, on the 5th of May, 10 captains came to the bridge, wearing feathered armor, diadems of feathers, and masks over their faces; they were also brandishing their spears and sounding a horn. They arrived at the entry of the bridge where I was, asking if I was the man who dared to come and speak to the Inca. I said yes, and to this they replied that it was not possible [to talk to the Inca] if I was fearful and if I was afraid, I should not go because he was a great enemy of cowards. To this I replied that if he were an elephant or a giant, then I would be afraid, but as he was a man like me, I was not afraid, and moreover, I would be very respectful. If he wanted me to enter under his word, I would do so, because I knew that he would honor it. They then took out two letters, one from a mestizo who is there, who is named [Martín] Pando, and the other from the Inca, and they threw them to me from the other bank.[4] At this time, some of the Indians who were with me fled. The letters both said they were very glad to have learned from the writ that [I] was not a spy, nor [did I] come to deceive them, [and] that they were pleased that I should enter, and that I should not stop until [I reached] a town named Arancalla and that [the Inca] would arrive there with his governor and *maese de campo*.

On the 6th of May, I and [the] seven Indians that I was bringing with me crossed to the other side of the river in a hand basket along a rope. The Inca's 10 Indians helped me to cross and accompanied me. That night I slept at the foot of a snowy mountain in a deserted town, called Condormarca, where in ancient times there was a bridge [by which] they crossed the Vitcos River to go to [Ollantay]tambo and Sapamarca and Picho,[5] which is in the land of peace.

On the 7th of May, as many as 100 Indians came to meet with me on the road to Maraniyo, a very rugged land full of forested mountains and marshes. They asked me if I was the one who had put up the handkerchief as a flag, which I have previously mentioned. I said yes and that I had done it as a sign that I came in peace. They replied to this that it was very bold to plant a flag next to the land of the Inca, and that if it were not that the Inca had ordered that I enter, they would have killed me there and then. And thus each one began to vaunt his strength, calling us bearded men, cowards, thieves. Others asked, "Do we not have permission to kill this bearded man in revenge for what his brothers have done to us?" I placated them, saying that it was true that at that time when the Spaniards entered this kingdom, they had done much ill but that now there was much justice and that the Indians were very much protected and had great liberty. To this they asked if I was from that time, or had I come recently from Spain? I replied to them that I had come from Spain 17 years ago,[6] and that in all times there were good and bad [people], and that if it were now [that the Spaniards first arrived], they would do them great honor, because they seemed to me to be good men. As for what the others had done, that was not my fault. And thus I gave them drink and I gave them some needles, beads and knives, and we became friends. And then I wrote to the Inca that I had entered his land, and that I would not stop until [I reached] where he was, and that as a sign of friendship I was sending him two glass pitchers and two dozen green glass buttons that looked like emeralds.

On the 8th of May we left a storage house of the Inca's called Maraniyo, and I traveled until I arrived at a town of Indians called Lucma, where four Indians came to see me on behalf of a captain, named Cayanbi, who is at that frontier. I sent him salt and knives and in return he sent me maize and *chicha*, beseeching me not to go on from there, because the Inca had not sent him any word about my arrival, and that he would come to sleep there that night and accompany me. And out of indignation at the miserable road and the effort of having come on foot and at finding that [I was] next to the town, [yet] they would not allow me to enter, I sent [the captain] word that they not come, that I wanted to return to Cuzco. I also sent the Indians marching in the direction from which we had come, and then I wrote to the Inca with much anger, saying that I had arrived at Lucma under his authority, and that one of his captains who was at the frontier had not wanted to receive me in his land. And with this [message] I sent him a hat with two feathers. When the captain saw my determination to return to Cuzco, he came to the road to implore me not to leave until a reply arrived from the Inca, and he brought me a lot of food from his land.

And I stayed there with the captain until the next day, when the reply came from the Inca, covering 40 leagues in two days. He said in his letter that he was very angry at his captain and that he would be severely punished. And thus he sent another [captain] in his place, who was named Vilcapari Guaman, with 100 Indians so that they [could] take account of what I needed [on my journey], and they lodged me in Arancalla, a town with as many as 100 Indians, two leagues from Lucma, in a rough land near snowy [mountains] and a very large fort.[7]

I arrived there on the 9th of May, where they built two houses for me on the outskirts of the town on a hill two long harquebus shots away. And then everyone from the town came and brought many things to eat, and they shared them with my Indians. Before anything else, he [i.e., the captain] begged me to show him what I was bringing in my loads, because he wanted very much to know. I [first] refused, [but] as it seemed to me that even if I did not want to, they were bound to find out, I thought it would be all right that they saw and I sent for [my loads]. So they looked at each thing individually. They saw that I brought a sword and dagger, and they said that, as they seemed to them to be good items, I should show them to the Inca, because he would be happy to see them. And later that day a servant of the Inca's came to visit me on his behalf with two baskets of peanuts. I received him well and gave him a headcloth and a small quantity of beads, and I gave him to give to the Inca two decks of cards and two pairs of scissors. It seemed to me that he came to see what kind of man he had [in his land] and to get information from those who had come with me about what they had seen me ask, say, and do. They left very content.

On another day, which was the 11th of May, I received another letter from the Inca in which he made grand offers to me because he had heard of my good repute in a report from Cuzco. [He said] that I was to go to another town further on that was called Pampaconas so that we could see each other sooner and that he would be there in two days.

Therefore, I left on the 12th of May and passed Vitcos, where the seven Spaniards [had] killed the Inca, [where] to this day their heads are still hanging. The Indians told me that those Spaniards had killed [Manco Inca] to take over the land and that while playing horseshoes, they decided to kill him. What's-his-name Méndez grabbed and hit [the Inca]; stabbing him four or five times in the back of his head with some scissors, until he killed him. [They told me] that [the Spaniards would have killed] Titu Cusi [Yupanqui] Inca, who is now [Inca], but he escaped into some cliffs that they showed me. Despite all this, they were able to stab him in the leg, of which he later showed me the scar. If they had wanted to kill some Indians, they could have done that, but their intent was to rebel and kill the Inca. There were many Indians and captains of the Inca in attendance, who grabbed and killed [the Spaniards].

On the 13th of May I sent two of my Indians on the road to the Inca with some refreshments, including raisins, figs, and other things for the journey, and the Inca received them well. He gave them two baskets of peanuts to bring to me and [sent word] that he would be there the next day so we would see each other soon [and our meeting] would not be further delayed.

On the 14th of May [I arrived in Pampaconas]. The Indians of Pampaconas had made a large house in a high fort surrounded by a wall, and below were the houses of the town, which contained about 200 citizens. The road leading there was very clean and [crossed] an expansive plain. Thus, with up to 300 Indians from the town with their spears, and [with the help] of others from the area, they had made, out of red clay, a large open platform for the Inca. They were awaiting his arrival there, and wanting to go out to receive him, I told them that I wanted to go out to the road. In response, they told me that those who were in the town had to wait on the plain, and that I should not move from the seat they showed me. Then they had two loads of straw brought and set them aside to their right, about half a stone's throw away, on a hill beyond where the other Indians were congregating. They told me to wait there, and that from there I would see the Inca's arrival but not to move until the Inca had me summoned.

During this time many spearmen emerged from behind a small hill, and messengers came saying that the Inca was arriving. Then the people with the Inca started to enter the plaza. The Inca came in front of everyone with a multicolored backplate of feathers and a silver breastplate. In his hands he carried a gold shield and a half spear [with an] iron [point] and gold ribbons and hooks wrapped around it. He wore feathered straps on his calves and wooden bells hanging on his ankles. On his head he wore a crown of many feathers, and, similarly, he wore another one around his neck. He had a golden dagger in the hand [with which he carried] the shield of Castille, and he was wearing a red mask that they [customarily] wear, sometimes green and sometimes various shades of purple, leading the march. On arrival at the plain where his seat had been placed, and where the townspeople and I [were], he looked toward the sun and made a [gesture] of reverence with his hand, which they call *mocha*, and then he took his seat. Accompanying him was a mestizo with a shield and sword, in Spanish dress, with cotton breeches, a tunic, and a very old brownish-gray cloak.[8] When the Indians were not watching, [the mestizo] looked toward me and lifted his hat. I then showed him an image of Our Lady that I wore upon my chest, and from there he knelt, and although some Indians saw him, they paid no heed. Two *orejones* came with the Inca with two halberds. They were also wearing feathers, crowns, and a lot of silver and gold ornaments. Both of these, who represented one faction, performed a *mocha* and bowed to the sun and then to the Inca. During all this, [the Inca] was standing up next to his seat; and thus they formed a circle around him in good order. Then his governor, named Yamqui Mayta, entered with his people, which must have been up to 50 or 60

Indians, with their silver breastplates and shields and all of them with their leather armor [adorned] with feathers and the spears wrapped in ribbons of silver and gold thread with iron from Spain and copper points, and the same [was true of] all those who had entered with the Inca. Then his *maese de campo* entered with the same number of Indians, like the rest, very gallantly dressed. And, as I say, they all made a [gesture of] reverence to the sun and then to the Inca, crying out to him, "Child of the sun, only you are the son of the day!" They arranged themselves along the [perimeter of] the entire plain, around the Inca. And then another captain named Vilcapari Guaman[9] entered with up to 30 Indians with spears adorned in very splendid multi-colored feathers, and likewise another 20 Indians with clubs and axes of iron [arrived]. When alongside the others they made a [gesture of] reverence to the sun like the rest, and they were similarly wearing feathers.

Everyone whom I have mentioned came wearing masks of different colors on their face. Next another Indian, a small man not worth half a cent, also entered, and after having made a [gesture of] reverence to the sun and to the Inca, he came toward me, brandishing his spear and leaping very bravely. I laughed upon seeing this performance. And he started to say in our Spanish language, "Get out! Get out!" and to thrust the spear at me. And [then] his captain called him. Then another captain named Cusi Poma[10] entered, with as many as 50 Indian archers who are A[n]des [Indians], who eat human flesh. Like the rest, they all had plumed armor, as I have described, and their spears had long and elegant feathers at the end. And during all this, the Inca had not sat down. And then all of them took off all of those feather harnesses, and each of them drove their spear in[to the ground at] their post. They all carried daggers made of iron or copper, as well as shields made of silver or leather or with feather[s]. Fully armed, each one went to bow to the Inca, who was seated, and they then returned to their places.

Later [the Inca] sent for me, and passing though that multitude of Indians, I took off my hat to him and I offered many greetings and I [told him] how I had come from Cuzco just to see, know, and serve him, and I made known that I brought a sword and a dagger to give to him and not to offend him. To this he replied that it was a man's right to carry arms, and not that of women or of cowards, and that is why he held me in high [esteem], and that he was grateful to me for the effort I had made in coming to see him from so far away; however, he also had come more than 40 leagues just to see me and talk to me.

Then he gave me a cup of *chicha*, begging me to drink it as a favor to him. I drank about a quarter of it, and because I did not know how to drink it, I began to make faces and clean myself with a handkerchief. He covered his mouth and started to laugh, realizing that I did not know how to drink this wine. Then I spoke with the mestizo, asking him how he was and [telling him] to remember our Lord Jesus Christ, that he would help him out of those difficulties, and [I asked] that he point out to me the governor Yamqui Mayta, [because I needed] to talk to him. And therefore he introduced me to him, and he embraced me, as the Inca had done, who was seated to his right.

With the Inca's permission I then returned to my seat, and he later sent me, through his governor, a macaw and two baskets of peanuts. Then the mestizo came with a small cup, about a fourth of a half of a *quartillo* of wine, and [said] that the Inca entreated me to drink, and that in all else, he considered me a friend and that when[ever] I wanted to we could discuss what I had come for. I took a sip and gave the rest to one of the Indians who had come with me; and I sent word to [the Inca] through the mestizo to rest, since he was tired and that it was late, and that the next day all that his grace commanded would be done. And then I sent him four pieces of glass and a basket of sweets, which was what the Judge Matienzo sent him, as mentioned in his letter to him. I also sent half an *arroba* of glass beads, pearls, seven silver bracelets, and a small [number] of earth-colored beads. I gave them to him, telling [him] that Judge Matienzo sent him the glasswork because it was highly valued among lords, and that just as the sweets gave pleasure upon touching the tongue, I hoped that my words would give him joy, and that [as for] the rest, I was coming to serve him as a messenger and ambassador. He received everything and was very pleased; and so that he would not hesitate to eat the sweets, I told him that they were very good, and so that he would know that they would not harm him, I wanted to eat some of them in front of him. Afterwards I gave his governor, Yamqui Mayta, two knives with sheaths, a headscarf, and other things. I also distributed [other gifts] among all the other captains whom the mestizo introduced to me, embraced them all, and returned to my seat.

The [residents] of the town then brought much food and presented it to the Inca and to everyone else who had come with him. The Inca does not eat on cloths, but rather on many green reeds, while the others [eat] on the ground. He is a man around 40 years [old], of medium height, dark-skinned with smallpox scars on his face. He had a rather serious and firm expression.[11] [He] was wearing a shirt of blue damask and a cloak of very fine cloth. [He] eats his food with silver and always has about 20 to 30 rather decent-looking women close behind him. He sent me [some] of what he, with his wives and his governor, were eating. The foods that they have there include maize, potatoes, beans, and the other foods that we have here, except that there is very little meat, and what there is includes deer, chickens, partridges, monkeys, which they eat baked or roasted, and parrots.

When night fell he sent for me and asked me if they had treated me [as they had] their captains. And I said yes. I said goodbye, and he went to the house that I have mentioned they had prepared for him, more or less in the same order in which they had arrived, with their silver flute music and trumpets as [they] had when they entered. That night they set up a watch of more than 100 Indians and they distributed candles to three quarters, and at the turn of each watch, every quarter played the flutes and drums in the best manner that they knew. That night they assigned to me a guard of 15 men, with their spears, at a house I have mentioned that was outside the encampment. It seemed to me that the total [number] of Indians who came with the Inca and those who were in the town was about 450.

Then on the morning of the 14th of May, the Inca summoned me to his house because it was raining that day, and he could not go out to the plaza. He was staying in a large thatched building, as I have said. Most of his people, all of those who could fit into the building, were seated around a large fire. [The Inca] was seated, dressed in clothes of crimson velvet and a cloak of the same [material]. They had all removed the masks that they were wearing on their faces the day before. As I entered, I greeted him, offering reverence, taking my hat off to him, and in his own language he too greeted me. The mestizo was seated on a bench in front of him. Then I gave him a very good crystal mirror, two coral necklaces from Castille, and two bundles of paper as gifts. He was very pleased with everything and he ordered me to move [my] seat slightly away from him, [such] that his governor and two other captains could fit in the middle. According to what I understood, [the Inca] had received information from one of his captains, who had come with me, of what I had spoken of and asked about. I also understood that he had come to know that I was unhappy with his Indians because of the little respect and the lack of shame that his Indians had [shown me].

Then he asked me about the letters that I was bringing, and what I had come for. I replied that he had already seen the letters, before I arrived, and that they referred to what I would now tell him. [He] said this was true. Then I said that I had to discuss with him matters of great importance for salvation of the body as well as for the soul; and so that he would see that I did not want to deceive him in any way with what I had to say, [I suggested he] send for the wisest men there, so that he would better understand what needed to be addressed. Although, since he was a man of such sound judgment, his understanding was enough to attain all that he could want. He replied that everyone was there and that I [should] tell him what I wanted so that [the] next day I could return to Cuzco with his reply. [He noted] that he had never given the Christians who had entered to see and speak with them more than a day's audience, and the next he turned them away because it was his belief that if they remained there longer, they would be killed due to his people's fear and terror; as some of [them] would disrespect [him and], without his permission, kill them. To this I replied that more than two days were needed to discuss and to reach a good decision on the points that I had come to negotiate, especially since I did not want to overwhelm him in telling him [so much] in such a brief time; instead my intention was to bring him happiness, not acrimony. [The Inca] was pleased and thanked me, and then he told me that he and his captains would not reply to anything that I told to him until everything that I had come for was explained, and in the end, they would reply with what was in their best interest.

Then I told the mestizo, who was the interpreter, to ask permission for me to say something in praise of God and our holy Christian religion. [The Inca] gave permission. I said many things that I had prepared for more than eight days, in some books that I was carrying [with me], but to avoid being excessively wordy, I am not writing them here. I have these written in another little book, [along] with other things.[12] The Inca and all his captains were glad to have heard it, and then I asked if there were any Christian Indians within the group of captives who were there. So [the Inca] ordered them to stand up; there must have been 20 to 25 *caciques*. I asked each one what his name was, and they all told me their Christian names. Then I asked the Inca permission to comfort them and console them, which he gladly gave. I told them that I had come for nothing more than to see them, to console them on behalf of our lord Jesus Christ, and that they should hold firm [to] what they had professed when they were baptized. [I also told them] to serve the Inca, as he was their lord, and that they remember God, creator of all things. I said many other things to them, with which I brought them all to tears, in the presence of all those captains of the Inca, [such] that even the Inca became misty-eyed upon seeing them. He [then] spoke to me very gruffly, [saying] that no Spaniard had dared to enter his land to discuss such matters or say praise to our lord Jesus Christ, not even in the time of his father. And that it was very impudent of me and that he was about to have me killed. To this I replied that I came as a man who must do such things [and having] confessed and received communion, and having done what a Christian should, death could not take me at a better time. Furthermore, [I reminded the Inca that] what I had said, I had said with his permission, and thus he calmed a little. Then I made a speech in praise of the truth and against lies and [stressing] that with what I needed to discuss with him, it was necessary to be very honest, as though it were said under oath. I then praised the Judge Matienzo, who was the one who had given me permission to enter and [had written] the letter for the Inca, as much as I could. I then told [the Inca] how fond I was of the Indians, and to support this I showed him some papers I was carrying,[13] so that it would be clear to him and so that he would not think that I had come as a spy, nor with any bad intentions, [and] so that he could understand what I had done for him here in [Matienzo's] absence. Since they thought that all the incursions into their land, by foot and by horseback, were in secret, [I told him] that they were in fact public knowledge and therefore spies were not necessary, and that I would later relate all of them to him, [but] that I first wanted to take up the earlier business.

In the middle of all this, three of his Indians arrived whom he had sent as messengers to the President [i.e., Lope García de Castro].[14] They brought him eight varas of yellow damask and half a dozen masks and a letter from the President, in which he said that if [the Inca] would come out peacefully to Cuzco, he would bestow upon him the *encomienda* of certain towns of Indians, which amounted to more than 15,000 pesos, which Treasurer [García de] Melo would show him, and he would send [the accounts] with the treasurer Melo in three or four days, so that he could show and explain what the Indians that we were giving to him, in name of Your Majesty, [paid in] tribute. Melo also wrote a copy [for the three Indians] of what was contained in the deeds of the Indians. He also sent [the Inca] another letter signed by the President, which was from the selfsame Melo, telling [the Inca] in his own [words] that that [second] letter had been written by the President, and stating that if the Inca did not want to accept the *repartimiento*, which he was giving him as a gift, he [needed] to reply promptly because there was a nobleman who intended [to make] a raid on behalf of the city of Cuzco [into Vilcabamba], to wage war on him; and [this matter] must be concluded immediately because he had given his word [to act].[15]

[Because] of these letters and because [the Inca] was told that the *caciques* of Jauja[16] and of the entire kingdom were imprisoned, and because the *cabildos* [municipalities]of Huamanga and of Cuzco wanted to wage war on him, [the Inca] and his captains were greatly disturbed. Right there in front of me the Inca fiercely stood up and said that they should not be afraid of us, that we were a bunch of cowards. He then made a speech, above all insulting the Spaniards and praising his Indians. All the Indians then got up and began to perform *mochas*. The Indian captains began volunteering themselves [to fight].

Waving iron and copper daggers, some said they would kill four Spaniards, others five, six, and ten. One of them, named Chinchero, asked [the Inca] what was he going to do with me and why did he not have me killed. He [said] that he wanted to stab me with the dagger he was holding. But the Inca fell silent and said nothing, so the Indian returned to his seat.

When it seemed to me to be dawn and they had drunk plenty, I asked the Inca permission to go to my house and eat, and [said] that the next day I would tell him everything that I had come for. So I left, leaving them angrily boasting, everyone very unsettled. They sent me at my lodging a sheep from Castille, many partridges, chickens, and food that they have in their land. I gave those who brought these things beads, needles, and things like that from Castille. Later the Inca had me summoned again. I went there, and I was there until nighttime without saying a word, whereupon I returned to my house. It seemed that they were [still] somewhat drunk from the *chicha*.

The next day, which was the 15th of May, during the morning, the Inca and all his men from the day before came out to the plain in the same order as before. He summoned me to the plaza. When I went, I found them having lunch and they gave me and the Indians who came [with me] a lot of food that they were eating. Then I asked [the Inca] permission to tell him what I had come for. I told [the Inca] through the mestizo, [who was] interpreting, how the President and Judges of the Royal Audiencia had been entrusted [by His Majesty] to make it a high priority to help [the Inca of Vilcabamba], wanting [them] to come out in peace, not by waging war or attacking the Indians in the land of peace. The President had been wholeheartedly entrusted by Your Majesty to grant [the Inca] and his captains many favors, and that was what Judge Matienzo had sent me to do; to find out [the Inca's] intentions and what he wanted. To this they [i.e., the Inca and his men] replied that they had been warned that [the Spaniards] wanted to wage war on [the Inca] from Cuzco and Huamanga,[17] and because they had previously attempted to, they had disturbed him; that was why he had entered the land of peace to rob and attack. Furthermore, [he knew] that Hurtado [de Arbieto][18] had also already asked for [permission to lead] incursion[s] against them during the time of the count.[19] It was because of this that [the Inca] had attacked Huamanga and Amaibamba. I replied that after that [incursion], in order to do him no ill or harm, [the Spaniards] put a stop to [waging war], not out of fear of his people but because the friars and clerics and the Lord Archbishop had interceded to help him. So they [would] not wage war.

The Inca replied that it was true and that he had heard as much, and [he wanted to know] if [the clergy] would now oppose war, as [they had] then.

I told him not [any longer] since [the Inca] had entered the land of peace and had burned churches, broken images, and burned crosses; furthermore, [despite] being a Christian, he made the Indians who were here with him worship the sun. Because of this, [neither] the clerics nor friars nor the archbishop supported him any longer.

[In response] to this, [the Inca] exonerated himself, saying that he had not ordered such [actions], because the first order that he gave his people every time he sent them to attack was that they were not to touch the churches or the crosses. Hearing this, I told him that there were many witnesses who had seen the mestizo and him [i.e., the Inca] take the images and that they had burned the church. [He replied] to this that it was true that he had taken the images, and that he had them there very well protected with the frontals,[20] and that he could have them brought out, but that they had never burned a church. I told him that I had seen a burned cross with which sheep had been cooked at Amaibamba. He replied that he had not personally gone on that raid, that his people had done it, and that [the news] greatly grieved him. He said that none of the friars, clerics, soldiers, or people of Peru could complain that he had killed anyone, although he could have done so many times. He could have easily killed the two Augustinian friars and two Spaniards, who were in a house in Curahuasi, and many others in many places, but he did not want to, and so he ordered his people not to kill them. Nor did he kill [any of] the Indians he brought [with him] and what's more, they had more freedom in his land than in the land of the Spaniards, and that he only took [back the] Indians who were his by ancestry.[21]

So I replied that here in Peru it was said that he was not the lord heir of the Incas in this kingdom, but rather the children and grandchildren of Atahualpa were, since at the time that the Spaniards entered this land, [Atahualpa] was in possession of the kingdom.[22] He responded to this saying that [Atahualpa] had been a tyrant and that he was a bastard and that he had killed Huascar Inca, who was the legitimate heir, and that after him [the legitimate heir] was his father, Manco Inca. To this I replied that it was also said that [Titu Cusi Yupanqui] was the bastard son of Manco Inca. He countered that among them, when there were no legitimate sons, customarily bastards inherited [the rule]. [Furthermore,] that he had been the high priest of their religion. This was because there was no other brother who was older than him. In this same way, he inherited the earthly domain, and now that he possessed it, the Incas who were with him obeyed him. If this were not [so], they would not obey him as they did, and that [as for the rest] he wanted to find out through [force of] arms and not through debate.

[The Inca said] that everyone who entered [Vilcabamba] tried to deceive him and that I should go back the following day, and that he would write to Judge Matienzo, [with his decision] that if he was given a good *encomienda* that he would come out in peace.[23] [He added] that he was shocked at my having had such audacity when speaking to him. With this I bade him goodbye and went to my house, where I spent the rest of the day. From the top of a small hill, I watched the festivities that they held for the Inca and [heard the] songs. The dances were [performed] with spears in hand, as in war, making thrusts at one another, from which one or two were wounded. I think that they did such things, and that they were acting foolishly, because of all the *chicha* they had drunk.

The Inca had me summoned in the afternoon, and I went against my will. He then ordered me to sit, and angrily started to tell me things; saying that he alone could kill 50 Spaniards and that they must kill all of the Spaniards who were in this kingdom. He grabbed a short spear, which he held in his hands, and a shield and started put on a show of bravado and then said in a loud voice, "Go now and bring me all the people who live behind those mountains of the Anti. I want to move against the Spaniards and I will kill them all [and] I want those [people] to eat them! Later a small number, around 600 or 700 Anti Indians, who are from there, came forward; all with their bows and arrows, clubs, and axes. They entered in order and made a [gesture of] reverence to the Sun and to the Inca and assumed their places. [The Inca] brandished his spear again, and said that the uprising of all the Indians in Peru was in his hands and it was in his power to order it [and] that they would do it [if so ordered]. Then all those Anti came to offer themselves to the Inca, and [he said that] if he wanted to, they would later eat me raw; they asked [the Inca]: "What are you doing with this bearded man who wants to deceive you? It would be better if we eat him right away." Then two renegade Inca *orejones* rushed toward me with spears in their right hands, thrusting at me and pushing the iron [points] against my ribs, saying: bearded men, our enemies! While I was laughing at all this, I also commended myself to God. I asked the Inca to grant me a favor: I wanted to go and equip myself and so I slipped away from these men and I hid until morning.

On the morning of the 16th of May he ordered me to come to the plaza, [where he had already] entered in his accustomed manner. When I arrived, I greeted the Inca and sat down. He and all the captains had a good laugh over what had happened the day before, and asked me what I thought of the party of the day before. I told them I thought it was good, except that I felt very badly about the Indians' having been injured, and they had treated me badly since I had come with words of peace, not of war. He replied that his father had taught them so, [and] that he could not change that bad habit of theirs. I then told him that since I had to leave, not having reached any agreement with him, we [needed to] agree upon some order or manner of peace that pleased them and would be for a fixed term because they would receive great benefits from this, since they had in their land many things from which they could earn a lot of money and be[come] very rich. They said that they wanted do so; however, they did not trust us. The Inca asked me what would be good peace terms. I told him that the king would give him food [i.e., an estate] and more than 15,000 pesos in [annual] income if he were to remain in Cuzco, or there in the Andes, provided that he agree to establish a town of Indians there in Vilcabamba. They replied that they thought this was good, because I told them that they could sell the herb [i.e., coca] or firewood to the Spaniards, [and] that they [should] settle there and they would be[come] very rich.

They [discussed] this matter for two days. Then the Inca told me that if Spaniards lived among them, they might, perchance, harm him, killing him, or he [might kill] the Spaniards [and war would ensure]. It was for this reason that he did not want there to be a town [in Vilcabamba] or for Spaniards to enter where he was. I told him that I [also] did not want that, [and] it would be for the best if he or his son came out to take possession of the Indians that the President had, in Your Majesty's name, given him. It would also be advisable for a corregidor to be [in Vilcabamba] to hold and maintain justice in that land, in Your Majesty's name. Furthermore, [it would be best] if they received the evangelical law and Holy Baptism, and that they would derive much good from this, and [in this way] they would own their houses and estates and would be very wealthy.

They agreed with this, on the condition, above everything else, that Your Majesty pardon them for all that they had done until now, and that [Your Majesty] would give those who [the Inca] had with him and who served him a new *encomienda* of the Indians, and likewise that [Your Majesty] grant [the Inca] the towns and lands that he and his father had depopulated next to the land of peace, as well as Amaibamba Valley; also that the Indians whom he had taken from there, and from the land of peace, be his and that he be given them in a new *encomienda*. Furthermore, [the Inca requested] that Your Majesty reward the people whom he has brought [with him] by giving them high status, like those of [noble] birth, so that they can enjoy their liberties and freedoms. [The Inca also agreed] that from then on, friars and clerics [could] enter to preach the Holy Gospel and that he would give obedience to Your Majesty. Also, because he is poor and could not come out in accordance with the status of his person, that his son [Quispe] Titu would come out and marry Doña Beatriz [Clara Coya], his niece. In the meantime, two friars or clerics were to remain as hostages until [the Spaniards] placed Doña Beatriz in his custody, because he is afraid they will marry her to someone else and that he and his son will be left without the *repartimiento* of the Indians who were given in *encomienda* to his brother Sayri Tupac. [Furthermore,] after one or two years, he would come out in peace, after having collected one or two [years' worth of] tribute. In this way he could buy the necessary things, so he could live in the Huamanga area or in Cuzco or where he most desired to, and that in the meantime his son [Quispe] Titu be in the custody of his governor, Yamqui Mayta. [All this] seemed proper to him, and, if necessary, he and his captains would swear to do this according to their law, and that I should leave [Vilcabamba] through Huamanga and that I [could] negotiate this with the President.

At this same time, a letter arrived from Judge Matienzo, in which he said that he would leave Cuzco in 10 days and, given that, I should leave and take the reply [detailing] what the Inca wanted. I told the Inca, for clarity and so that the Christians would understand that what he had agreed upon was true, to give me permission to gather together the Christian Indians, raise a cross, and preach to them the law of our lord Jesus Christ and the Holy Gospel. He replied [that] this was good, and he then ordered poles be brought to build a very tall cross. So that negotiations could proceed better, I pleaded and beseeched him to confirm one truth, and it was that I had seen in a baptism book in the main church [in Cuzco] that he had been baptized and that he was named Don Diego.[24] He said that this was true, that he was a Christian, that he confessed it [to be] thus in front of his Indians, and that they had poured water over his head, and that he did not remember his [baptismal] name. Then as many as 120 Christian Indians gathered together. And [when they were] all together at the foot of the cross, [including] the Inca himself with the Christian Indian captives, I told them to kneel and take their *llautos* off their head and to kneel, and that all who were Christian should be together, and those who were not should move away and watch what we were doing. [Then] I and four Indians who were helping me took the cross and placed it in the plaza. There I spoke a great deal about our holy Christian religion and the salvation of their souls. Then I told them to kneel and ask God for mercy, and to deliver them from their current hardships. So they kneeled three times, crying out in a loud voice, mercy, mercy, mercy! [and] clasping their hands and looking toward the sky. Afterward I asked the Inca to grant me the favor [of allowing me] to preach to those who were not Christian like himself. He approved and ordered them to step forward. I preached to them and said that the things God had created were for the service of man, and that the sun and moon were his creations, and that God had created them to give light and to serve man. Then after they had crossed themselves and worshiped the cross, they went to the plaza. I told [the Inca] that it would be good for me to write to Judge Matienzo telling him how they wanted to receive the Holy Gospel, to have peace, and to send me to Lima by way of Huamanga to finalize [the agreement]. They sent two Indians, and I [sent for] two others of those who had come with me, and we wrote down the above.

Then on the 17th of May, [the Inca] sent some parrots and baskets of peanuts to Treasurer Melo and Judge Matienzo. So I told him that it would be very prudent and [best] for his security to send 30 captains to the city of Cuzco so that they could see how well [the Indians] were treated and that they were free to travel throughout the land. [I agreed that] I would stay in custody [in Vilcabamba] until they returned, and that [in this way] he could reply to the letters from Judge Matienzo and from Melo, so that they would clearly understand his intention. He told me that, if I wanted them to go, to look at him closely, for if [the Spaniards] caused even the smallest harm to any of his Indians, he would strangle me. I told him that I was content with that risk and to send them. So he sent the 30 captains, who were to arrive within six days, and [they] were to send news of how they were treated [in Cuzco] within five days [of their arrival]. He ordered them to go straight to the main church and worship the most holy sacrament and from there to the house of Judge Matienzo. [The Inca] wrote to the friars of Our Lady of Mercy and to the Franciscan friars [requesting] that they preach to them and that two of them come to their land and that they would give them things they had in their land in payment for [preaching] the doctrine. He also wrote to Judge Matienzo, thanking him for having sent me there, and [saying] that I had conveyed the law of our lord Jesus Christ to them very well. [The Inca also requested] that he then send two friars, [saying]that they wanted to be Christian and that they understood well that what they had worshipped until then was a mockery. Also, since His Grace had written him [indicating] that he wanted to first see him in the land of peace, he was pleased to do so, because of what I had asked him, as long as no more than three Spaniards came with him, and that they would see each other at the bridge of Chuquichaca on the day that His Grace advised him to be there.

During this interim, I preached to them and told them of the Christian doctrine every morning, and they came to hear it. Since the Indian messengers who went to Cuzco did not return at the appointed time, [the Inca] believed that they had been hanged in Cuzco. One morning I found them very sad, and the first words that his governor, Yamqui Mayta, said to me were [to ask] if I had committed some sin in Peru, because of which they sent me [into Vilcabamba] for them to kill me. [He said] that before I arrived, they had decided to descend on all the towns that were on their frontier with 700 Anti [Indians] who were there and another 2,000 [who would later join them] and take as many Indians as they could and kill all the clerics, friars, and Spaniards that they could. But they had abandoned [this plan] out of respect for me, and [said] that although they had received the evangelical law, I had deceived them. And if the reply [explaining] what had happened to the captains did not arrive within two days, they would lead a raid into the land of peace, as they had planned.

On the 20th of May, the reply came [recounting] how his captains had been received and treated very well. Out of happiness, they played many drums and trumpets and held a great party, and they called for me and told me that I had brought them much truth. Then the letters from Judge Matienzo were read, and in them he said that he wanted to come see the Inca, and that he would leave Cuzco on the last day of Easter, and that he would make haste to be at the bridge by Friday or Saturday, and that he would bring 14 or 15 men with him, which were the guard that Your Majesty granted to accompany him.

The Inca was undecided about this [news], not wanting to make a decision, saying that he wondered if [Matienzo] was coming with his guard to kill him and his Indians, but that I should tell him the truth, as he trusted me. I told him not only to trust the word of the judge in going to Chuquichaca but, moreover, he could go to Cuzco, and that even if [Matienzo] brought one hundred men with him, it was not to offend him but rather to serve him, and that all who would come with [Matienzo] would come on terms of friendship and to serve him. Furthermore, if the king of Spain wanted to conquer him, the strength of all the Indians of this land, or of 10,000 more, would not be enough against the power of the king. But he [had] decided against it, thinking that [the Inca] would come out in peace and would accept God, and in this way the Spaniards would have no pretext to enter their land and seize their children, wives, and property. [The Inca] replied that even if the power of the king was great and he held as many nations subject as I claimed, including black or Moorish, in those mountains he would be able to defend himself, just as Manco Inca, his father, had done, with only a few [Indians]; however, since I told him to go, he had decided to do so. He then sent to Vilcabamba for more men.

On the 25th of May, a general of his arrived [from Vilcabamba] with as many as 300 Indians, with spears and wearing feathers, as I have described.

They entered the plaza, where the Inca was with all his people, and they offered reverence to the sun and then to the Inca. Then 100 of the captains who came from Vilcabamba got up and went to where the governor Yamqui Mayta was, and asked him how he could consent to placing a cross in that land. If during the time of Manco Inca no [cross] had been placed, why did they put one now? Was it true that the Inca had ordered it, and if not, they wanted to kill me. To this the Inca replied that he had ordered it, and that it was good that they receive the cross of the creator of all things. So they settled down and went to their seats, and a very solemn festivity was held, like the others.

On the 28th of May, we left for the bridge of Chuquichaca to meet the judge, who had already told us he was coming. [The Inca] left 200 Indians at the garrison of Arancalla but took the rest. We arrived for our meeting on Saturday, the night before the Trinity, at the bridge of Chuquichaca. There we received news that the Judge Matienzo had arrived at the bridge of Amaibamba with 30 Spaniards, 10 black men, 20 harquebuses, and 150 spear-carrying Cañari Indians. We then received a letter from Judge Matienzo himself, in which he said that this group was coming and that the Inca should cross to the other side [of the Urubamba] to see him. Also for [the Inca's] security he would give [as hostages] the treasurer [García de] Melo, a cleric, another Spaniard, and myself. The Inca wanted to do it, but his captains did not agree.

[The Inca] then wrote to Judge Matienzo that he should come with all his men to the bridge site.[25] In the meantime, the bridge would be [re]built so that His Grace could cross to the other side, and that [the Inca] would send his governor and *maese de campo*, to be held in custody as hostages, and [Matienzo could] then cross to this side. Then [the Inca] had 300 Indian warriors spread out across the area to observe what was happening, to make sure. I told him that Judge Matienzo would not do this, because he did not have a mandate from the king, but that he should first write to him [anyway, requesting] that he cross to the other side with all the men he was bringing as a guard, as well as the Indians, black men, and Spaniards, and that they could see one another and discuss whatever they wanted in a large open area. [The Inca agreed with this] and he wrote him. Then [the Inca] had some litters covered with silver and gold ornaments prepared. He also had 25 harquebuses brought out and had them distributed among those who knew [how to use them]. He told me that, since I was his friend, he wanted to show me a secret. He then brought out more than 300 old tunics and trousers of the men who had died. [The Inca] then made a speech, saying that they had killed all those who once wore those clothes, and that if the Spaniards attempted to harm them, each should do as any good soldier [should do] in defense of his lord.

At that moment Judge Matienzo arrived at the bridge, which had already been [re]built as noted above. Then García de Melo, the cleric, and another Spaniard crossed, and they explained the writ of the President to the Inca. He said that he understood it, but that he would give the reply to Judge Matienzo; that he would cross to the other side as he had said. [In response] to this, they told him that the bridge was treacherous and [reminded him] that he was having trouble with his legs because of a fall that he had sustained, and that he would not be able to cross. And [the Inca] then sent me with his governor and two other captains so that they could remain in custody along with the 30 captains who had gone to Cuzco [and] who were still on the other side [of the river] with the judge. I took the judge aside and told him about all that had happened but the people who were with him hardly allowed us to speak in private. I began to understand that there would be no final results because of things I sensed from the many *chapetones* [newcomers to America] who were with him, since they made unreasonable demands, and the Indians took much note of it. [Matienzo] replied that he did not want to [cross the bridge].

I returned with the governor and all the Inca's captains. I beseeched him to cross to the other side, and explained the line of reasoning to him. As I was advising him, he agreed that he would do it, against the will of all his captains. Thus, they all came out to the bridge, all [wearing] many feathers with their masks on their faces and [their] weapons in good order. They went straight to a cross that had been placed on that side of the river, next to the house of the Inca, and they all revered it in order. They all went down accompanying the Inca, and in all there must have been as many as 600 Indians.

Then I went down and crossed, and told Judge Matienzo to go down to the bridge by himself, apart from his people, so that he and the Inca could speak without being overheard by those who had come with him. So he went down with a mestizo [named] Porras as interpreter. They were armed with coats of chain mail, swords, and harquebuses, and the Inca had his [weapons], as I have recounted above.

[The Inca] crossed to the other bank with his governor, *maese de campo*, general, 10 captains, and the mestizo. He then threw himself at the feet of the judge, crying, telling of the hardships he and his father had been made to endure, how Juan Pizarro had kept [his father] in prison on a collar like a dog in Cuzco, to make him give them a house chest of gold, and how they killed one of his sisters and his mother in the valley of Tambo. His father had retreated into those mountains, and Orgóñez, Hernando Pizarro, and Juan Pizarro had come to conquer him four times on behalf of the marquis, and during these [battles] many Spaniards and Indians had died. Furthermore, for having hosted seven

Spaniards, who had been sheltered because of [the rebellion] of Don Diego de Almagro, well, they killed his father. And [the Inca] related many other things, saying it was for these reasons that he did not trust us. He also said that he wanted peace as they had negotiated, which is described above. Then he sent for some small baskets of feathers and gave them to the judge.

The judge told [the Inca] to leave with him in peace, and that he would authorize everything that he asked in the name of Your Majesty, except for the Indians that he had taken from the citizens of Cuzco; they had to be returned. The Inca said that he would come out later as long as [Matienzo] later authorized them [i.e., the Indians from Cuzco] along with all the rest. The judge replied that that was not possible. [The Inca] said that he wanted to discuss this with his captains, and that he would later return to give him the reply. The judge implored him to come out, and [the Inca] replied that he was poor and could not afford it. To this the judge stated that he would have him paid a year's tribute, which was 15,000 pesos, in advance. [The Inca] replied, speaking with his captains: so they come to see me but they do not bring me anything, [and] with three citizens [having] arrived with the judge, it is even less likely that they will fulfill what they say. The judge continued to implore him to give him his son. But [the Inca] gave as an excuse that [his son] was in the Andes, which were 60 leagues from whence he had come, and that the judge would have to wait over a month for them to bring him. It was true that he was there. So the judge said that he would wait in Cuzco.

At this point the harquebusiers, who were with Judge Matienzo, were moving closer to hear and smell what was being said, ignoring that he was calling out to them to stop and return, because the Inca was afraid of them and wanted to leave. Reason did not prevail, but instead turned into chaos. The Inca said goodbye, stating that he wanted to discuss [matters] with his captains, and he went back. And I crossed over [the bridge] four, five times to find out from him what had been decided, because the judge wanted to go back. And the Inca answered that they were very afraid since he came in such a hurry, and because of this they believed that he wanted to deceive them. I went and spoke to the judge, [arguing] that he not leave that day because it was already very late and he could not return to Amaibamba, because it was more than three leagues away and he would not be able to make it before sunset, and that he should wait to see what the Inca decided. He therefore waited until morning, watching over all the Indians and Spaniards keeping guard over the bridge, each from his own side. The Indians lit many fires and played trumpets and their whistles. In the morning, the *maese de campo* crossed over to this side and told me that the Inca beseeched me, since I could cross, to go there so he could [give me his] reply to the judge and tell me his opinion of the negotiations. [However,] the judge did not want [me to], and he sent the Inca a letter with instructions to reply to him later in writing, indicating what he had decided, because he wanted to leave. If he did not want to come in peace, that he should order the bridge demolished and that we would do the same on our [side]. To this, the Inca replied that, having received the abovementioned writs from me, he would comply with his agreement with me and that he was also ordering the bridge taken down from his side. So it was taken down, and we returned and they left.

This is the true account of what happened on this journey, being brief in all [my descriptions] so as not to be excessively wordy, because it is true that it happened in front of me, [and] I signed it in my name.

NOTES

1. García de Melo had begun to negotiate with Titu Cusi Yupanqui much earlier, perhaps in 1563, and it was he who suggested that Titu Cusi Yupanqui could gain access to the Yucay *encomienda* through the marriage of his son with Beatriz Clara Coya. For a review of the complex negotiations that occurred between the Spaniards and Titu Cusi Yupanqui, see Hemming (1970: 288–304), Titu Cusi Yupanqui ([1570] 2005: 128–134), and Guillén Guillén ([1977] 2005: 541–588).

2. The document is held in the Berlin State Library and was first published by Richard Pietschmann ([1565] 1910). We have relied on Pietschmann's transcription for this translation. The first English translation was published by Markham (1913).

3. The fires set by the two sides may have been a way to ward off the mosquitoes.

4. Martín Pando had been asked to enter the Vilcabamba region in 1560, along with Juan de Betanzos, by Polo de Ondegardo to explain the circumstances of Sayri Tupac's sudden death. Pando began serving as secretary and advisor to Titu Cusi at that time (Guillén Guillén [1977] 2005: 580). He remained in Vilcabamba until his death in 1571, when he was falsely accused of causing Titu Cusi Yupanqui's death.

5. This is one of the few early colonial references to the site of Machu Picchu.

6. That is to say, around 1548.

7. This large fort was the town of Vitcos, which is a short walk from the town of Huancacalle.

8. This is the only extant description of Martín Pando.

9. This is the captain who escorted Rodríguez de Figueroa from Lucma to Pampaconas.

10. Cusi Poma was one of the most important Inca captains and is mentioned by a number of other writers.

11. This is one of the very few surviving descriptions of Titu Cusi Yupanqui.

12. Unfortunately, these field notes have been lost.

13. These papers may have been related to the fact that Rodriquez de Figueroa had been appointed Defender of the Indians by the viceroy.

14. Lope García de Castro was interim viceroy of Peru (1564–1569).

15. According to information provided below, the nobleman was Martín Hurtado de Arbieto.

16. The Spaniards had discovered what they believed to be a plot to rebel and arrested the *cacique* of Jauja along with many others (see Hemming 1970: 294–297).

17. The final 1572 raid into Vilcabamba was launched from Cuzco and Huamanga as well as from Curamba, which lies between the two.

18. Martín Hurtado de Arbieto was to lead the 1572 raid into Vilcabamba. Apparently he had been planning such a raid for a long time.

19. Diego López de Zúñiga y Velasco, fourth count of Nieva.

20. A frontal is a cloth placed over the front of the altar to protect it.

21. Titu Cusi Yupanqui had brought back several hundred Indians following raids into different areas bordering Vilcabamba. The *encomienda* holders of those areas were angered by what they saw as the theft of their peasantry.

22. Here Rodríguez de Figueroa is questioning Titu Cusi Yupanqui's bloodline. Titu Cusi Yupanqui was the son of Manco Inca, a half brother of Atahualpa.

23. This phrase literally reads, "que dándole él muy bien de comer, que él saldria de paz" (that [if] he fed him well, that he would come out in peace).

24. Titu Cusi Yupanqui was captured during the first Spanish raid into Vilcabamba. He was taken to Cuzco and sent to live with Pedro de Oñate (Titu Cusi Yupanqui [1570] 2005: 118), but he escaped and returned to Vilcabamba in a few years. Apparently, he was baptized during his time in Cuzco.

25. Matienzo ([1567] 1910: 193–198) also describes the Chuquichaca meeting in detail.

Document 4

Antonio Bautista de Salazar
and the Fall of Vilcabamba

Sometime around 1596 Antonio Bautista de Salazar wrote a history of Spanish activities in Peru. Like so many of the colonial chroniclers of Peru, Bautista de Salazar began his work with the arrival of Francisco Pizarro in Cajamarca and continued the narrative until his own times. While much of his chronicle has been lost, two parts—the first detailing the activities of Viceroy Francisco de Toledo (from 1569–1581) and the second discussing the actions of Viceroy García Hurtado de Mendoza (from 1590 to 1596)—have survived in the Biblioteca Nacional de Madrid. Bautista de Salazar was especially knowledgeable of Toledo's rule since he journeyed with Toledo during the latter's general inspection of Peru, traveling from Lima to Cuzco to Potosi and then back to Lima (Porras Barrenechea 1986: 724–725).[1] Bautista de Salazar also appears to have had access to important archival documents since he provides direct quotes from several of Toledo's letters as well as field reports (Guillén Guillén 1977a; Levillier 1940, 1:328–330). Most important for this work, Salazar was with Toledo during the fall of Vilcabamba and may have personally witnessed the execution of Tupac Amaru. Our translation of Antonio Bautista de Salazar's ([1596] 1867) writings begins with Toledo's attempts to understand what events had transpired in Vilcabamba during the year 1570 and ends in September of 1572 with the death of Tupac Amaru.

DOI: 10.5876/9781607324263.c006

CHAPTER 26

The tasks carried out by the viceroy to find out the state of the
Province of Vilcabamba and to peacefully draw out the Inca

As stated in the history of the Marquis Don Francisco Pizarro,[2] after the defeat of Manco Inca, and following [the] long siege of Cuzco, the leader [i.e., Manco Inca] of the kingdom retreated to the province of Vilcabamba. [Vilcabamba] was the wealthiest [province] in gold and silver minerals that [the empire] contained throughout its long governance and great rule as is described in the chapter discussing this governance. He took with him all his wives, household, and family, and more than 60,000 Indians, and his idol and god named Punchao, whom they adored, and his children, including Sayri Tupac Inca Yupanqui and Titu Cusi Yupanqui, among others who have died. And in the said province he sired Tupac Amaru, Don Felipe Quispe Titu,[3] and others.

Manco Inca was a close friend of Don Diego de Almagro, the elder, and later of his son, Don Diego de Almagro, the younger, [who were] governors of New Toledo. And when Don Diego de Almagro, the elder, was defeated near Cuzco in the battle they call Las Salinas, Captain Diego Méndez, with 13 or 14 soldiers, fled to Vilcabamba, where Manco Inca was. [The Inca] received and hosted them as soldiers of his friend the *adelantado* Don Diego de Almagro, the elder. They were with him for nearly three years and were well treated in every way. The Inca was very acculturated to Spanish ways, and he knew the games that the Spanish played, which included ninepins, dominoes, and chess. One day while he was playing with Captain Diego Méndez, they had a disagreement over the game, which some say was chess [and] others ninepins, such that in anger and with little thought and [even] less restraint, the guest said of the Inca and lord: "Look at the dog!" [At this] the Inca lifted his hand and slapped him. The captain [then] drew a dagger and stabbed [the Inca], from which [wounds] he later died. His captains and Indians came seeking vengeance and tore that Diego Méndez to pieces, along with all the Spaniards who were with him in the province.

[Manco Inca's] son, Sayri Tupac Inca Yupanqui, succeeded him in the office and position of Inca. He married Doña María Cusi Huarcay, his sister, with dispensation from His Holiness, which I mentioned in the history and discussion of the government of the Viceroy Marquis of Cañete, Don Andrés Hurtado de Mendoza, to whom he came out in peace to pledge obedience, so I will not return to repeat [it here].[4] Titu Cusi Yupanqui Inca remained in the province, with the office and duties [of Inca]. He was determined to do harm to the Christians after learning of the death of his brother, robbing

Yucay, [Ollantay]tambo, and other valleys, such that there was no security for the natives along the road or [at the] entrance to the bridge over [the] Chuquichaca River. He would emerge along the mountain road at Curamba, Pincos, Marcahuasí, Mollepata, and the Apurímac River.[5] Not being content with taking the Indian men and women of the towns, [the Inca and his men] would rob the pack trains that were traveling from this city [i.e., Lima] to Cuzco and other places. His boldness, defiance, and audacity went so far that he would kill Spaniards who were coming and going on the roads from Cuzco to Lima and from [Lima] to Cuzco. Because of these [raids], the trade, transactions, and overland commerce of the cities of Huamanga and Cuzco suffered and were severely damaged.

And in that province there was a cleric of the Order of Saint Augustine, who indoctrinated [the inhabitants], named Fray Diego Ortiz, and a highlander, [an] interpreter, named Martín Pando, and a great Spanish miner, named Antonio Romero [who were all killed]. As the viceroy wanted to know the state of the province, he requested information from various people. The viceroy was careful and diligent, although the man who was Inca at the time, and his captains, were doing all that was humanly possible to hide [news from Vilcabamba] so that no one would learn about it. They did not allow anyone to leave or enter [the province]. The viceroy agreed to deal somehow with the Inca so that he, [with] his captains and his people, would come out in peace. For that [purpose], [the viceroy] sent a cleric of the Order of Santo Domingo, named Fray Gabriel de Oviedo, a person of letters and a pastor, and licentiate [Diego] Rodríguez [de Figueroa], a lawyer, with considerable authority to make a peace agreement and provisions for pardoning past crimes. And thus the viceroy himself wrote a letter to the Inca, the tenor of which was that [the viceroy] wanted to publically announce their agreement, as he had done with others.

Copy of the letter that the viceroy wrote to the Inca, who was in Vilcabamba, so that he would come out in peace and pledge obedience to His Majesty
Most magnificent lord son:
Several days ago, understanding [your] oversight in not coming out to the road to meet me when I came to this city, nor after I arrived here, and in recognition of the service you owe to God and His Majesty, the king, my lord, [and as I am] fulfilling the obligations of a father because of the faith that you have given God and the king, my lord, I ordered that licentiate [Diego] Rodriguez [de Figueroa] and Father Fray Gabriel de Oviedo, prior of the convent of Santo Domingo of this city, be sent with letters from myself and from His Majesty, King Felipe, my lord. These contained instructions and correspondence that would benefit

the service of God and the king's majesty. And for your own good [and] security they establish what we have [already] outlined and agreed upon. [I] have now learned from those people who traveled for that purpose [i.e., Oviedo and Rodríguez de Figueroa] that they sent prominent Indians via the Acobamba River. They report that [the Indians] crossed [the river] in rafts with those letters in which my order and mandate was made known to you. [However,] they did not return and the rafts were found washed up in a bend of the river. [Oviedo and Rodríguez de Figueroa] returned by way of the Chuquichaca road. Notwithstanding, the bad taste that this has left me with, to better explain what is in the best interest of the authority of the king, my lord and yours, I wanted you to be advised by Atilano de Anaya, through letters that I had sent you, and through this one of mine since they are going to the Chuquichaca Bridge, so that if you have, as you say you have, the fidelity and zeal for serving God and the king, my lord, you will show it by coming out to meet with [Anaya and his men] and to learn what they have to say and to communicate to you on behalf of His Majesty, the king, and myself. Otherwise, we will become disillusioned, which [will, nevertheless,] give us the benefit of knowing how to proceed. For your benefit and so that you will have more security when you comply, I tell you through this, my letter, [the conditions] that are subject to royal authority [in contrast to] what you may have been told through other channels filled with false lies and news, such as you tell among yourselves. So you can see what your role in this negotiation should be and you will carry out what I tell you with the obedience you owe to all that is important to you, and to your security and that of your sons, brothers, and captains. I am telling and advising you about this, as a father, for your own good and for your safety. And as soon as possible you are to dispatch Atilano de Anaya, whom I have sent with this message. May our Lord protect your very magnificent person to better serve him. From Yucay, on 16 October of the year 1571. From the hand of the viceroy.

"At the service of your grace, lord son—Don Francisco de Toledo." It is addressed: "To the very magnificent lord, my son, Don Diego Titu Cusi Yupanqui Inca, in the Andes"—It is from the viceroy.

CHAPTER 27

Of what happened to Atilano de Anaya, who took
the aforementioned letter to the Inca

On seeing that sending Fray Gabriel de Oviedo and licentiate Rodríguez [de Figueroa] had been of no avail, Atilano de Anaya, who had been in that province on other occasions and had been the [Yucay] majordomo of the Inca, offered to take the letter and communiqués from the viceroy, [stating that] he would return with [the Inca's] reply and information about what was taking place in that province. He and everyone [else] were unaware not only of the fact that Inca Titu Cusi Yupanqui was dead and had been succeeded by Tupac Amaru Inca, [but] also [of] the harm and murder that the Inca had ordered of the Augustine friar [Diego Ortiz], [Martín] Pando, and [the miner] Romero. Anaya was able to enter [Vilcabamba] by the bridge they call Chuquichaca. After he spoke and reasoned with some of the Inca's Indians, he on this bank of the river and they on the other, they promised him [safe] passage on behalf of the Inca, as long as it was he alone. He did so, leaving his servants at the river's edge. When he reached the other bank, the Indians made space for him in a storeroom and brought him some things to eat. They told him, on behalf of the Inca, to wait there for three days without going further, that there they would provide him what was necessary, although they also gave him what was not necessary. He spent the day sitting on a rock next to his hut, in such a way that he could be seen by a black servant of his, whom the Indians had not allowed to cross with him. That night, they stabbed [Anaya] with spears and dragged him out [of the hut], and threw him down into a gully. At daybreak, not seeing his lord at his accustomed post, nor any Indians, the black man, who had heard noises there, crossed the bridge, [and] went to the hut. He did not find his master's bed or his personal items and following a trail, he saw him dead, thrown into a gully.

After he confirmed that [Anaya was dead] and afraid that they would do the same to him, he crossed back over the bridge. Taking the road to Cuzco, [he] went all the way, telling the news of the death of his lord, especially in Amaibamba, which is the closest town to where the body was. The parish priest sent Indians for [Anaya], who brought him, and [the priest] buried him. In Cuzco they did not want to believe the black man about the death of Anaya, although he went tearfully to inform his wife before anyone else. She cursed him, telling him to get out of her sight, and saying that he was a lying scoundrel and that he had fled, leaving his master rather than serving him. The black man then went to Dr. Gabriel de Loarte, *alcalde de corte*. Although [the slave] told what he had seen, the wife of the deceased sent word that she could not believe it and asked that [Loarte] pay no heed to the black man, since he was a liar, but rather that [Loarte] have him arrested. The alcalde did so; however, [the slave] was set free two days later when news arrived from the priest of Amaibamba that he had retrieved the deceased and buried him.

CHAPTER 28

Of the measures the viceroy took and decisions he
made following the abovementioned news

Knowing the above, the viceroy took very great care to learn through all means: the power of the Inca, the condition and characteristics of the land, the entrances and roads to the province, which [provinces] bordered it, the number of Indians that must be there and in the neighboring [provinces] that could support the Inca, where he could escape to and hide [if he were] defeated, what forces they had, and the difficulties of the treacherous passes where [the Inca] had so often defeated the Spanish captains and forces who attempted to enter [the region]. And having obtained the aforementioned information from those who had gone with the [Spanish] captains and from other people who had entered [the province] many times, they discussed the matter with the city council, and throughout several days [the viceroy] sought the advice of various citizens and gentlemen who [were] the most experienced and who had the best information and intelligence. These [individuals] described the difficult areas along the roads and the rough passes as well as the mountains where [the natives] had many boulders that they threw at the army as they passed. It was with these that [the Incas] had defeated the Spaniards in the past.[6] [These same citizens also] told him that the Andes Indians, the Opataries, and [the Indians] of the Manarí, Pilcosuni, and Momorí provinces, and the Satis and Zapacatís, and others that bordered these [provinces], with whom the Inca had contact, could have joined the Inca. When the viceroy received information from Dr. Loarte, alcalde of the court, that the Incas and Indians of this kingdom were in agreement and conspiring, and seeing how insurrections and uprisings had occurred on many occasions, [he decided to proceed]. The final goal and intent was always, if things did not go as [peacefully] as we hoped, to attack the Inca, from [whose territory] no one would be able to oust us.

CHAPTER 29

Of the resolution that the viceroy made to wage all-out war against the Inca

With the approval and agreement of the most prudent and intelligent people there were in Cuzco, and with votes of the municipality, it was resolved to put an end to that robbery and fright and to wage all-out war against the Inca, as apostate, turncoat, murderer, rebel, and tyrant. First, [the viceroy] mustered the military for a general inspection of the soldiers who were in the city at the time, to see their numbers as well as to see the quantity and types of their weapons. Having thoroughly seen and assessed [their military forces], [the viceroy] announced a war of fire and blood. He sent Captain Juan Alvárez Maldonado, [who was already named] the governor and *adelantado* of the province of Opatarí by the King, our lord, to go with some harquebusiers of the army, members of the royal guard of this kingdom, and others to take the bridge crossing of Chuquichaca, so that the Indians of these kingdoms would not be able to send information to that province, nor could information reach here from there. For the raid into and conquest of Vilcabamba, beginning at the bank of that bridge, the [viceroy] also named as his lieutenant general Martín Hurtado de Arbieto, a longtime and very prominent citizen of Cuzco, [who was] *encomendero* of the Indians of Guancallo and others. And as captains, [he named] Martín García Oñaz de Loyola, a knight of the Order of Calatrava and the captain of his guard; Martín de Meneses, a longtime citizen [and] *encomendero* of the *repartimiento* of Guaiqui and others; and Don Antonio Pereyra, also a citizen and *encomendero* of the *repartimiento* of Combapata, Parcartambo, and others. [He named] Juan Alvárez Maldonado as *maese de campo*, Juan Ponce [de León] as *alguacil mayor*, Orgóñez de Valencia as captain of artillery, [and] Pedro Sarmiento de Gamboa as *alférez real*.[7] [He also assigned] the other officials and ministers as was suitable and necessary. When the winter was over, since the province where they were going was mountainous, [and it would have been] difficult to achieve the purpose and desired goal during the [winter season], the men set out from Cuzco at the end of April. No *encomendero* of Indians remained behind, nor were any excuses accepted for failing to fulfill their obligations [on account of being] old or young. The noblemen also went, armed with spears and harquebuses, and a number of other knights. They needed nothing more than to know that this was in the service of the king, our lord, and the pleasure and satisfaction of his viceroy, to offer their persons and to spend their wealth in order not to tarnish the nobility from which they descended. There were many Indians, some of them Cañaris. This military force entered through the bridge of Chuquichaca. [The viceroy sent] another of group, [led by] Gaspar [Arias] de Sotelo, a longtime resident and citizen of Cuzco, an *encomendero*, to enter through Abancay and take the pass from the Inca. He carried out [these orders] with more than 70 chosen soldiers. [The viceroy also commanded] Don Luis de Toledo Pimental to enter through the Mayomarca Valley, which is in the district of the city of Huamanga, with 50 inhabitants of Huamanga, to take the pass of Osambre, in order to prevent the Inca from escaping through it. He went; however, he arrived late.

CHAPTER 30

Of the battle and ambush that the Inca's captains
fought against the royal force and army

The viceroy told the captains and general concerning what they should do, [the duties they were to] fulfill and carry out over the course of the journey. [The instructions were] so shrewd and on the mark that one day, when [the officers] did not comply [with the order] that the army was never to march without first taking the heights, out of fear that [the Indians would again throw] boulders with which they had inflicted [such] damage and routed [the army, as] previously discussed, that that [day] the Indians fought a battle against them. Not only did [the Indians] drive many of them away, but they came with spears, *macanas* [clubs], and arrows with such great courage, vigor, and determination as the most skillful, brave, and experienced soldiers of Flanders could have done.

That day, it was Loyola's turn to be in the vanguard, which in the end was fortunate [for two reasons]: first, for his skillfulness, [a trait] of no small importance in captains; the other, for the great valor and courage that comes from the noble blood from which he descended and the military order of the Knights of the Order of Calatrava, to which he had been admitted. Another reason [was] on account of the chosen men of his company, who were mostly aspiring *hidalgos* [gentry men] and who offered their services to the viceroy, considering it dishonorable, in the event of war, to not participate, [wanting to] serve the majesty of the King, our lord. Another part of this company consisted of illustrious servants of the viceroy; although they all volunteered themselves, he could not do without those who were requisite and necessary for his service. Another [part consisted] of soldiers chosen from the companies of Captains Martín de Meneses and Don Antonio Pereyra, who were well versed in military [matters] and sons of the first conquistadors, with experience and accustomed to hardships, wars, and raids, [eager] to live up to their fathers' examples.

The Indians fought this battle next to the river they call Cayaochaca, which in our language means "river of willows," even though there are none.[8] The location was very opportune for the Indians, because their opponents could only march in single file, as the path was very narrow, with two rough mountains on either side, between which flows the said great river, which swells in winter. The Indians were lying in ambush in various places on the upper slope, and along the lower [slope] there were others with spears to descend on those who fell; and in case anyone escaped from their hands, they had Indian archers on the other [bank]. They started blaring their *tarquis*, which resemble trumpets. As soon as [the Spaniards] heard this signal, the Indians were upon them with their spears and pikes and others with *macanas*, giving them chase and fighting with such fervor that [the Spaniards] wished they had more hands, if it were possible, as their feet did them no good, for fleeing from Scylla they ran up against Charybdis,[9] as between [the two they heard] the sound of the *combas*, which are the boulders. [The Indians] charged into the mouths of the harquebuses, not afraid of the injury they might sustain, just to fight hand to hand.

And there was a certain [man] who grabbed hold of Captain [García Oñaz de] Loyola, and struggled with him for a considerable time to push him down the ravine. [Then] one of [Loyola's] Indians unsheathed a sword he was carrying and cleaved clean through one leg and then through the other. The captain, escaping this [danger], [began] fighting with his sword and shield, as did his soldiers because, seeing their enemies among them and unable to take advantage of their harquebuses, they cast them aside. Grasping their shields and unsheathing their swords, fighting hand to hand to save their lives, it was necessary for them to take [the lives] of their opponents, who did not seem to value [their lives] at all, as they approached to fight with their *macanas*, stones, spears, and arrows, which were the weapons with which they defended themselves or planned to defend themselves. Furthermore, the courage of the captain and his brave soldiers put those barbarians to shame, such that the general, who was [named] Atahualpa Inca, and the *maese de campo*, a brave and courageous Indian named Curi Paucar, gave the signal to retreat, which his soldiers obeyed. Not only did they retreat, but they disappeared without being seen until a while later they positioned themselves on a small, barren hill. Although some of our [soldiers] were wounded, only three died, crushed by the boulders, [but] a great number of the Indians [were killed]. I will not describe in detail the feats of some of these brave soldiers, to avoid offending others by not mentioning them, as it would make for a long story.

I will only say that Don Francisco [Ordoño de] Valencia, son of Dr. Valencia, *alcalde del crímen* of the Royal Audiencia, of the company of royal pikemen, [whose services were] offered to the viceroy for this conquest, was the first to fire his harquebus in this skirmish and killed two Indians with that shot. The rest of the army was unable to come to the aid of the vanguard, which was in the thick of the battle, due to the narrowness of the trail where the Indians waged the battle. Although Captain Juan Ponce [de León] came to help with great determination and courage, as I have said, he was not, in effect, able to [do so].[10] [However,] the Indians became so afraid that they lost their nerve and never appeared again. The captains and the other Indians with their wives and children first fled, [among them] the Inca, although he was not present [at the battle], nor do I believe he even gave the order.

The army marched without any opposition, and every day more [Indians] deserted with their wives and children to our army, where they were welcomed and treated with kindness.[11] They stated that the Inca Tupac Amaru, Quispe Titu, General Atahualpa, Captain Curi Paucar, and others were hiding in the mountains. Thus, arriving at the place and site [of Vilcabamba], they did not find the Inca or the [other] aforementioned [individuals] or [any] other prominent Indians. And every day more [Indians] would return [to the town of Vilcabamba]. And since the journey would serve no purpose without capturing the Inca, who was the cause of all these problems, Captain [García Oñaz de] Loyola offered to go in search and pursuit of [the Inca], even though it was in enemy territory, being [the lands of] the Momorí and Capacatis. So he put [the plan] into effect, with more than 20 select soldiers, including some extremely good harquebusiers and some highlanders who were accustomed to mountains, as this was.

According to the trail they were following and their guides, they learned that the Inca had fled downriver in rafts, so it was necessary for them to do the same in another [set of] rafts to the place where they had heard the Inca had disembarked. They then followed the trail on land for about three days. Some of the Indians who were with the Inca started deserting him, [and] they told where he was. In the end, Captain [García Oñaz de] Loyola came upon the Inca and his wives and children and captured him. Being greatly pleased with the fortunate end and conclusion of this expedition, he returned to the army, where he was very well received by the general and everyone else. And during the time that [Loyola] was in pursuit [of the Inca], [other] army commanders and captains would go out with [their] troops, making forays in search of the other [Inca nobles] who had escaped. And every day they returned with [additional] captives, including the general [Atahualpa] and others. [They also returned] with other high-ranking Indians, the idol of the Sun, the embalmed bodies of Manco Inca and Saytri Tupac Inca, and spoils. The last Indian taken prisoner was Captain Curi Paucar.

Understandably, the viceroy was anxiously waiting [to hear] the outcome of the raid and the expedition of Captain [García Oñaz de] Loyola. Especially since news of what had happened to him and his soldiers and how he had fared was late [in arriving], even though General Martín Hurtado de Arbieto sent word at every opportunity of what was happening; including on the day that the said captain [Loyola] had left in pursuit of the Inca into the land of unconquered Indians. [Then] at nearly nine at night, or later, a [man] named Francisco Ruiz de Navamuel, who was one of the *hidalgos* who had volunteered [their services], uncle of the secretary of the *gobernación* of these kingdoms, Álvaro Ruiz de Navamuel, arrived [in Cuzco] with correspondence from the general [Hurtado de Arbieto] and Captain [García Oñaz de] Loyola on the successful end to the conquest.

We owe thanks to God, who granted [our wishes] in everything, and to Your Excellency, who, with his good counsel, discretion, and great wisdom in government, finished what so many had attempted without being able to achieve. We did not fail in the first [point], that of giving thanks to God, because thanks were given and offered the next day, and [on] many other days, with great care in the main church [and in] the parishes and convents. [The viceroy] gave a gift of an *encomienda* of Indians, to the man who brought the news, not only as a reward for bringing the good news, [but also because] he deserved it for his services on that expedition and others in which he had participated in [the service of] His Majesty, fulfilling his obligations as *hidalgo*. [The viceroy] also granted favors to those whom the general and captains reported were deserving. [The viceroy] ordered the general [Martín Hurtado de Arbieto] to stay in the province as governor, and [named him] as *encomendero* of its Indians. [Martín Hurtado de Arbieto] remained along with the conquistadors, granting them land and fields.[12] [The viceroy also ordered] that the captains, citizen *encomenderos,* and other soldiers leave for Cuzco with the Inca Tupac Amaru, the general [Atahualpa], and the other captains who were most to blame, which they did.

The viceroy ordered that the city [of Cuzco] be on vigil for the entire duration of this expedition because it was known that the Indians of the [city] had an agreement and were conspiring with the Inca and those of that province. The [city] council summoned all the people of the city [to attend] the triumphant entry of the captains with their prisoners; naming a captain to bring [each of the prisoners] out. It was very splendid, although the soldiers of the conquest looked better in the military and mountain garments in which they came, reflecting the purpose of their journey. Each brought one of the notable captives that they had caught: one [Spaniard] [brought] a captain, another [Spaniard brought] someone else, another [brought] the *maese de campo* [i.e., Curi Paucar], and another [brought] the general [Atahualpa]. Captain [García Oñaz de] Loyola came last with the Inca, Tupac Amaru, who was imprisoned with a gold chain around his neck. [They] were paraded by the houses of Doña Teresa Orgoñez, where the viceroy was staying, who could see what he wanted from a window without being seen. All of them were taken to the fortress, where they were left well guarded and in good custody. Proceedings were initiated against them, assigning them defenders until they were condemned to death, and Doctor Gabriel de Loarte, *alcalde del crimen*, was [assigned as] counsel. The sentences against them and against Tupac Amaru were carried out. On the day that the Inca was executed, there was a scaffold in the public plaza that had been built to behead him, [and there] were more than 100,000 Indian men and women, wailing for their king and lord.

[Tupac Amaru] was so disheartened that he could barely speak. On the verge of such a harsh end, having asked to be baptized and having been baptized on that very platform, [he] took the named Don Pablo. It seems that the Lord exercised his divine mercy on him, giving courage and strength to he who was so lacking, so that he would declare the error with which they had deceived their subjects for so many years. [While] the Indians were protesting, as previously mentioned, [the Inca] stood up, because he had been on his knees for some time commending himself to the true God, creator of heaven and earth, through Father [Alonso de] Barzana, of the Order of the Jesuits, a great servant of His and very knowledgeable in the [Quechua] language, and Father Cristóbal de Molina, of the Order of San Pedro, who was also [an expert], and *bachiller* [Francisco] Vélez, priest of the main church, and other clerics.[13]

CHAPTER 31

Of what the Inca Tupac Amaru said from the gallows before they beheaded him

[Tupac Amaru] lifted both hands, making a sign with them such as the Indians customarily make to the *apus* [lords], and he turned his face toward the largest group of *curacas*. He, who was at death's door and a moment before could hardly be heard by those who were next to him, said out loud, in his language, "*Oiariguaichic* [listen to me]!" The cries, weeping, and clamor ceased at once, and everyone breathed a great sigh and a hush fell over the crowd, as if [not a] soul were alive in the plaza, such was the command and grandeur of the Incas and the subjection in which their subjects were held. And, in summary, what he said in his language, verified in the statement of the interpreters, who, as I have said, were on the scaffold, and others who were near them, from whom statements and depositions were [later] taken, is the following:

"*Apus*, who are here from all of the four *suyos* [regions],[14] know that I am Christian and [that] they have baptized me and that I want to die in the law of God, and I must die. And [know that] all that we have told you until now, I and my Inca ancestors, that you should adore the sun, Punchao, and the *huacas*, idols, rocks, rivers, mountains, and *vilcas* [holy objects], is all falsity and lies. And when we told you that we entered to speak with the Sun, and that he said that you should do as we said and that he spoke, this was a lie, because it did not speak, rather we [did], because it is a piece of gold and cannot speak. And my brother Titu Cusi told me that, when I wished to say something to the Indians, I should enter alone to the said idol Punchao, and that no one should enter with me, and that the said idol Punchao would not speak to me, because it was [just] a small piece of gold. Afterward, I should go out and tell the Indians that it had spoken to me and that it said whatever I wanted to tell them, so that the Indians would more willingly do what I would order them, and so that they would venerate what was inside the sun, Punchao, which is made from the hearts of the Incas, my ancestors."[15]

Having said this, Don Pablo Tupac Amaru[16] turned to tell them that it was all falsity and lies, and that they should believe in only one true God, the creator of all things, because he was dying for all the sins he had committed, and that he wanted to die a Christian. [He asked] that they pardon his deceptions, in which he had [mis]led them until that moment, and that they pray to God for him. Even though he was a prisoner, Don Pablo Tupac Amaru said all of this with a royal authority and majesty; [it was] not disingenuous or artificial, but rather very natural, and he acted as I have described [even though it was a] critical moment. It seemed that the Lord had given him new strength to speak, [after] having been faint and trembling, hardly able to say an audible word to those who were helping him to die well. [But] these [words] were heard by many, not only those around the scaffold and gallows, but also by others who were further from him.

Then they took him away to the site and place where they were going to behead him, which was done, [and] they showed his head to all the surrounding people. The lamentations and weeping of the Indians, which had begun with the end of the speech, grew [louder upon seeing] the spectacle. [It was] something that must be seen to be believed. They placed the head on the gallows, where it remained for only one more day, until nightfall, [when] the Viceroy ordered it be taken down, because a great crowd of Indians were in the plaza *mochándola* [worshiping] and adoring it there, without eating or wanting to part with it. The [royal] Indians were held in such great veneration that, even in death, they were treated like this. Some of the other [members of his family] were sent to this city [i.e., Lima] and other areas that are not important to detail. I will only say that there was an investigation against Don Carlos Inca, son of Paullu Inca, a loyal and great servant of His Majesty, as I have mentioned in the [history of] the life of the Marquis Don Francisco Pizarro. This investigation was conducted into some charges of what appeared to be a conspiracy and other things; Francisco Jimenez, a linguist [and] a highlander, [acted] as interpreter.

It later became clear that this was not the case, and [Carlos Inca's] honor and estate were restored to him. [He was] married to Doña María de Esquivel, who is alive today, [and] with whom he had Don Melchor Carlos Inca, whose godfather, by baptism in Cuzco, was Don Francisco de Toledo.

Don Melchor is the only remaining direct descendant of the past Inca kings, and it is evident in his personal valor; as a descendant of theirs, he embodies the [best] qualities of their generation, and in his Spanish [traits] to the nobility and *hidalgo* status of his mother, who raised him and had him instructed in all the exercises of virtue that princes customarily have and learn. He has turned out to be not only a good pupil but a renowned master. He married Doña Leonor Arias Carrasco, daughter of Pedro Alonso Carrasco, knight of the Order of Santiago, citizen of Cuzco, *encomendero* of the *repartimientos* of Yanaoca, Camata, and others. [His wife was] the granddaughter of one of the first conquistadors and Doña Isabel Fernández Cabeza, daughter of licentiate Alonso Pérez, a prominent and noble man.

NOTES

1. Antonio Bautista de Salazar was also treasurer of the Real Hacienda in Lima during the viceroyalty of García Hurtado de Mendoza.

2. These chapters of Bautista de Salazar's work have been lost.

3. This statement is not correct; Felipe Quispe Titu was the son of Sayri Tupac.

4. This section of Bautista de Salazar's writings has been lost.

5. All of these places are along the major road that connected Cuzco with Huamanga.

6. This is a reference to the battle of Chuquillusca (1539), during which Gonzalo Pizarro and his forces took heavy losses. This part of Bautista de Salazar's chronicle is lost.

7. Pedro Sarmiento de Gamboa was the standard-bearer for the army. There are two important documents produced by Pedro Sarmiento de Gamboa concerning Vilcabamba. The first records the arrival of the Spaniards in the town of Vilcabamba (see Guillén Guillén 1977a). The second is his testimony in support of Juan Alvárez Maldonado's services to the king of Spain during the Vilcabamba campaign (Guillén Guillén 1980).

8. Various other early colonial writers also describe the battle of Cayaochaca.

9. Scylla and Charybdis were two mythical sea monsters between which sailors needed to pass. The modern English expression might be "between a rock and a hard place."

10. Juan Ponce de León would later become the brother-in-law of Martín Hurtado de Arbieto.

11. Here Salazar jumps several days forward in time. He does not describe the taking of Vitcos, the joining of Gaspar de Sotelo's forces with those of Martín Hurtado de Arbieto at Pampaconas, or the fall of the Huayna Pucará and Muchu Pucará forts on the trail to the Inca city of Vilcabamba. Nor does he describe the actual fall of the city.

12. General Martín Hurtado de Arbieto was given the *encomienda* of Vilcabamba for two lifetimes in return for the successful capture of the Inca and his immediate family. He remained as governor of Vilcabamba until his death in 1598.

13. Both Barzana and Molina are also mentioned by Ocampo as being eyewitnesses to the death of Tupac Amaru.

14. The Inca Empire was divided into four subregions that radiated outward from Cuzco.

15. The center of the Punchao held a paste made from the hearts of the dead Inca rulers.

16. When he was baptized, Tupac Amaru took the Christian name of Pablo.

Document 5

The Death, Interments, and Miracles of Fray Diego Ortiz (Vilcabamba, Peru)

In 1571 the leader of the collapsing Inca state, Titu Cusi Yupanqui, died suddenly while in the remote town of Vitcos.[1] Protected deep within Inca-controlled territory, Titu Cusi Yupanqui had been healthy the day before his death and took part in a religious celebration. But as the evening wore on, the Inca grew sick and by the next morning he was dead. His loyalists suspected poisoning and detained the two foreigners who were near Vitcos: Diego Ortiz and Martín Pando. Ortiz was an Augustinian priest who had been evangelizing in the Vilcabamba region for about three years while Pando was a mestizo who had worked as the Inca's scribe, translator, and advisor for over a decade. Pando was quickly killed; however, because of his higher status as a priest, Ortiz was kept alive. The Inca loyalists demanded that Ortiz, in accordance with his many sermons, hold a mass and resurrect Titu Cusi Yupanqui. When the mass failed to provide the desired results, Ortiz was forced to walk for several days toward the Inca stronghold of Vilcabamba before being killed. Approximately a year later, Spanish-led forces invaded the Vilcabamba region and brought an end to indigenous rule in the Andes.

The complex events that surround the deaths of Titu Cusi Yupanqui, Martín Pando, and Diego Ortiz have long held the attention of writers. Ortiz's near contemporaries, Martín de Murúa ([ca. 1616] 1987, [ca. 1616] 2008) and Antonio de la Calancha ([1638] 1981), both highlight his torture and "martyrdom" in their

DOI: 10.5876/9781607324263.c007

chronicles, while more contemporary scholars have placed these events within the larger contexts of the fall of the Inca Empire (Hemming 1970). However, how we have come to know about what occurred in the distant region of Vilcabamba during that chaotic week of death and revenge killings and what eventually became of Ortiz's remains after the Vilcabamba area was seized by the Spaniards has not been widely discussed.

In this chapter we draw upon two little-known investigations dating to 1595 and 1599–1600 that the Augustinian Order in Cuzco conducted into the death of Ortiz (Bauer et al. 2014). While the investigations began more than twenty years after the dramatic events took place, several eyewitnesses were still living and were interviewed by the Augustinians. The investigations reveal new details of Titu Cusi Yupanqui's and Ortiz's deaths and highlight the Augustinians' determination to elevate Ortiz's death to an act of martyrdom, worthy of a Christian saint.

JERÓNIMO NÚÑEZ'S 1582 INVESTIGATION INTO THE HISTORY OF THE AUGUSTINIAN ORDER

Following the "pacification" of the Vilcabamba region in 1572, at least three different Augustinian priors conducted investigations into the death of Ortiz. The first inquiry was led by Jerónimo Núñez in September of 1582, a little more than a decade after Ortiz was killed. Núñez was writing a history of the Augustinian Order in Peru and, as such, wanted information on their missionary work in the Vilcabamba region. Although Núñez's investigation remains unpublished, Levillier (1935: 342–344, 359) provides some insights into its contents.[2] It appears that the inquest took place in Cuzco and focused on several veterans of the Vilcabamba campaign and other noteworthy gentlemen of Cuzco.[3] During the inquiry, at least two questions concerning the Vilcabamba region were asked. One question centered on the actions of Fray Juan de Vivero, the founder of the Augustinian Order in Cuzco, who had traveled into the Vilcabamba region for a short time period in 1568 to baptize Titu Cusi Yupanqui. The other question concerned whether the Inca who succeeded Titu Cusi Yupanqui (i.e., Tupac Amaru) had ordered the death of Diego Ortiz. Levillier (1935: 342–344) writes that Gomez de Tordoya and Juan Pérez de Prado, both of whom were veterans of the 1572 Vilcabamba campaign, indicated that the death of the priest was ordered by Tupac Amaru, while Garcia de Melo, the crown's former envoy between Cuzco and Vilcabamba, stated that it was widely believed that Ortiz was killed spontaneously by the men who had captured him.

THE 1595 AND 1599–1600 INVESTIGATIONS
INTO THE DEATH OF DIEGO ORTIZ

Two additional investigations into the death of Diego Ortiz took place in 1595 and 1599–1600. Both of these studies were held by the Augustinians with the hope that the sufferings and miracles associated with Ortiz would be officially recognized and that he would be canonized as a Christian saint. This study focuses on the documents produced during these two investigations.

The 1595 hearings were conducted under the direction of Fray Pedro de Aguilar, who was then the procurator of the Augustinian convent in Cuzco. Although this investigation took place more than twenty years after Ortiz was killed, it included an impressive array of both Andean and European interviewees. Furthermore, many of the interviews took place in different communities in the Vilcabamba region, and they included many eyewitnesses, such as two of Titu Cusi Yupanqui's former wives, the former wife of Martín Pando, and various Inca loyalists who could still remember the dramatic events of 1571. The interviewees also included several Spaniards who had participated in the 1572 raid on Vilcabamba and a number of longtime Spanish residents of the Vilcabamba region who had heard about the killing of Ortiz and who had seen the miracles attributed to Ortiz after his death. Nevertheless, the testimonies did not provide enough information to convince a group of secular judges in Cuzco that Ortiz should be considered for beatification.

After the 1595 investigation failed, a subsequent Augustinian prior in Cuzco, Diego de Arenas, requested permission from the Bishop of Cuzco in late 1599 to begin another investigation. Over the course of the next several months, interviews were conducted again in the Vilcabamba and the Cuzco regions. These interviews included a combination of individuals who had already testified in 1595 and new witnesses. On 18 August 1600, the bishop of Cuzco gave his final ruling on the case: while the bones of Ortiz could be placed in the Augustinians' church in Cuzco, the Augustinians were to make it clear to their parishioners that Ortiz was not officially canonized and was not a saint. Sometime after 1606 the proceedings and interview notes from the 1595 and 1599–1600 investigations were bundled together in Cuzco and a clean, well-ordered document was sent to the Augustinian Order in Rome (Aparicio López 1989; Bauer et al. 2014).

Over the next four decades the information collected in the 1595 and the 1599–1600 investigations was copied and disseminated within three different chronicles. First, in 1616, Martín de Murúa ([ca. 1616] 1987; [ca. 1616] 2008) completed his magnum opus, *Historia general del Perú*, which includes detailed descriptions of Titu Cusi Yupanqui's and Ortiz's deaths. It is clear that Murúa had access to the records of the 1595 and 1599–1600 investigations since he copied large parts of several testimonies and paraphrased information from several others in his work.[4]

The circumstances of Ortiz's cruel death became more widely known after 1638, when Antonio de la Calancha ([1638] 1981) completed his massive history of the Augustinian Order in Peru titled *Corónica moralizada del Orden de San Agustín en el Perú* (The Righteous Chronicle of the Order of Saint Augustine in Peru). As an Augustinian, Calancha also had access to the Ortiz files, and he too copied large sections of several testimonies into his narrative. Later much of Calancha's information on Ortiz was included within an introduction to Garcilaso de la Vega's ([1609] 1723) *Primera parte de los Commentarios reales . . .*, and thus Ortiz's ordeals became even more widely known. Recent research in the Biblioteca Nacional in Lima and the Augustinian archive in Rome has yielded the original documents from which Murúa and Calancha gained their information.

THE BIBLIOTECA NACIONAL (LIMA) AND THE AUGUSTINIAN ARCHIVE (ROME) DOCUMENTS

Since Murúa's work was not published until the 1940s, Calancha's text has become the most widely cited document on the deaths of Titu Cusi Yupanqui and Ortiz. We now know, however, that parts of the field manuscripts from the 1595 and the 1599–1600 investigations have survived in a badly damaged document titled "Ynformacion del Padre Fray Diego que mataron en Vilcabamba" in the Biblioteca Nacional in Lima and that the complete final version of the report is held within the Augustinian Archivo de la Postulación General in Rome under the title "Declaraciones ante notario publico de varios testigos sobre el martirio del V.P. Diego Ortiz."[5]

A few pages of the Ortiz file in the Biblioteca Nacional were published a century ago (Romero and Urteaga 1916). They are grouped, however, along with several other documents as appendixes to a transcription of Titu Cusi Yupanqui's 1570 narrative. These appendixes include the mistakenly combined 1595 testimonies of Angelina Llacsa Chuqui and Alonso de la Cueva as well as the complete 1600 testimony of Baltasar de Ocampo Conejeros.[6] Romero and Urteaga (1916) also included Fray Diego de Arenas's 1599 petition to begin a new investigation of Ortiz's death and the bishop of Cuzco's positive response as appendixes.[7] Unfortunately, as these appendixes were published without any background information or catalog references, few readers knew the historical context in which the documents were written or even where the source documents could be found. Nevertheless, it is fortunate that Romero and Urteaga published part of the Ortiz papers held in the Biblioteca Nacional because this manuscript is badly damaged, and most of the published sections have now been lost (figure 7.1).

The Ortiz materials in the Biblioteca Nacional contain sixty-four folios, representing about half of the original manuscript. Most but not all of the 1595 testimonies have been lost, while the majority, but not all, of the 1599–1600 testimonies are preserved.[8] The folios that remain in the Biblioteca Nacional are written in many different hands[9] and include many irregularities in spelling, abbreviations, and grammar (figures 7.2 and 7.3). It is made even more difficult to read because of its many rips, holes, and burned areas. The folios are numbered in pencil; however, this seems to have been a rushed affair since the numbers do not always follow the original page order.

It is important to note that the first part of the Lima document represents a copy of declarations made in 1595 by witnesses living in the Vilcabamba region. The copy was made by Antonio de Olave in San Francisco de la Victoria on 17 March 1595 before he left the region to return to Cuzco. This part of the document originally contained thirteen testimonies as well as five administrative letters; however, a fire destroyed most of these, and only the incomplete testimonies of Felipe Pomaunga, Angelina Llacsa Chuqui, and Antonio de la Cueva have survived (folios 27, 24, 25, and 26). The rest of the folios within the Lima document appear to be originals, since they are signed by witnesses and some include rubrics.

In 1989 the Augustinian historian Teófilo Aparicio López (1989) published a transcription of the official copy of the complete beatification investigation resulting from the 1595 and 1599–1600 inquiries, which he found in the Augustinian Archivo de la Postulación General in Rome. The official copy was produced in Cuzco by scribe Juan de Olave on 4 January 1607 at the request by Friars Diego Verdugo, prior of the Convent of San Agustín in Cuzco, and Fray Alonso Domínguez, procurator of the same convent. Upon completion the copy was notarized by Diego de la Carrera Ron, Gaspar de Prado, and Miguel Mendo and then sent on to Rome.

The Augustinian Archive document provides insights into the deaths of Pando, Ortiz, and Titu Cusi Yupanqui that were not known before, and it allows us to better understand the fragmented portions of the manuscript stored in the Biblioteca Nacional. The complete document also assists in the reconstruction of the 1595 and 1599–1600 field investigations of the Augustinians in detail and to follow the progression of the petitions as the documents moved from one official to another in Cuzco.

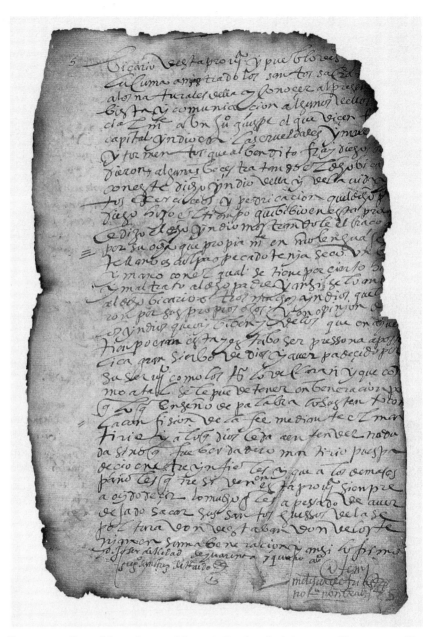

FIGURE 7.1. *Part of the testimony of Gregorio Sánchez de Aedo, vicar of Lucma, 1599. Note the poor state of the manuscript with its burned edges. Courtesy Biblioteca Nacional de Lima SM 110: fol. 5.*

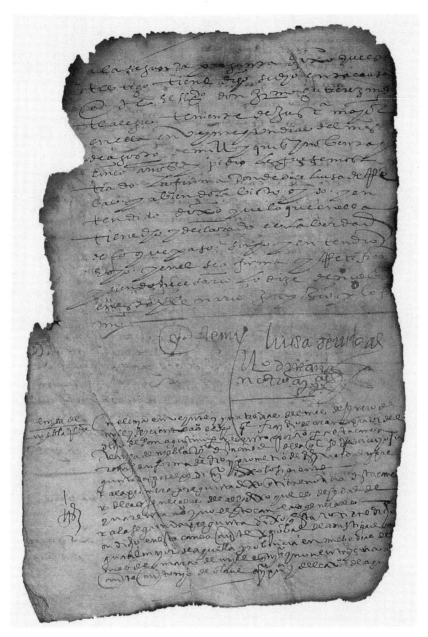

FIGURE 7.2. *The ending of Luisa de Ribas's testimony and the beginning of Luisa de Niebla's testimony, 1600. Note the different calligraphy styles attributable to different scribes as well as Luisa de Ribas's signature. Courtesy Biblioteca Nacional de Lima SM 110: fol. 9.*

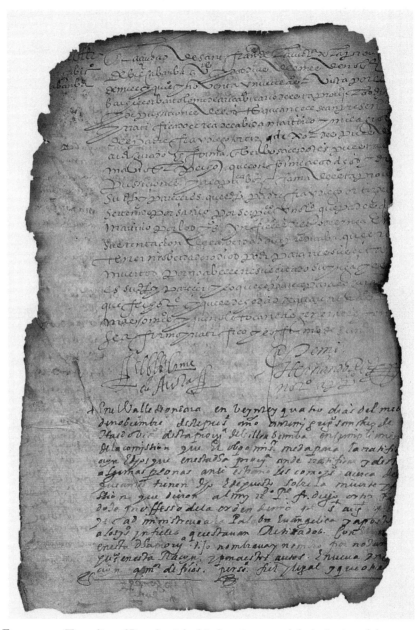

FIGURE 7.3. *The ending of Bartolomé de Arica's testimony and the beginning of the appointment of Melchor Frías as the public notary, 1599. Note the different calligraphy styles attributable to different scribes. Courtesy Biblioteca Nacional de Lima SM 110: fol. 13.*

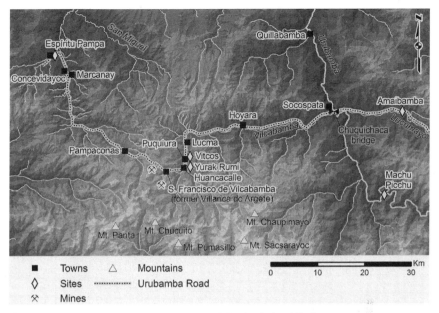

	Towns	△	Mountains
$\diamond$	Sites	┄┄┄	Urubamba Road
$\times$	Mines		

FIGURE 7.4. *The Vilcabamba region in 1595. Map by Gabriel E. Cantarutti.*

OVERVIEW OF THE 1595 INVESTIGATION BASED ON THE BIBLIOTECA NACIONAL (LIMA) AND THE AUGUSTINIAN ARCHIVE (ROME) DOCUMENTS

The 1595 investigation formally began on 22 January in the mining center of Villa Rica de Argete[10] in the Vilcabamba region, with a hearing before the corregidor and Supreme Justice of Vilcabamba, Don Antonio de Monroy Portocarrero (figure 7.4). At that time, a petition was presented by Fray Pedro de Aguiar, the procurator of the Augustinian Order in Cuzco, to interview various residents of the region. The goal of the interviews was to demonstrate that Friar Diego Ortiz, through his holy works and the manner of his death, was worthy of being canonized as a saint. Monroy Portocarrero accepted the petition and named Juan de Peralta as the official Quechua-Spanish interpreter.

It took several days to organize the investigation and to assemble the first witnesses. On 25 January 1595, Fray Aguiar interviewed four witnesses, all of whom were Quechua speakers living in the nearby town of Lucma. The first person to be interviewed was Felipe Pomaunga, an elderly leader of the town. Pomaunga, who could remember Fray Marcos's name but not that of Ortiz, indicated that he had been in the town of Vilcabamba when he heard of the

Inca's death. He was still in Vilcabamba several days later when he learned of the killing of Ortiz. The second person interviewed was Angelina Llacsa Chuqui, a former wife of Titu Cusi Yupanqui. Her testimony is one of the most detailed, and thus most important, of the collection. In her testimony Llacsa Chuqui describes the death of Titu Cusi Yupanqui and notes that immediately afterward another of the Inca's wives, named Angelina Polan Quilaco,[11] accused Ortiz and Pando of being involved his death.[12] Llacsa Chuqui, like many others who were to testify after her, mentions the failed mass of Ortiz to raise the dead Inca and how Ortiz was forced to walk to the town of Marcanay before he was killed. Her account reads as follows:

> And later that day, month, and year [i.e., 25 January 1595], to provide more information, Fray Pedro Aguiar presented a native woman of Lucma, named Angelina Llacsa Chuqui, as a witness. Aided by the interpreter, she swore in accordance with [the] law to tell the truth before the corregidor. When she was asked about the subject in question, she said she knew the father Fray Diego of the Lord of Saint Augustine Order, and that he had been in this province indoctrinating the natives and instructing them in the holy Catholic Faith, with much love and willingness. This was about two years before this province was conquered by the Spaniards. Accompanying him was also another father from the same order, named Fray Marcos, who was greatly hated by Cusito Yupanqui [i.e., Titu Cusi Yupanqui], the lord of the province at that time, because he [Marcos] felt free to reproach what he though was done incorrectly and what offended God. After arguing on one occasion with the Inca, Fray Marcos left for Cuzco without having taken leave. As soon as he [the Inca] learned this, he sent some natives after him and they brought him back. The Inca asked him why he was leaving without his permission, and said that if he wanted to leave, he could go. Having been dismissed by the Inca, Fray Marcos left for the city of Cuzco. Only Fray Diego stayed in the province indoctrinating the natives, and he was in this ministry for around six to seven months, until he died.
>
> The Inca suddenly died with a swollen tongue and mouth, coughing up clotted blood while he was visiting the town of Puquiura. The natives agreed that he was poisoned, and after he died, one of the wives of the Inca named Angelina [Polan] Quilaco started yelling that Fray Diego and that Pando guy, a mestizo who was the secretary of the Inca at that time, should be captured because they had murdered the Inca. The natives then caught Fray Diego, tied his hands behind his back, and went on slapping and kicking him during the night. They did many other cruel things to him, insulting him and asking him to bring back and resurrect their Inca that he had murdered.

[She said] that in the morning of the next day, [Father Ortiz] was commanded to get dressed, say mass, and to resurrect the Inca, since [the Inca] had died. So Father Diego, with much patience and commending himself to God, got dressed and said his mass with much devotion. Having said the mass, the natives grabbed him again and tied his hands in back. They tied a rope to his neck, whipped him hard, and dealt him many kicks, slaps, and punches, demanding that he bring back their Inca, since he had murdered him. To this Fray Diego, with much patience and humbleness, kneeling on the ground, answered that he was a sinner and he could not resurrect the Inca, that only God could do that. [He told them] that he would receive all the torments that they were willing to give him, hoping that God could give him the strength to suffer and then the glory. She said that she heard all of this in public from the many natives that came in and spent some time where the dead Inca was. She was with the [Inca's] body because she was a former wife, and [they] would tell her everything that was happening and what was being done with the father.

[She said] that after a while, this witness [i.e., Angelina Llacsa Chuqui] emerged onto a *cancha* or patio, where she saw five natives carrying Fray Diego to Vilcabamba, [with] his hands tied in back and a rope on his neck. [She] saw the Father walking sad and defeated, with his eyes staring at the sky commending himself to God. About eight days later, this witness heard that the natives had finished killing Fray Diego in the town of Marcana. He was hit with a copper axe in the neck and he died after receiving the second blow. Once he was dead, he was dragged along the road by the grass rope that was tied to his neck. They took him to a place called Navaguanungo [i.e., Mananhuañunca, Quechua for "he will never die"], where they dug a deep hole, and put him in upside down. Once there, a long and sharp stick was driven in his anus and through his body. He was covered with dirt and stones and left buried there.

A year and a half or so later, the Spaniards conquered this land. Approximately a year after settling the city of San Francisco de la Victoria, the general Martín Hurtado de Abierto ordered that they search for the bones of the father, and father Diego López de Ayala, the vicar of that city, buried them in the church. Before that, he said mass, and this vicar came out with the governor to receive [the bones] in a procession with many natives and all the citizens of the city. The bones of the deceased were carried with much sorrow and veneration. They were buried in the city church. They first laid them in a box that was then placed under the ground, where they remain until the present.

This witness was present during the procession and the funeral, and what she has said is the truth as she knows it, following the vow she has taken. Judging from her appearance, she seemed to be around 50 years old. She did not sign, because she did not know how to. [The testimony] was signed by the corregidor and interpreter Don Antonio de Monrroy [Portocarrero], [and] Juan de Peralta, before me, Antonio de Olave, scribe of the district. (Bauer et al. 2014: 63 65; authors' translation)

Juan Gualpa, then a carpenter by trade, was the next person to be interviewed.[13] Gualpa had served as a captain under Titu Cusi Yupanqui and at the time of his testimony was married to Angelina Llacsachuqui. He is especially critical of Fray Marcos's harsh treatment of converts and describes the friar beating the father of a young boy who was improperly baptized. Gualpa also describes in unusual detail the two friars' journey to Vilcabamba during the rainy season of 1570 and their return to the town of Puquiura about three weeks later; perhaps indicating that he was with them during their trip. Gualpa also adds some interesting details concerning the circumstances of Titu Cusi Yupanqui's sudden death in Vitcos. He states that the Inca had been fencing with Pando on the afternoon before his death and that in the middle of the night Pando and a servant of Titu Cusi Yupanqui's, named Gaspar Sulcayana, gave the Inca a whipped egg white to help him recover from his illness. Gualpa, like the speaker before him, also indicates that Angelina Polan Quilaco had turned the crowd against Pando and Ortiz after the Inca had died. He also states that he made the coffin for Ortiz when he was laid to rest in the church of San Francisco de la Victoria de Vilcabamba.

The final person to be interviewed on 25 January 1595 was Angelina Polan Quilaco. She had been a wife of Titu Cusi Yupanqui and was baptized along with him in the town of Puquiura in 1568. Polan Quilaco must have been under considerable pressure, since the two individuals who spoke before her on that same day indicated that her panicked reaction to Titu Cusi Yupanqui's sudden death had played a role in the deaths of Pando and Ortiz. In what is the shortest statement of the 1595 and 1599–1600 investigations, Polan Quilaco stated that she knew nothing specific about the matters under investigation.

Three more interviews were held with Quechua speakers from Lucma two days later, on 27 January. Alonso Tisspo was interviewed first. Tisspo stated that seven or eight days after the death of Titu Cusi Yupanqui, he had seen the captured Ortiz being led by angry Inca loyalists in a place called Matipampa, half a league from Marcanay, as he was traveling on the trail from Vilcabamba to Vitcos. Tisspo states that he later heard that the friar had been killed, and he offered the names of the five Inca captains who were responsible for beating and killing Ortiz—Curi Paucar,[14] Guandopa,[15] Canarco, Tumi, and Atoc.[16] Although Tisspo's testimony suggests that he had only witnessed the beating of Ortiz, other individuals who were interviewed later placed him among the leaders responsible for Ortiz's death.

Juan Quispe was the second inhabitant of Lucma to be interviewed that day. He suggests that both of the Inca's wives, Angelina Llacsachuqui and Angelina Polan Quilaco, had incited the crowd against Ortiz and Pando. Quispe also states that while he had seen Ortiz dragged from the village in the direction of Vilcabamba after the failed mass to resurrect the Inca, he played no part in these actions since he was involved in the preparation of the Inca's mummy.[17] It is important to note that Juan Quispe does not mention hitting Ortiz in the face nor does he refer to his own disabled arm. These absences are intriguing since many later witnesses accused him of striking Ortiz and suggest that God caused his right arm to wither as a result of this act.

The third person to be interviewed on 27 January 1595 was Francisco Haravaca. His testimony adds the interesting detail that colored *chicha* was poured over the grave of Ortiz. The final testimony from Villa Rica de Argete was taken more than a month later.[18] On 2 March 1595 the Quechua-speaking Francisco Condorpuri, who had been an eyewitness to the beating and killing of Ortiz, was interviewed. He suggests that saltpeter was also sprinkled on top of Ortiz's grave.

The following day Fray Pedro de Aguiar requested that another official be named to hear additional witnesses who were residing in the valley of Hoyara, as the corregidor Monroy Portocarrero could not make the journey due to his duties in Villa Rica de Argete. Monroy Portocarrero granted the request and authorized Cristóbal de Aróstegui, *alguacil mayor* of the Vilcabamba province, to carry out this function on his behalf.[19] With this new appointment, the tribunal slowly began to work its way back toward Cuzco, stopping occasionally to take new testimonies.

A deposition was taken on 7 March 1595 in the sugar mill of Chuquillusca[20] from Martín Pérez de Aponte, the first Spaniard to be interviewed by the tribunal. Pérez de Aponte notes that he had lived in the Vilcabamba region for eighteen or nineteen years and that he had frequently heard people discuss the death of Ortiz. Pérez de Aponte is also the first witness to tell the story of a man named Quispe, whose arm was said to have immediately withered after he struck Ortiz in the face.[21] Interpreted as a divine act, the punishment of Quispe was later repeated in many other testimonies, and the story holds a prominent place in both Murúa's ([ca. 1616] 2008) and Calancha's ([1638] 1981) chronicles.

Two more Spaniards, Maria de Villalobos and Luisa de Niebla, were interviewed on 9 March 1595 at a hacienda in the Hoyara Valley. Villalobos, who must been one of the first Spanish women to enter the area, states that she had arrived twenty-two years before. She also adds the interesting detail that *chupas* (coca bags) were made from Ortiz's clothes after his death. Niebla arrived in the Vilcabamba region about the same time as Villalobos. She states that much of her information came from Doña Maria de Riveros (the wife of Jerónimo de Costilla[22]), who had spoken with Fray Marcos after he returned to Cuzco as well as from Juana Guerrero.[23] Niebla's testimony includes the intriguing statement that the earth from beneath where Ortiz had prayed and held mass was dug up after his death and thrown into a river.

Two days later, two additional testimonies were recorded in Socospata, a small village located near the Chuquichaca Bridge over the Urubamba River, the traditional entrance into the Vilcabamba region. The first interview was provided by Juana Guerrero, who had been the wife of Martín Pando and was living with him at the time of the Inca's death. Guerrero's testimony is especially important since it is rich in details not provided by other witnesses. For example, she tells of Garcia's and Ortiz's difficult journey to the town of Vilcabamba at the height of the rainy season.[24] She also describes an unusual event that occurred while the two Augustinians visited Titu Cusi Yupanqui in the town of Vilcabamba. Guerrero states that several pairs of lowland women, dressed as friars, came to where the Augustinians were staying and the priests believed that these provocative actions were meant to humiliate them. While the true intent of the women is difficult to decipher, it is possible, as noted by Hemming (1970), that the women were simply dressed in their traditional white cotton tunics and the priests misunderstood their motivations. Guerrero also recalls the priests' return to Puquiura, the burning of the Yurak Rumi shrine (also called Chuquipalta), and the death of a Spanish miner named Romero who entered the Vilcabamba region several months later. Furthermore, as an eyewitness to the events, she provides very detailed descriptions of the deaths of Titu Cusi Yupanqui and Ortiz. Guerrero's testimony is a detailed and rich description of the events. It is long but worth quoting in full:

> On 11 March of 1595 in the settlement of Socospata, which is under the jurisdiction of the city of San Francisco de la Victoria in this province of Vilcabamba, Father Pedro de Aguiar presented a citizen of that city, Juana Guerrero, as a witness to provide information. She swore in accordance with law to tell the truth before the Alguacil Mayor. When she was asked about the subject in question, this witness said that she has lived in the province since three years [before] it was conquered by the Spaniards, [and] that she lived there with

Martín Pando, her first husband, who served as secretary of the Inca. During that time in the province, she knew Fathers Fray Marcos and Fray Diego of the Lord of Saint Augustine Order, who [both] preached and indoctrinated the Inca and his followers; catechizing and baptizing them. In this way, Fray Marcos baptized Cusitito [i.e., Titu Cusi] Yupanqui, who was at that time Inca and lord of this land.

After some time, Fray Marcos decided to leave for Cuzco having received permission to do so by his prelate. After which he started his journey [but] the Inca learned of this and sent [people] after him. [The Inca] said how he [Marcos] was leaving without his permission, and ordered him not to go before someone else came to fill in his place. Fray Diego arrived a few days later, and after a month or so, the Inca took them from Puquiura, where he lived, to the town of Vilcabamba. Following the road, he made them enter a river that they needed to cross, where the water reached to their waists. This was done openly to make them think how difficult the road and the land were, so that they would not have the will to remain there.

When [the Fathers] arrived at Vilcabamba, the Inca ordered the Inca women that were in the town to go and talk to the religious men in pairs and dressed like friars, as a way of mocking and scorning them. On arriving at the town, he [i.e., the Inca] housed them outside of it, so that they could not see the rituals and *mochaderos* [that were in it]. They stayed there for about eight days, and later they returned to the town of Puquiura with some of the natives that had come with them, while the Inca remained in the town of Vilcabamba. All that this witness has said so far, she heard it from her husband, Martín Pando.

A month or so after the Fathers returned to the town of Puquiura, this witness saw that some natives came looking for them and told them [that] near Vitcos, in a place called Chuquipalta, there was a white stone above a spring from which many dreadful death curses were cast upon them, because the Devil was there and because when they past it they no [longer] prayed to it nor gave it offerings as they had in the past. And they asked the fathers who were there to exorcise it and deliver them from that evil. And so those Religious went there with a number of Indians and young men carrying firewood and they exorcised and burned it. And since that was done, no harm has come to any Indian. Around eight days later, Fray Marcos left the province and only Fray Diego remained administrating the sacraments to the natives. During this time, a Spaniard named Romero entered the province saying that he was a gold miner, and he requested permission from the Inca to look for [gold]. He left with [the Inca's] permission to do so, and as requested he brought [gold] to show to him. As soon as [the Inca] saw [the gold], the Inca ordered him beheaded, and they threw him into the river. The Father [Diego] learned of this when he noticed a disturbance at the house of the Inca, and he ran to [see] what was happening. When the Inca saw [Father Diego], he sent word to him that he should go to his house and to let him kill that man [Romero]; if not, [the Inca] would also kill him. So the Father turned back grieving and crying as he realized that he could not redress the [situation]. [Later] he sent a boy of the doctrine to the Inca to ask him for mercy [and] to give him the corpse so that he could be buried. [But the Inca said no.] During the night the Father went to the river searching for the corpse so that he could bury it, but he never found it. Having learned this, the Inca sent word to the Father to stop searching for the corpse of the man, [and] if he went out to do so the following night that he would be killed.

Five days after the death of Romero, the Inca suddenly died because of a pain in his side or drunkenness, bleeding from his mouth and nose. This [agony] lasted less than twenty-four hours. It was openly known that the Inca had gone to the *mochadero* where his father was killed and that when he grew weary of crying, he returned to his house, sweating and tired, where he drank wine and ate, which caused him pain, and he died that night, as stated above.

Following the death of the Inca, his captains captured Fray Diego. His hands and arms were tied behind his back in such a way and so hard that his ribs became dislocated. He was kept in this way during the entire night [near] a bonfire under careful vigilance. In the morning, around eight or ten, he was untied, ordered to say mass and to resurrect the Inca, since he had preached that his God was capable of doing this. He [Fray Diego] answered them that although he was a sinner, in his mass he would pray to God to grant [the Inca good] health if he was alive, and if he was dead, that he would be sent to serve His Majesty. Since the Father was extremely exhausted due to the torments he had been put through and he was not able to move [because] of the dislocated bones in his chest, one of his torturers threw him to the floor, stepped on top of his chest, and pulled him up with his hands, while kicking him hard, which caused him much suffering.

Later he went to the church, got dressed, [and] started his mass with much devotion, stopping [at times] for long interval[s]. When he was [reading] the gospel and the words of the canon, so many tears flowed from him that they soaked the missal and the corporals [i.e., the communion clothes]. Having finished the mass, the natives tied him up again screaming and shouting; and questioning him why the Inca was not resuscitated. [He answered that it] was not God's will to resuscitate him.

Then a rope was put around his waist and he was tied to a cross that was brought from the cemetery, and was told to walk inland. He asked for something to eat, and they brought him two hard biscuits that the Father kept in his *petaca*. After eating them, he asked for some water, and he was brought urine and saltpeter mixed with other bitter concoctions. When he tasted its bitterness, he refused to drink. The captains approached him and threatened him with spears [saying] that he would drink; if not, they would kill him. So the Father drank it. On finishing drinking, he raised his eyes to the sky and said: "For the love of God!" He was untied from the cross and from there he was taken toward Marcanay. He was slapped, hit with sticks, shoved, and they spit in his face. To all this the Father said: "For the love of God! What else do I deserve?"

This witness saw all that has been said [above] with her own eyes. She [also] saw when he [Fray Diego] was untied from the cross, and an ignorant and shameless native named Quispe slapped him to show off. Because of this, his hand and entire arm withered. He still lives in this province with his withered arm and hand. It is openly known among the natives that while the Father was tortured in the way described, the captains ordered all the sorcerers to gather and foretell what would happen, and how it would all end if the Father died. Having consulted among each other and the devil, they answered that the blood of the blessed Father would claim [justice] before God, and that soon because of that the offspring of the Inca would be devastated. About a year later, the Spaniards entered in this land. They conquered and won it, and the Inca was beheaded.

This witness [also] heard in public from the natives that, as they were carrying him [Fray Diego] to Marcanay, where he was killed, at each camp where they spent the night he was whipped, beaten with sticks, and subjected to many other ill treatments. On arriving at Marcanay, and after being pulled [along the way], he was hit in the neck with an axe and killed. He was buried in a hole upside down, and a palm stick was driven through his anus. After he was buried, they threw saltpeter, leaves, and red *chicha* over [the grave].

[She said] that after this land was conquered [by the Spaniards], this witness saw Alonso de la Cueva, who is her current husband, and other soldiers bringing [back] the body of the blessed Father on orders from the governor. [People] came to receive [Fray Diego's remains], making a procession that started in the city of San Francisco de la Victoria. [Fray Diego] was brought inside the church, and after Father Diego López de Ayala, who at that time [was the] vicar, said mass, [Fray Diego] was placed in a casket and buried.

This witness saw the natives rip the habits and clothes of the father, and she learned that some *chuspas* and tunics that the natives were carrying had been made out of the habits. They did this because the habits and church clothes were given [to the natives] when they caught the Father to martyr him. Three or four months after [Fray Diego] was brought back [to San Francisco de la Victoria], they took them [i.e., the *chuspas* and tunics] away. This was openly known, and later they took [all] this to the place called the Gallows of the Inca, where they stamped on them and left them.

This is the truth and [all] that she knows following the vow she has taken. She said she was around 45 years old. She did not sign because she did not know how to. It was signed by the Alguacil Mayor, Cristóbal [de] Aróstegui, before me, Antonio de Olave, public scribe. (Bauer et al. 2014: 80–84; authors' translation)

Juana Guerrero's testimony is also intriguing for what is not said. As noted above, she was married to the Inca's scribe, Martín Pando, who was killed by Inca loyalists following the death of the Titu Cusi Yupanqui. Yet there is no mention of Martín Pando's death in her testimony.

The second person interviewed on 11 March 1595 in the village of Socospata was Alonso de la Cueva (figure 7.5).[25] He was a member of the 1572 expedition that invaded Vilcabamba and was one of the soldiers that retrieved Ortiz's body from its burial place. He was married to Juana Guerrero when the testimonies were recorded. It is also worth noting that de la Cueva refers to the Inca as *el inca único*. This is a translation of the Quechua term Sapay Inca (the unique Inca), suggesting the de la Cueva may have had a greater grasp of Quechua than many of his Spanish contemporaries.

De la Cueva received much of his information on the deaths of the Inca and Ortiz through conversations with Diego Aucalli, who was an Inca captain at the time of the deaths and who appears to have been in charge of the mummification of the Inca. Apparently, Aucalli also told de la Cueva a unique story of seeing a large snake slither through the remains of a burning building soon after the death of Ortiz. Aucalli believed that this was an evil omen foretelling the fall of Vilcabamba and the end of the Inca kings.

After the interviews were conducted in Socospata, the delegation returned to the town of Vilcabamba de la Victoria. On 17 March 1595 a complete copy of all the testimonies so far collected and the various documents from local officials was made by the Augustine scribe Antonio de Olave at the bequest of Antonio de Monroy in San Francisco de la Victoria de Vilcabamba. The original testimonies were most likely retained by the local scribe, Díaz de Bermudez, when the delegation left the town. Antonio de Olave took the notarized copy with him and returned to Cuzco.

On his return to Cuzco, Fray Pedro de Aguiar informed the lieutenant corregidor of Cuzco, Jerónimo Gutiérrez de Montealegre, of the information he

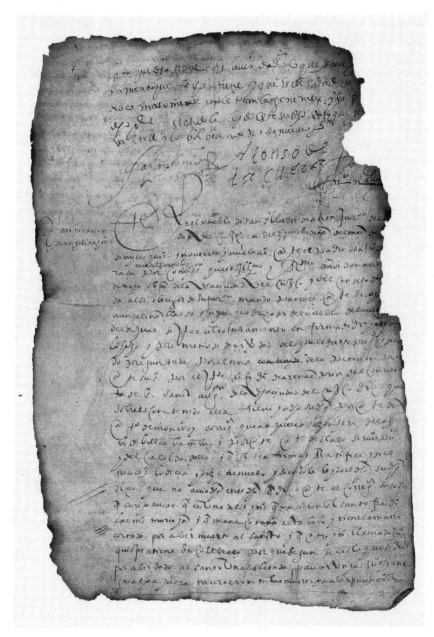

FIGURE 7.5. *The final part of Alonso de la Cueva's testimony and the first part of Angelina Llacsa Chuqui's testimony, 1599. Note de la Cueva's simple and trebling signature. Courtesy Biblioteca Nacional de Lima SM 110: fol. 7.*

had collected on the death of Diego Ortiz and the miracles that were associated with him. Aguiar also requested and received permission to conduct additional interviews in Cuzco. He began these interviews, in the presence of Gutiérrez de Montealegre, in Cuzco on 17 and 18 August 1595. Aguiar first interviewed Juana de Ayala Ponce de León,[26] the widow of Martín Hurtado de Arbieto, the general who led the raid into the Vilcabamba region in 1572 and who had been given the governorship of the province by the crown in return for his work. Aguiar also interviewed two of Juana de Ayala Ponce de León's daughters (Leonor Hurtado de Mendoza[27] and Mariana Hurtado de Mendoza[28]) and two daughters of Luisa de Ribas (Leonor de Ojeda and Lorenza de Ojeda).[29] Besides outlining the basic events that occurred during the death of Ortiz, these women indicate that Juana de Ayala Ponce de León's toothaches were cured and that the eyesight of Mencia Salcedo de Arbieto, an illegitimate daughter of Hurtado de Arbieto, was restored after they prayed at Ortiz's remains.[30] Three days later, on 21 August, Luisa de Ribas repeated nearly the same information.

The final interview took place in Cuzco on 29 August 1595 with Juan de Valdivieso and concerned the miraculous healing of a young boy after he visited the grave of Ortiz. Sometime after this interview, the case was reviewed by a set of secular judges in Cuzco; they concluded that the case did not merit further action by the church.[31] This must have come as a hard blow to the Augustinians who had spent great efforts developing the case and preparing the documents.

It is critical to point out, however, that one important event that occurred during the 1595 investigation in the Vilcabamba region was *not* recorded by the Augustinians. At the end of his investigation in the Vilcabamba region, Fray Aguiar asked the township for permission to move the bones of Ortiz from the local church to the Augustine monastery in Cuzco. When his request was turned down, Fray Aguiar arranged for Luis Hernández Castillo, a citizen of San Francisco de la Victoria de Vilcabamba, to steal the bones in the middle of the night.[32] Hernández Castillo and Fray Aguiar then met outside of town around two in the morning, and the friar carried the remains to Cuzco. The theft of the religious relics was noticed the following day since Hernández Castillo left both the church door and the burial crypt open.[33] The removal of Ortiz's bones from the Vilcabamba region caused considerable outrage among its citizens, especially since their removal was perceived to have caused the sudden return of mosquitoes to the region.

THE 1599–1600 INVESTIGATION

The Ortiz case was reopened four years later on 8 November 1599 when Fray Diego de Arenas, then the prior of the Augustine monastery in Cuzco, petitioned the bishop of Cuzco, Antonio de Raya (1594–1606), to grant permission for a commission of ecclesiastical officials to review the previous findings. In his petition Fray Arenas expresses concern that the secular judges who previously heard the case did not fully appreciate its gravity.

In preparation for this new investigation, the members of the Augustinian Order had already met on 22 September 1599 and authorized two friars, Lucas Gasco and Patricio Melez, to carry out various tasks, including collecting funds, calling witnesses, hearing testimony, and requesting written evidence. These appointments appear to have been premature since Gasco authorized Fray Alonso de Figueredo to take his place on the same day that the bishop received the petition for the new investigation; Melez is not mentioned again in the documents (figure 7.6).

Having received permission to renew the investigation from the bishop of Cuzco, Figueredo arrived in the town of San Francisco de la Victoria de Vilcabamba on 16 November 1599. He presented his credentials to Bartolomé de Arica, the priest in charge of the province, and began taking testimonies two days later. Over the course of the next week seven people were interviewed. Three of these seven, Francisco Condorpuri, Juan Quispe, and Martín Pérez de Aponte had been interviewed in 1595 and reconfirmed their earlier testimonies that were read to them. New testimonies were taken from Antonio de Vibanco, Luis Hernández Castillo, Francisco Pérez Fonseca, and Pedro Gómez Mañón. The latter two had been members of the 1572 raid into Vilcabamba.

Although the witnesses provided few new details on the death of Ortiz, all of their testimonies contain bitter complaints against Fray Aguiar for stealing the bones of Ortiz from the local church four years earlier, which they blamed for the subsequent return of mosquitoes to the region. So what had begun as a review of the three-decades-old murder of the cleric quickly became a forum in which the inhabitants of the Vilcabamba region could vent their anger against the Augustinians.

On 23 November, Figueredo began his journey back to Cuzco. Along the way he tried to find individuals who had been involved in the 1595 investigation. The following day Figueredo arrived in the Hoyara Valley, where he, along with a local priest named Gregorio Sánchez de Aedo,[34] reinterviewed Alonso Tibiso, Maria de Villalobos, and Juana Guerrero.[35] Each of these individuals simply reconfirmed their 1595 testimonies.[36]

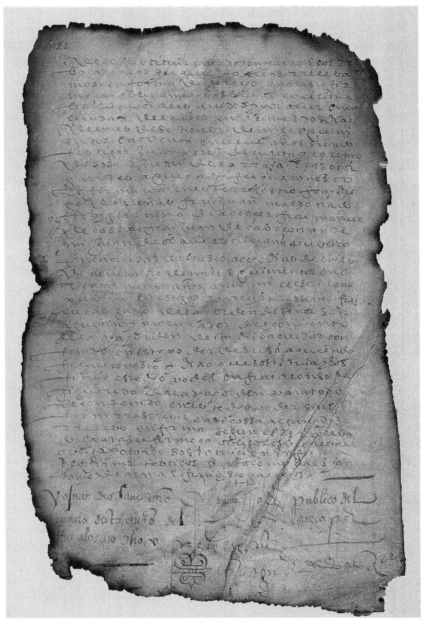

Figure 7.6. *Fray Lucas Gasco's authorization for Fray Alonso de Figueredo to assume investigative powers, 1599. Note the rubric used by Juan de Olave, public scribe. Courtesy Biblioteca Nacional de Lima SM 110: fol. 20.*

On 29 November 1599 the investigators arrived at the town of Amaibamba, where with the help of the local priest named Antonio de Solorzano and a local citizen named Francisco Gallegos they were able to find Alonso de la Cueva. He also reconfirmed his previous testimony.[37]

A month later Angelina Llacsachuqui was interviewed by a commission member, Juan de Lizarazu, in the town of Anta. The former wife of the Inca reconfirmed her four-year-old testimony and added the observation that many of the Inca captains who had participated in the death of Ortiz had come to bad ends. This was taken as further proof of divine intervention.

Additional interviews were conducted by Fray Diego de Arenas in Cuzco on 16, 22, and 24 January 1600. These included a new statement from Francisca de Arbieto, a daughter of Martín Hurtado de Arbieto, as well as reconfirmations of previous statements by Leonor Hurtado de Mendoza, Juan de Valdivieso, Lorenza de Ojeda, Luisa de Ribas, and Luisa de Nieblas. The penultimate testimony was provided on 20 February 1600 by Baltasar de Ocampo Conejeros, who would later write his own history of the Vilcabamba region (Ocampo Conejeros [1611] 2013; see document 2 this volume). The final interview involved Antonio Álvarez, one of the participants in the 1572 campaign. It was conducted on 8 March 1600.

Later that same year, Fray Diego de Arenas petitioned Bishop Raya to have Ortiz's remains, which were still being housed in the Augustine convent in Cuzco, transferred to an eminent place until he was canonized by the Holy Apostolic See. On 20 August 1600 Bishop Raya granted permission for Ortiz's bones to be reinterred on the right side of the main altar of the Augustine convent. However, at the same time, the bishop denied further action on Ortiz's canonization and ordered that the Augustinians inform their parishioners that Ortiz was not a saint. The reinterment was delayed but finally occurred on 4 January 1607.[38]

The final eyewitness account related to these unusual events was written by Baltasar de Ocampo Conejeros who participated in the 1600 investigation. In a long account written to the viceroy in 1611, in which he describes his life in Vilcabamba, Ocampo confirms that the remains of Ortiz were buried in Cuzco. He writes: "[Ortiz's remains are] presently in a tabernacle in the convent of Saint Augustine in the city of Cuzco, on the gospel side of the main chapel, next to the cross" (Ocampo Conejeros [1611] 2013: 30).[39] The Augustinians left Cuzco around 1840 after their convent was destroyed amid civil strife (Azevedo 1982). The current whereabouts of Ortiz's remains are unknown, and mosquitoes continue to plague the Vilcabamba region.

NOTES

1. This study was originally published in Spanish along with the transcriptions of the described documents in Bauer et al. (2014).

2. Levillier indicates that part of the report is housed in the AGN in Lima (Levillier 1935: 359) under the title "Información hecha a instancia de Fray Jerónimo Núñez, Prior del Convento de San Agustín del Cuzco, de los servicios hechos a S. M. por su religión en el Perú. Septiembre de 1582 A de I (71–3–24. Leg. 316)."

3. Testimonies were taken from García de Melo, Martín de Olmos, Damián de la Bandera, Jerónimo Costilla (who was also interviewed in 1595), Sancho Ortiz de Orúe, Gómez de Tordoya, Juan Pérez de Prado, García Rodríguez, Juan de Castañeda, and Pedro de Córdoba Mecía (Levillier 1935: 342–344).

4. It is worth noting that an early version of Murúa's chronicle, dating to about 1590, does not mention Ortiz (Murúa [ca. 1590] 2004). This suggests that Murúa learned the details of Ortiz's and Titu Cusi Yupanqui's deaths only after the Augustinian investigations.

5. The testimonies taken in the Vilcabamba region in 1595 were copied on 17 March 1595 by Antonio de Olave, the public scribe of Vilcabamba, and the authenticity of the new document was verified by Juan Díaz de Bermudez, the public scribe of Villa Rica de Argete (also written as Hargete), before they were sent to Cuzco. Long after the close of the 1599–1600 investigation, the Ortiz documents were again copied (on 4 January 1607, the day that they were interred) by a public scribe in Cuzco named Diego de la Carrera Ron. This final version was sent to Rome and is now housed in the Archivo de la Postulación General (see Aparicio López 1989; Bauer et al. 2014).

6. The first half of this publication is from Angelina Llacsa Chuqui's testimony while the second half is from Alonso de la Cueva's testimony. The misnumbering of the folios most likely occurred after the fire that destroyed much of the document.

7. The Lima copy of Baltasar de Ocampo Conejeros's testimony has since been lost.

8. In short, it appears that a fire destroyed much of the first half of the manuscript but spared parts of the second half.

9. From the handwriting on the folios, we estimate that fourteen different scribes were involved in the production of the Lima document as it now exists; many others would have been involved in the production of the complete document.

10. Villa Rica de Argete, formerly known as Oncoy by the indigenous population, was a small settlement established by the Spaniards around 1586, near the headwaters of the Vilcabamba River, to exploit newly found silver deposits. This mining center grew in importance, and around 1596 the town of San Francisco de la Victoria de Vilcabamba was moved, from its original location near the modern town of Hoyara to Villa Rica de Argete, to better support the mining operations of the region. With this

move the name Villa Rica de Argete slowly ceased to be used, and the new community was referred to as San Francisco de la Victoria de Vilcabamba.

11. Angelina Polan Quilaco was baptized by Prior Juan de Vivero at the same time as Titu Cusi Yupanqui.

12. Parts of Llacsa Chuqui's testimony was first published by Romero and Urteaga (1916: 133–138).

13. In a much later testimony (17 January 1600), Francisca de Arbieto suggests that Juan Gualpa delivered the death blow to Ortiz; however, this statement is not supported by other eyewitnesses.

14. Curi Paucar is also mentioned by Ocampo Conejeros ([1611] 2013: 32, 39). He was hanged in Cuzco in 1572 before Tupac Amaru was executed.

15. Perhaps this is a reference to Huallpa Yupanqui, the uncle of Tupac Amaru, who was hanged in Cuzco in 1572 before Tupac Amaru was executed.

16. Murúa ([ca. 1616] 1987: 262) notes that, following Manco Inca's death, Atoc Supa was appointed as the leader of Vilcabamba until Sayri Tupac came of age. This information was later copied by Cobo ([1653] 1979: 176).

17. Juan Quispe was interviewed again in 1599.

18. It is not clear what the commission did during the month of February.

19. Antonio de Olave continued to serve as scribe.

20. Battles between the Incas and the Spaniards took place at Chuquillusca in 1539 and 1572. Its exact location is not known, but may have occurred near the modern town of Lucma at the site of Pincollunca (Bauer, Fonseca Santa Cruz, and Aráoz Silva 2015: 31, 32)

21. Within the testimonies it is noted that Quispe was still living as late as 1600 and that his unusually long life was granted by God, so that all could see what happened to those who would strike His earthly representatives. Calancha ([1638] 1981) states that Quispe lived until 1624.

22. Jerónimo Costilla was a powerful landowner who lived in Cuzco.

23. Juana Guerrero was interviewed two days later.

24. Martín Pando, and perhaps Guerrero herself, was in the town of Vilcabamba at the time of the Augustinians' visit.

25. Because both of these testimonies are unusually long and detailed, they were used extensively by Murúa ([ca. 1616] 2008) and Calancha ([1638] 1981) in their retellings of the death of Ortiz.

26. Juana de Ayala Ponce de León suggests that Diego Ortiz gave the Inca an egg with a little pepper on the evening that he died, while Leonor de Ojeda suggests that the Inca was given an egg with sulfur.

27. At the time of her interview, Leonor Hurtado de Mendoza was married to Diego de Gamarra. Her testimony is notable for the fact that she refers to the Inca city of Vilcabamba as Vilcabamba la vieja (Vilcabamba the old).

28. At the time of the interview, Mariana Hurtado de Mendoza was married to Luis Catano de Cazana. Her testimony supports the 1595 testimony of Juan Gualpa, who suggests that Pando and Titi Cusi Yupanqui were fencing ("jugó a las armas") on the day of his death.

29. These women suggest that Martín Pando was involved in the killing of Ortiz, an accusation that is not supported in other testimonies.

30. The recording of miracles in association with Ortiz's remains was an important part of the canonization process. Other miracles, or at least signs of God's favoring of Ortiz, included the observation that his body did not decompose even though it was buried for more than a year in the Vilcabamba region before it was recovered, that two red roses that seemed to spill blood had grown on his face while he was buried, and that mosquitoes disappeared from the region at his death and then returned when his bones were stolen. Furthermore, there were several incidents of healings associated with visitations to his body, including those of Juana de Ayala Ponce de León, Mencia Salcedo Hurtado de Arbieto, and an unnamed five-year-old boy.

31. It is believed that Ortiz's nomination for sainthood did not gain momentum partly because he had been killed, along with Martín Pando, for his incorrect association with the death of Titu Cusi rather than being martyred for his Christian beliefs alone (Hemming 1970).

32. In an interview in 1599 Hernández Castillo himself admits that he entered the church and removed the bones from Ortiz's coffin, placing them in a large sack

33. The removal of the bones was first noted by Francisco Sicha.

34. Gregorio Sánchez de Aedo, who had been the priest in the town of Lucma for more than three years, also gave a brief statement concerning Juan Quispe's withered arm.

35. Lucas de Sagartequieta served as translator.

36. Melchor de Frias served as the notary, and Lucas de Sagartequieta worked as the translator.

37. Francisco Gallegos served as the notary.

38. The scribe Juan de Olave witnessed the transfer of the remains to their new location, as ordered by the bishop of Cuzco.

39. "... como al presente está, en un sagrario en el convento del Señor San Agustín en la ciudad del Cuzco, en el lado del Evangelio de la capilla mayor, junto al crucero." The convent was recently converted into a Marriott hotel.

Acosta, José de. (1590) 2002. *Natural and Moral History of the Indies*. Edited by Jane E. Mangan, with an introduction and commentary by Walter D. Mignolo. Translated by Frances López-Morillas. Durham: Duke University Press. http://dx.doi.org/10.1215/9780822383932.

Adorno, Rolena. 2008. "Censorship and Approbation in Murúa's *Historia General del Piru*." In *The Getty Murúa: Essays on the Making of Martín de Murúa's "Historia general del Piru,"* edited by Thomas B. F. Cummins and Barbara Anderson, 95–124. J. Paul Getty Museum Ms. Ludwig XIII 16. Los Angeles: Getty Research Institute.

Albornoz, Cristóbal de. (ca. 1582) 1984. "Instrucción para descubrir todas las guacas del Pirú y sus camayos y haziendas," edited by Pierre Duviols and included in "Albornoz y el espacio ritual andino prehispánico," by Pierre Duviols. *Revista Andina* 2 (1): 169–222.

Aparicio López, Teófilo. 1989. *Fray Diego Ortiz, misionero y mártir del Perú: un proceso original del siglo XVI*. Valladolid, Spain: Ed. Estudio Agustiniano.

Azevedo, Paulo Ormindo D. de. 1982. *Cusco, cuidad histórica: Continuidad y cambio*. Cuzco: Promoción Editorial.

Barriga, Victor M. 1942. *Los mercedarios en el Perú en el siglo XVI: Documentos del Archivo General de Indias de Sevilla 1518–1600*. Vol. 3. Arequipa, Peru: Colmena.

Bauer, Brian S., Teófilo Aparicio López, Jesús Galiano Blanco, Madeleine Halac-Higashimori, and E. Gabriel Cantarutti. 2014. *Muerte, entierros y milagros de Fray Diego Ortiz: Política y religión en Vilcabamba, S. VXI*. Cuzco: Ceques editores.

DOI: 10.5876/9781607324263.c008

Bauer, Brian S., and Antonio Coello Rodríguez. 2007. *The Hospital of San Andrés (Lima, Peru) and the Search for the Royal Mummies of the Incas.* Fieldiana Anthropology, n.s., no. 31. Chicago: Field Museum of Natural History.

Bauer, Brian S., and Madeleine Halac-Higashimori. 2013. *Baltasar de Ocampo Conejeros y la Provincia de Vilcabamba.* Cuzco: Ceques editorial.

Bauer, Brian S., Lucas C. Kellett, and Miriam Aráoz Silva. 2010. *The Chanka: Archaeological Research in Andahuaylas (Apurimac), Peru.* Los Angeles: Cotsen Institute of Archaeology, University of California.

Bauer, Brian S., Javier Fonseca Santa Cruz, and Miriam Aráoz Silva. 2015. *Vilcabamba and the Archaeology of Inca Resistance.* Los Angeles: Cotsen Institute of Archaeology, University of California.

Bauer, Brian S., Miriam Aráoz Silva, and George S. Burr. 2012. "The Destruction of the Yurac Rumi Shrine (Vilcabamba, Cusco Department)." *Andean Past* 10:195–211.

Betanzos, Juan de. (1557) 1996. *Narrative of the Incas.* Translated and edited by Roland Hamilton and Dana Buchanan. Austin: University of Texas Press.

Bingham, Hiram. 1912a. "The Ascent of Coropuna." *Harper's Monthly* (March): 489–502.

Bingham, Hiram. 1912b. "Preliminary Report of the Yale Peruvian Expedition." *Bulletin of the American Geographical Society* 44 (1): 20–26. http://dx.doi.org/10.2307/199739.

Bingham, Hiram. 1912c. "A Search for the Last Inca Capital." *Harper's Monthly* (October): 695–705.

Bingham, Hiram. 1912d. "Vitcos, the Last Inca Capital." *Proceedings of the American Antiquarian Society* 22 (April): 135–196.

Bingham, Hiram. 1914. "The Ruins of Espiritu Pampa, Peru." *American Anthropologist* 16 (2): 185–199. http://dx.doi.org/10.1525/aa.1914.16.2.02a00010.

Calancha, Antonio de la. (1638) 1981. *Corónica moralizada del Orden de San Agustín en el Perú.* Edited by Ignacio Prado Pastor. Lima: Universidad Nacional Mayor de San Marcos, Editorial de la Universidad.

Cobo, Bernabé. (1653) 1956. "Historia del Nuevo Mundo." In *Obras de P. Bernabé Cobo de la Compañía de Jesús,* edited by P. Francisco Mateos. Biblioteca de Autores Españoles, vols. 91 and 92. Madrid: Ediciones Atlas.

Cobo, Bernabé. (1653) 1979. *History of the Inca Empire: An Account of the Indians' Customs and Their Origin together with a Treatise on Inca legends, History, and Social Institutions.* Edited and translated by Roland Hamilton. Austin: University of Texas Press.

Cook, David Noble, ed. 1975. *Tasa de la visita general de Francisco de Toledo.* Lima: Universidad Nacional Mayor de San Marcos, Seminario de Historia Rural Andina.

Covey, R. Alan. 2006. *How the Incas Built Their Heartland: State Formation and the Innovation of Imperial Strategies in the Sacred Valley, Peru.* Ann Arbor: University of Michigan Press.

Covey, Alan, and Donato Amado Gonzáles. 2008. *Imperial Transformations in Sixteenth-Century Yucay, Peru: Memoirs of the Museum of Anthropology* Studies in Latin American Ethnohistory and Archaeology, vol. 6. Ann Arbor: University of Michigan Press.

Cueva, Alfonso de la. [1595] 1916. "Testimony on the Death of Diego Ortiz (Socos-pata: 1599, incomplete)." In *Colección de libros y documentos referentes a la historia del Perú,* edited by Carlos A. Romero and Horacio H. Urteaga, ser. 1, vol. 2, appendix E, 135–137. Lima: Sanmarti.

Garcilaso de la Vega, Inca. (1609) 1723. *Primera parte de los comentarios reales, que tratan, del origen de los Incas, reyes, que fueron del Perù, . . .* Edited by Andrés González de Barcía Carballido y Zúñiga (under the pseudonym Gabriel Daza de Cardenas). Madrid: La Oficina Real.

Garcilaso de la Vega, Inca. (1609) 1970. *Royal Commentaries of the Incas and General History of Peru, Parts 1 and 2.* Translated by H. V. Livermore. Austin: University of Texas Press.

Guaman Poma de Ayala, Felipe. (ca. 1615) 1980. *El primer nueva crónica y buen gobierno.* Edited by John V. Murra and Rolena Adorno. Translated by Jorge I. Urioste. 3 vols. Mexico City: Siglo Veintiuno.

Guillén Guillén, Edmundo. 1977a. "Documentos inéditos para la historia de los Incas de Vilcabamba: La capitulación del gobierno español con Titi Cusi Yupanqui." *Historia y Cultura* (Lima) 10:47–93.

Guillén Guillén, Edmundo. 1977b. "Vilcabamba: La última capital del estado imperial inca." *Scientia et Praxis* (Lima) 10:126–155.

Guillén Guillén, Edmundo. 1979. *Visión peruana de la Conquista: La resistencia incaica a la invasión española.* Lima: Editorial Milla Batres.

Guillén Guillén, Edmundo. 1980. "'El Testimonio del Capitán Pedro Sarmiento de Gamboa.' Excerpt from the document 'Probanza de méritos de Juan Álvarez Maldonado . . . ,' included in the article 'El Testimonio del Capitán Pedro Sarmiento de Gamboa y el itinerario de la campaña española contra Thupa Amaro Inka: 1572.'" *Boletín de Lima* (9):22–40.

Guillén Guillén, Edmundo. 1981. "Titu Cusi Yupanqui y su tiempo." *Historia y Cultura (Lima)* 13–14:61–99.

Guillén Guillén, Edmundo. 1994. *La guerra de reconquista Inka: Historia épica de como los Inkas lucharon en defensa de la soberanía del Perú o Tawantinsuyo entre 1536 y 1572.* Lima: R. A. Ediciones.

Guillén Guillén, Edmundo. [1977] 2005. *Los Incas y el trágico final del Tawantinsuyo.* Lima: UAP and AHPA.

Hemming, John. 1970. *The Conquest of the Incas*. New York: Harcourt Brace Jovanovich.

Hyland, Sabine. 2003. *The Jesuit and the Incas: The Extraordinary Life of Padre Blas Valera, S. J.* Ann Arbor: University of Michigan Press.

Julien, Catherine J. 2006. Introduction to *History of How the Spaniards Arrived in Peru*, by Titu Cusi Yupanqui, i–xxix. Translated by Catherine Julien. Indianapolis: Hackett Publishing.

Las Casas, Bartolomé de. (1552) 1992. *The Devastation of the Indies: A Brief Account.* Translated by Herma Briffault. Baltimore: Johns Hopkins University Press.

Lee, Vincent R. 2000. *Forgotten Vilcabamba: Final Stronghold of the Incas*. Las Vegas: Empire Publishing.

Levillier, Roberto. 1925. *Gobernantes del Perú. Cartas y papeles, siglo XVI*. Vol. II. Madrid: Sucesores de Rivadeneira.

Levillier, Roberto. 1935. *Don Francisco de Toledo, supremo organizador del Perú: Su vida, su obra (1515–1582)*. Vol. I, *Años de andanzas y de guerras*. Buenos Aires: Biblioteca del Congreso Argentino.

Levillier, Roberto. 1940. *Don Francisco de Toledo, supremo organizador del Peru: su vida, su obra (1512–1582)*. 3 vols. Buenos Aires: Espasa-Calpe, S.A.

Lohmann Villena, Guillermo. 1941. "El Inga Titu Cussi Yupanqui y su entrevista con el oidor Matienzo, 1565." *Mercurio Peruano* 166:3–18.

Markham, Clements, ed. 1907. *Account of the Province of Vilcabamba and a Narrative of the Execution of the Inca Tupac Amaru by Captain Baltasar de Ocampo.* Supplement to *History of the Incas*, 203–247. Works Issued by the Hakluyt Society, ser. 2, vol. 22. London: Hakluyt Society.

Markham, Clements. 1913. "Narrative of the Route and Journey Made by Diego Rodríguez from the City of Cuzco to the Land of War of Manco Inca." In *The War of Quito and Inca Documents*, by Pedro de Cieza de Leon, 170–199. Works Issued by the Hakluyt Society, ser. 2, vol. 31. London: Hakluyt Society.

Markham, Clements. 1923. "Descripción y sucesos históricos de la provincia de Vilcabamba, por Baltasar de Ocampo." In *Las posesiones geográficas de las tribus que formaban el imperio de los incas*, 154–196. Lima: Sanmarti.

Matienzo, Juan. [1567] 1910. *Gobierno del Perú: Obra escrita en el siglo XVI por el Licenciado Don Juan Matienzo*. Buenos Aires: Compañía Sudamérica de billetes de banco.

Maúrtua, Victor M., ed. 1906. *Juicio de límites entre el Perú y Bolivia*. Vol. 7, *Vilcabamba*. Barcelona: Henrich y Comp.

Millones, Luis. 1990. *El retorno de las huacas: Estudios y documentos sobre el Taki Onqoy siglo XVI*. Lima: Instituto de Estudios Peruanos.

Molina, Cristóbal de. 2011. *Account of the Fables and Rites of the Incas.* Translated by Brian S. Bauer, Vania Smith, and Gabriel E. Cantarutti. Austin: University of Texas Press.

Murúa, Martín de. (ca. 1616) 1987. *Historia general del Perú*. Edited by Manuel Ballesteros Gaibrois. Crónicas de America, no. 35. Madrid: Historia 16.

Murúa, Martín de. (ca. 1590) 2004. *Códice Murúa: Historia y genealogía de los reyes incas del Perú del padre mercedario Fray Martín de Murúa: Códice Galvin*. Edited by Juan M. Ossio. Madrid: Testimonio Compañía Editorial.

Murúa, Martín de. (ca. 1616) 2008. *Historia General del Piru*. Los Angeles: Getty Research Institute. (Previously known as the Wellington manuscript.)

Nowack, Kerstin. 2004. "Las provisiones de Titu Cusi Yupanqui." *Revista Andina* 38:139–79.

Nowack, Kerstin, and Catherine Julien. 1999. "La campaña de Toledo contra los señores naturales andinos: el destierro de los Incas de Vilcabamba y Cuzco." *Historia y Cultura* (Lima) 23:15–81.

Ocampo Conejeros, Baltasar. (1611) 2013. "Descripción de la provincia de San Francisco de la Victoria de Vilcabamba." In *Baltasar de Ocampo Conejeros y la Provincia de Vilcabamba*, edited by Brian S. Bauer and Madeleine Halac-Higashimori, 19–56. Cuzco: Ceques editorial.

Oricain, Pablo José. (1790) 2004. *Compendio breve de varios discursos sobre diferentes materias, y noticias geográficas, comprensivas, a este obispado del Cuzco, que claman remedios espirituales*. Lima: Ministerio de Relaciones Exteriores del Perú.

Ossio, Juan M. 2008a. "Murúa, Martín de." In *Guide to documentary sources for Andean Studies 1530–1900*, edited by Joanne Pillsbury, 3:436–441. Norman: University of Oklahoma Press.

Ossio, Juan M. 2008b. "Murúa's Two Manuscripts: A Comparison." In *The Getty Murúa: Essays on the Making of Martín de Murúa's Historia General del Piru, J. Paul Getty Museum Ms. Ludwig XIII 16*, edited by Thomas B. F. Cummins and Barbara Anderson, 77–94. Los Angeles: Getty Research Institute.

Pietschmann, Richard, ed. (1565) 1910. "Bericht des Diego Rodriguez de Figueroa über seine Verhandlungen mit dem Inka Titu Cusi Yupanqui in den Anden von Villcapampa." In *Nachrichten von der Königlichen Gesellschaft der Wissenschaften zu Göttingen, Philologisch-historische Klasse*, 79–122. Berlin: Weidmannsche Buchhandlung.

Pizarro, Pedro. (1571) 1921. *Relation of the Discovery and Conquest of the Kingdoms of Peru*. Edited and translated by Philip Ainsworth Means. New York: Cortés Society.

Pizarro, Pedro. (1571) 1986. *Relación del descubrimiento y conquista de los reinos del Perú*. Lima: Pontificia Universidad Católica del Perú.

Porras Barrenechea, Raúl. 1986. *Los Cronistas del Perú (1528–1650)*. Lima: Banco de Crédito del Perú.

Regalado de Hurtado, Liliana. 1992. *Religión y evangelización en Vilcabamba 1572–1602*. Lima: Fondo Editorial de PUCP.

Rodríguez de Figueroa, Diego. (1565) 1910. "Relación del camino e viaje que
. . . hizo desde la ciudad del Cuzco a la tierra de Guerra de Manco Inga." In
*Nachrichten von der Königlichen Gesellschaft der Wissenschaften zu Göttingen,
Philologisch-historische Klasse*, edited by Richard Pietschmann, 90–112. Berlin:
Klasse aus dem Jahre.

Rodríguez de Figueroa, Diego. (ca. 1565) 1913. "Narrative of the route and journey
made by Diego Rodriguez from the city of Cuzco to the land of War of Manco
Inca who was in the Andes in insurrection against the service of His Majesty, and
of the affairs touching which he treated with the object of establishing peace, as
well as to induce the people to receive the evangelical doctrine of our Lord Jesus
Christ." In *The War of Quito and Inca Documents*, edited by Pedro de Cieza de León,
170–199. Translated and edited by Clements R. Markham. Works Issued by the
Hakluyt Society, ser. 2, vol. 31. London: Hakluyt Society.

Rodríguez de Figueroa, Diego. 1965. "Carta y Memorial de Diego Rodríguez de
Figueroa al Virrey Don Martin Enríquez sobre cosas tocantes a este reino y
mina de Potosí." In *Relaciones geográficas de Indias: Perú*, by Marcos Jiménez de la
Espada, ed. José Urbano Martínez Carreras, 1:63–67. Madrid: Ediciones Atlas.

Romero, Carlos A., and Horacio H. Urteaga. 1916. *Relación de la conquista del Perú
y hechos del Inca Manco II por D. Diego de Castro Tito Cussi Yupangui Inca. Notas
biograficas y concordancias del texto por Horacio H. Urteaga. Biografia de Tito Cusi
Yupangui por Carlos A. Romero*. Lima: Sanmarti.

Salazar, Antonio Baptista de. (1596) 1867. "De virreyes y gobernadores del Perú." In
*Colección de documentos inéditos, relativos al descubrimiento, conquista y organización
de las antiguas posesiones españolas*. Transcribed by Luis Torres de Mendoza,
8:212–293. Madrid: Imprenta de Frías y Compañía.

Sarmiento de Gamboa, Pedro. (1572) 2007. *The History of the Incas*. Translated and
edited by Brian S. Bauer and Vania Smith; introduction by Brian S. Bauer and
Jean Jacques Decoster. Austin: University of Texas Press.

Savoy, Gene. 1970. *Antisuyu: The Search for the Lost Cities of the Amazon*. New York:
Simon and Schuster.

Stirling, Stuart. 1999. *The Last Conquistador*. Sutton, UK: Thrupp.

Titu Cusi Yupanqui, Inca Diego de Castro. 1916a. "Cuenta Corta." In *Colección de
libros y documentos referentes a la historia del Perú*, edited by Carlos A. Romero and
Horacio H. Urteaga, ser. 1, vol. 2, appendix D, 125–132. Lima: Sanmarti.

Titu Cusi Yupanqui, Inca Diego de Castro. 1916b. Letter from Titu Cusi Yupanqui
Dated November 24, 1568. Written in Pampaconas. In *Colección de libros y docu-
mentos referentes a la historia del Perú*, edited by Carlos A. Romero and Horacio H.
Urteaga, ser. 1, vol. 2, appendix D, 121–122. Lima: Sanmarti.

Titu Cusi Yupanqui, Inca Diego de Castro. 1916c. Letter from Titu Cusi Yupanqui, Dated December 23, 1568. Written in Pampaconas. In *Colección de libros y documentos referentes a la historia del Perú*, edited by Carlos A. Romero and Horacio H. Urteaga, ser. 1, vol. 2, appendix B, 119–121. Lima: Sanmarti.

Titu Cusi Yupanqui, Inca Diego de Castro. [1570] 2005. *An Inca Account of the Conquest of Peru by Titu Cusi Yupanqui*. Translated by Ralph Bauer. Denver: University of Colorado Press.

Toledo, Francisco de. (1574) 1899a. "Merced a Antón de Álvarez." *Revista de Archivos de Bibliotecas Nacional* (Lima) 1:112–114.

Toledo, Francisco de. (1575) 1899b. "Merced a Antón de Álvarez de 400 pesos en los indios de Mudca y Pariaca de Chuquinga." *Revista de Archivos de Bibliotecas Nacional* (Lima) 1:114–116.

Toledo, Francisco de. (1575) 1899c. "Merced a la ciudad de Vilcabamba de los dos novenos pertenecientes a Su Magestad y de las faltas de doctrina que hicieron los sacerdotes en la dicha provincia." *Revista de Archivos de Bibliotecas Nacional* (Lima) 1:17–18.

Toledo, Francisco de. (1575) 1899d. "Merced de gentiles hombres lanzas a Juan de Ortega y Juan de Abierto y Alonso Juárez y Francisco Pérez Fonseca residiendo en la provincia de Vilcabamba." *Revista de Archivos de Bibliotecas Nacional* (Lima) 1:20–23.

Toledo, Francisco de. (1576) 1899e. "Para que los oficiales reales paguen de la Real Hacienda a los sacerdotes que doctrinaren en Vilcabamba." *Revista de Archivos de Bibliotecas Nacional* (Lima) 2:349–350.

Toledo, Francisco de. (1580) 1899f. "Provisión de S. E. por donde manda se descuenten las fallas que hiciere el Gobernador Martin Hurtado de Arbieto, de la provincia de Vilcabamba." *Revista de Archivos de Bibliotecas Nacional* (Lima) 1:419–420.

Toledo, Francisco de. (1575) 1899g. "Situación al Gobernador Martín de Arbieto de 1000 pesos en los indios de Tinta y Moyna." *Revista de Archivos de Bibliotecas Nacional* (Lima) 1:123–128.

Toledo, Francisco de. 1906. "Carta del Virrey D. Francisco de Toledo a S. M. sobre asuntos de guerra, acompañado una relación de los indios fronterizos (20 March 1573, written between Potosí and Tucuman)." In *Juicio de limites entre el Perú y Bolivia*, 1:79–103. Barcelona: Henrich y Comp.

Toledo, Francisco de. (1573) 1975. *Tasa de la visita general de Francisco de Toledo*. Edited by David Noble Cook. Lima: Universidad Nacional Mayor de San Marcos, Seminario de Historia Rural Andina.

Urteaga, Horacio H. 1916. "Titu Cusi Yupanqui, Inca Diego de Castro 'Relación de la conquista del Perú y hechos del Inca Manco II.'" In *Colección de libros y documentos referentes a la historia del Perú*, edited by Carlos A. Romero and Horacio H. Urteaga, ser. 1, vol. 2, 115–151. Lima: Gil.

Varese, Stefano. 2004. *Salt of the Mountain: Campa Asháninka History and Resistance in the Peruvian Jungle*. Norman: University of Oklahoma Press.